ANNIVERSARY ESSAYS ON
JOHNSON'S *DICTIONARY*

Samuel Johnson's *Dictionary of the English Language*, the first great English dictionary and one of the most famous books in the English language, appeared in April 1755. To commemorate the 250th anniversary, this volume brings together fourteen original essays by international scholars representing several disciplines: literature, lexicology, linguistics, and bibliography. The essays explore familiar and unfamiliar aspects of Johnson's masterpiece, ranging from the history of patronage to the book's typographical design, from the political background to the treatment of compound words. Challenging the myths surrounding the book and offering the most comprehensive and wide-ranging study of the *Dictionary* ever attempted, these essays present the latest scholarship on the *Dictionary* and open up new perspectives and directions for future research.

JACK LYNCH is Associate Professor of English at Rutgers University. He is the author of *The Age of Elizabeth in the Age of Johnson* (Cambridge, 2003).

ANNE MCDERMOTT is Senior Lecturer in English at the University of Birmingham. She has edited Johnson's *A Dictionary of the English Language on CD-ROM* (Cambridge, 1996).

ANNIVERSARY ESSAYS ON JOHNSON'S *DICTIONARY*

EDITED BY

JACK LYNCH AND ANNE McDERMOTT

CAMBRIDGE
UNIVERSITY PRESS

423
ANN

PUBLISHED BY THE PRESS SYNDICATE OF THE UNIVERSITY OF CAMBRIDGE
The Pitt Building, Trumpington Street, Cambridge, United Kingdom

CAMBRIDGE UNIVERSITY PRESS
The Edinburgh Building, Cambridge, CB2 2RU, UK
40 West 20th Street, New York, NY 10011–4211, USA
477 Williamstown Road, Port Melbourne, VIC 3207, Australia
Ruiz de Alarcón 13, 28014 Madrid, Spain
Dock House, The Waterfront, Cape Town 8001, South Africa

http://www.cambridge.org
Information on this title: www.cambridge.org/9780521848442

© Cambridge University Press 2005

First published 2005

Printed in the United Kingdom at the University Press, Cambridge

Typeface Adobe Garamond 11/12.5 pt.   *System* LATEX 2ε   [TB]

A catalogue record for this book is available from the British Library

ISBN-13 978 0 521 84844 2 hardback
ISBN-10 0 521 84844 X hardback

Contents

Illustrations

Contributors

GEOFF BARNBROOK is a Lecturer in English Language in the Department of English at the University of Birmingham. His principal research interests lie in the development and application of corpus linguistic analysis within both modern and historical linguistics. His most recent publication is *Defining Language: A Local Grammar of Definition Sentences* (John Benjamins, 2002).

ROBERT DEMARIA, JR. is the Henry Noble MacCracken Professor of English Literature at Vassar College. He is the author of many articles and three books about Samuel Johnson: *Johnson's "Dictionary" and the Language of Learning* (University of North Carolina Press, 1986); *The Life of Samuel Johnson: A Critical Biography* (Blackwell, 1993); and *Samuel Johnson and the Life of Reading* (Johns Hopkins University Press, 1997). He is also the editor of *British Literature 1640–1789: An Anthology* (Blackwell, 2nd ed., 2001); *Gulliver's Travels* (Penguin Classics, 2nd ed., 2002); and, with Gwin Kolb, a forthcoming volume in the Yale Edition of the Works of Samuel Johnson, *Johnson on the English Language*.

CATHERINE DILLE is Research Fellow at the University of Birmingham on the Johnson Dictionary Project, which will produce a Web-based edition of Johnson's *Dictionary* in 2005. She has previously worked on Johnson's unpublished revisions for the fourth edition of the *Dictionary* and has published on Johnson's reception in the nineteenth century.

R. CARTER HAILEY teaches medieval and early modern literature at the College of William and Mary, Williamsburg, Virginia, and publishes on lexicographic and textual matters. He also has designed and produces the COMET portable optical collator.

NICHOLAS HUDSON, Professor of English at the University of British Columbia, is author of *Samuel Johnson and Eighteenth-Century Thought* (Clarendon Press, 1988); *Writing and European Thought, 1600–1830*

(Cambridge University Press, 1994); *Samuel Johnson and the Making of Modern England* (Cambridge University Press, 2003); and many essays on eighteenth-century literature, thought, and culture.

PAUL J. KORSHIN, Professor of English at the University of Pennsylvania, is co-editor of *The Age of Johnson: A Scholarly Annual*. An earlier comment on Johnson and language is his "Reconfiguring the Past: The Eighteenth Century Confronts Oral Culture," in *The Yearbook of English Studies* (1998).

IAN LANCASHIRE is Professor of English at the University of Toronto. He does research into how early print and manuscript lexicons contribute to the growth of early modern English vocabulary.

PAUL LUNA is Professor of Typography and Graphic Communication at the University of Reading, UK. He is involved in teaching the practice, theory, and history of the subject, and his research centers on the design of complex texts such as dictionaries. He was a book designer and design manager at Oxford University Press for twenty years and designed the second edition of the *OED*, as well as Oxford's range of English language and bilingual dictionaries, introducing the Nimrod and Swift typefaces for dictionary typesetting. He has recently designed the fifth edition of the *Shorter Oxford English Dictionary*, and is now working on a research project to improve the design of children's dictionaries.

JACK LYNCH is Associate Professor of English at Rutgers University in Newark. He is the author of *The Age of Elizabeth in the Age of Johnson* (Cambridge University Press, 2003) and editor, with Paul J. Korshin, of *The Age of Johnson: A Scholarly Annual*. He is now at work on a study of forgery and fraud in eighteenth-century Britain.

ANNE MCDERMOTT is Senior Lecturer in English at the University of Birmingham, and editor of *A Dictionary of the English Language on CD-ROM* (Cambridge University Press, 1996). She is currently working on a scholarly edition of Johnson's *Dictionary*, containing among other things the sources of all the illustrative quotations, which will appear online in 2005.

NOEL E. OSSELTON has held chairs of the English Language in both Holland and England, and was a founding member of the European Association for Lexicography. He is the author of *Chosen Words: Past and Present Problems for Dictionary Makers* (University of Exeter Press, 1995), and co-editor of *The New Routledge Dutch Dictionary* (2003).

ALLEN REDDICK is Professor of English Literature and former departmental chair at the University of Zürich. The revised edition of *The Making of Johnson's Dictionary, 1746–1773* (Cambridge University Press) appeared in 1996.

JOHN STONE is a PhD candidate and Associate Lecturer in the Department of English and German Philology at the University of Barcelona. He has edited and helped translate a Catalan translation of Johnson's Preface to Shakespeare; published on Johnson, topics in seventeenth-century literature, and film studies; and is currently engaged in a study of Johnson's reception in Spain.

HOWARD D. WEINBROT is Vilas and Quintana Research Professor at the University of Wisconsin, Madison. He is author, most recently, of *Britannia's Issue: The Rise of British Literature from Dryden to Ossian* (Cambridge University Press, 1993), and has co-edited *Eighteenth-Century Contexts: Historical Inquiries in Honor of Phillip Harth* (University of Wisconsin Press, 2001).

Abbreviations and cue-titles

1755	Samuel Johnson, *A Dictionary of the English Language*, 2 vols. (London, 1755).
1773	Samuel Johnson, *A Dictionary of the English Language*, 4th ed., 2 vols. (London, 1773).
1825 *Works*	*The Works of Samuel Johnson*, 11 vols. (Oxford, 1825).
Bibliography	J. D. Fleeman, *A Bibliography of the Works of Samuel Johnson: Treating His Published Works from the Beginning to 1984*, 2 vols. (Oxford: Clarendon Press, 2000).
Letters	*The Letters of Samuel Johnson*, ed. Bruce Redford, 5 vols. (Princeton: Princeton University Press, 1992–94).
Life	James Boswell, *The Life of Samuel Johnson, LL.D.*, ed. G. B. Hill, rev. L. F. Powell, 6 vols. (Oxford: Clarendon Press, 1934–64).
OED	*The Oxford English Dictionary*, 2nd ed., 20 vols. (Oxford: Oxford University Press, 1989).
Yale *Works*	*The Yale Edition of the Works of Samuel Johnson*, ed. John H. Middendorf *et al.* (New Haven: Yale University Press, 1958–).

Entries in reference works, including Johnson's *Dictionary*, are cited by headword, followed by part of speech and numbered sense when necessary.

Introduction

Jack Lynch and Anne McDermott

When James H. Sledd and Gwin J. Kolb marked the bicentenary of Samuel Johnson's *Dictionary of the English Language* in 1955, they summarized the features that were part of the established pattern of contemporary research on Johnson's *Dictionary*. It is remarkable, fifty years on, how many of these have remained with us, some having hardened into clichés:

> Johnson's word-list is criticized as bookish, a little remote from the crudities of everyday life, sometimes almost un-English; but it may equally be praised for its inclusiveness. It is noted that though Johnson marked the accents of words, he said little about pronunciation, and his etymologies and his fussy remarks on usage are treated as rather ludicrous but typical of his age. To Johnson's definitions, his careful distinction and classification of the different senses of words, the historian gives high praise, but praise a little tempered by reference to tart Johnsonian humor or stilted Johnsonese. Unlimited praise is given to his industriously collected illustrative quotations, which are represented, with his definitions, as his grand contribution to the technique of English lexicography.[1]

Their aim was to bring to bear on Johnson's *Dictionary* new knowledge that had been gained in the previous fifty years about English philology, grammatical traditions, theories of language, and the development of lexicography in England, so that the established pattern might be "clarified, modified in some of its details and enriched with some new lore" (pp. 3–4).

The "new lore" may be different now, but our aim in this volume is very similar to theirs. We hope to bring to bear on Johnson's *Dictionary* the most recent research carried out in the distinct fields of literary scholarship, bibliography, textual criticism, corpus linguistics, and historical lexicography. In the process we hope to disturb some received ideas about the *Dictionary* and to suggest new avenues for research that have so far been neglected.

The *Dictionary* can hardly be called a neglected work. In the 250 years since it first appeared on 15 April 1755, Johnson's work has appeared in at least 52 editions, 13 adaptations, 120 abridgments, 309 miniature versions,

7 printed facsimile editions, 4 sets of selections, and 2 CD-ROMs. It has been the subject of more than 350 published works, including at least 28 books and a book-length bibliography. It even features in an episode of a television sitcom. The pace, moreover, seems to be quickening: fully half the published commentary has appeared in the last three decades. The number of passing references in general books about Johnson, English literature, the English language, or dictionaries generally is probably beyond the power of anyone to count.

And yet, despite the mountains of criticism, much of the *Dictionary* remains unfamiliar, even to scholars. This is because the book has led a kind of double life in which it is at once very familiar and very unfamiliar. The "familiar" *Dictionary* is a paradoxical one: it is presumed to have been written as part of a widespread effort in the eighteenth century to codify the language, to establish a standard form of English, and to stigmatize and marginalize the vulgar, the regional, the oral, and the dialect. In this account Johnson's *Dictionary* is seen as a centralizing, class-based, Anglocentric, and nationalist document of high culture and dogmatic authoritarianism.[2] It has at the same time been widely read as idiosyncratic and wayward, reflecting and presenting Johnson's own very individual prejudices and political outlook. Knowledge of this *Dictionary* comes from Boswell's *Life of Johnson*, from Johnson's statements in his Preface, and from a few well-known entries for such words as *whig* and *tory, oats* and *lexicographer*. This *Dictionary*, at once authoritative and idiosyncratic, is the *Dictionary* that has entered the world of legend.

The "unfamiliar" *Dictionary*, on the other hand, has emerged only from deep and sustained research into the book's content. The most recent stage of this research began in earnest in 1986 with Robert DeMaria's investigation of the illustrative quotations in the *Dictionary*, many of which were traced back to their source texts.[3] A picture began to emerge of a much more scholarly Johnson than had been presented by those who relied on the literal truth of his self-effacing comment in the Preface: "The examples, thus mutilated, are no longer to be considered as conveying the sentiments or doctrine of their authours . . . it may sometime happen, by hasty detruncation, that . . . the divine may desert his tenets, or the philosopher his system" (1825 *Works*, vol. v, p. 39).

DeMaria's discoveries were complemented by the groundbreaking research of Allen Reddick, whose *Making of Johnson's Dictionary* (1990) charted in unprecedented detail the genealogy and gestation of the *Dictionary* from manuscript to printed book.[4] This study gave us new knowledge about how the *Dictionary* was compiled, including the astounding discovery that some of the material from the original notebooks in which Johnson started his *Dictionary* had survived in the form of slips containing illustrative quotations that were reused in revisions to the fourth edition of 1773. Previous work on the *Dictionary* had focused almost exclusively on the first edition, but the new light shed by Reddick's immensely detailed scholarly and bibliographic scrutiny of the text has resulted in renewed study of the fourth edition.

DeMaria and Reddick inaugurated a new stage of serious study of the *Dictionary*, but much remains to be done. Most notably, there has still been relatively little attention to Johnson's *Dictionary* as a dictionary. Compared with the attention paid to literary texts, dictionaries in general have received very little bibliographical, textual, stemmatic, critical, theoretical, or historiographical scrutiny. And most of those who have written about the *Dictionary* are literary scholars, who tend to regard Johnson as a literary lexicographer. They give primacy in their readings of the *Dictionary* to the fact that it was written uniquely by *Johnson*, rather than a part of both English and Continental traditions of lexicography or the result of collaborative effort, both synchronically and diachronically. Many articles have been written about Johnson's use of his source texts, for example, making the claim that Johnson shaped the text according to certain ideological, political, moral, or cultural forces, without always considering that his reasons for selecting and editing the quotations may have been driven by *linguistic* considerations – whether, for example, they sufficiently illustrate or exemplify the meaning of a word.

Linguists and lexicographers have developed a rather different picture. Viewed as a milestone in the history of language and lexicography, rather than in the context of Johnson's life and works, the *Dictionary* has been seen as a culmination of an earlier tradition of English lexicography and as a precursor of the *OED*. But whereas literary scholars have generally celebrated Johnson's *Dictionary*, many lexicographers have reacted against it: the *Dictionary* has been demonized by Noah Webster, then by Richard Chevenix Trench and the early editors of the *OED*, and subsequently by modern lexicologists whose preference for descriptive and non-judgmental recording of the language is seen as running counter to Johnson.

In linguistic scholarship too, however, there have been recent developments, resulting from close detailed reading of the text, and these new insights have revised received wisdom. There have been studies of his principles of word selection (his treatment of lemmas, technical terms, calques or loan words, and ad-hoc coinages); his treatment of morphological

variants, compound words, participles, and phrasal verbs; his definitions
and explanations, particularly his treatment of polysemy; and his attempts
to trace the semantic history of words. This work has served to alter our
conception of Johnson the lexicographer: he is now seen to address some of
the central issues in lexicology, linguistics, and the philosophy of language.
Patrick Hanks, formerly editor at Oxford English Dictionaries, even goes so
far as to claim that "Johnson crisply addresses theoretical issues which were
subsequently neglected for some two hundred years . . . until philosophers
such as Russell and Wittgenstein, and pedagogical theorists such as C. K.
Ogden took them up independently in the twentieth century."[5]

  In this collection we have tried to reflect the current state of research
by including work by scholars engaged in linguistic, literary, editorial,
bibliographic, and lexicographic criticism of Johnson's *Dictionary*. More
importantly, we have tried to bring these diverse approaches together, out
of a conviction that only a variety of critical methods can do justice to a
work of this magnitude. The first edition of the *Dictionary* alone contains
roughly three million words of text; no one person can claim to know
it thoroughly, and no one approach can hope to treat every aspect of it.
Despite the divergent approaches, though, all the contributors to this volume share a few fundamental convictions. The first is the importance of
examining evidence critically, whether literary, linguistic, biographical, or
bibliographical. They have not been content, as so many other commentators on the *Dictionary* have been, to base their judgments on a handful
of famous entries and stories from Boswell. Their concern, in other words,
is with the "unfamiliar" *Dictionary*.

One reason this volume places so much attention on the unfamiliar
Dictionary is that much conventional wisdom about the familiar *Dictionary* is wrong. There is no shortage of legends about Johnson's work,
beginning with the "first English dictionary" myth – a surprisingly hardy
falsehood. A recent article in the *New York Times*, for instance, refers to
"Dr. Johnson's 1755 dictionary, the first in the English language."[6] Few readers of this volume are likely to make that mistake, but many other fables
continue to circulate even among professional critics. The volume therefore
opens with Paul J. Korshin's discussion of the myths that have developed
around Johnson the man, which portray him as an "unreal buffoon, bully,
and bigot," and around the *Dictionary*. Korshin revisits many scholarly
commonplaces, from the notion of the towering but impoverished genius
laboring alone in the Gough Square attic to the story of Frances Brooke
looking for all the "naughty words," and challenges readers to pay careful

attention to the nature of their sources. He advises us to resist the urge to circulate dubious stories simply because they are enjoyable.

A similar spirit of skepticism and caution informs the other essays in this volume. For more than a decade Johnson's politics has been a subject of often heated debate, and evidence from the *Dictionary* has been adduced to support positions on Johnson's political thought. Rarely, however, have the various partisans paused to reflect on how, or indeed whether, the *Dictionary* can be considered a political work. Ian Lancashire, Howard D. Weinbrot, and Nicholas Hudson therefore consider the *Dictionary* in various political contexts, each of them suggesting that the book's political uses to date have been too simplistic. Lancashire's interest is the history of patronage, and his goal is to examine Johnson's famous clash with Lord Chesterfield in that light. He argues that English dictionaries had traditionally been collaborative efforts of the lexicographer, the printer-publisher, and the patron. Johnson's renunciation of his patron – "a wretch who supports with insolence, and is paid with flattery" – is well known, but Lancashire re-examines this episode and the whole issue of patronage and control in the context of the traditional two-tiered patronage system in operation in early modern lexicons.

Weinbrot notes that the *Dictionary* has variously been claimed by the Right, the Left, and the Center, and argues that each has misinterpreted (or perhaps over-interpreted) the text according to this political point of view, paying insufficient attention to the fact that it is, above all, a dictionary. Johnson's main concern in selecting his quotations, Weinbrot insists, was not political, theological, or otherwise polemical, but linguistic. He points out that Johnson's sources were often polemical, even violently so, but that Johnson himself went out of his way to omit the most egregiously sectarian expressions in these texts. The *Dictionary* is a dictionary of the English language, not of Johnson's language.

Like Weinbrot, Hudson remarks that Johnson is often depicted either as a villain or a hero according to commentators' own political affinities, and that "his *Dictionary* seems to take on a different ideological shade as illuminated by political lights of different colors." He offers an argument that Johnson's *Dictionary* emerged out of a complex and amorphous political group, the "Broad-bottom" coalition, which developed after the fall of Walpole and championed the elimination of party difference and the non-partisan promotion of men of merit, as opposed to the rewarding of political favorites. A key figure in this group was Robert Dodsley, whom Johnson regarded as his patron for the *Dictionary* as well as the renounced Lord Chesterfield, and Hudson offers the intriguing suggestion that it was

Chesterfield's reneging on the principle of promoting men of merit that caused this renunciation.

Robert DeMaria turns his attention to what may be the most unfamiliar parts of the *Dictionary*, the Grammar and History of the English Language. From these usually neglected works he derives a lesson about Johnson's working methods. Among DeMaria's most important contributions to *Dictionary* scholarship is his portrait of Johnson as a serious scholar, deeply immersed in humanist traditions of learning, writing a book with a coherent moral and pedagogical purpose. And yet in this essay he offers some salutary advice not to overestimate the degree of control Johnson exerted over his work. "There seems to be a spontaneous, extempore quality to the *Dictionary* as well as a design," he discovers, and he shows a number of instances in which Johnson seems to have departed from his stated plans.

Some of the most pointed debates over dictionaries in the last half-century have concerned the merits of descriptive versus prescriptive lexicography, but there has been little extended consideration of where Johnson's work fits along this continuum. Geoff Barnbrook uses the methods of corpus linguistics to sort through more than ten thousand usage notes in both the first and fourth editions, and argues that roughly a quarter of them can be called prescriptive. He summarizes his results by stating that "the prescriptive approach promised in the *Plan* and detailed, though with reservations, in the Preface, informed the construction of the *Dictionary* to a significant extent." Anne McDermott, on the other hand, agrees that "The mood of the times certainly favored a prescriptive attitude to the language," but she thinks it reasonable to ask "whether the prescriptive expectation was carried out in practice." Likening Johnson's use of his "authorities" to the English common law tradition, she examines his expressed attitudes toward language and concludes that Johnson "seems unwilling to exercise the kind of prescriptive jurisdiction that was expected of him."

Jack Lynch picks up on DeMaria's hints in *Johnson's "Dictionary" and the Language of Learning* about "the encyclopedic qualities of his book," and explores the often permeable boundary between dictionaries and encyclopedias even after the older topically organized reference works had virtually disappeared as a coherent genre. In observing that Johnson's *Dictionary* contains more encyclopedic information than most general dictionaries, he argues that Johnson's approach to what is now often called the "lexicon–encyclopedia interface" is pragmatic rather than principled, and he notes that Johnson carefully reworks his source material to make it more useful to the common reader.

John Stone is also concerned with Johnson's use of earlier encyclopedic reference works, and focuses specifically on dictionaries of law, a subject close to Johnson's heart. The standard accounts of the English monolingual dictionary have traced its origin to "the hard-word tradition," while slighting the parallel tradition of topical dictionaries and encyclopedias. In drawing our attention to Johnson's use of legal reference works, Stone urges readers to recognize "the extent of the general monolingual dictionary's debt to its more specialized counterparts."

Noel E. Osselton draws on his experience as both a historian of lexicography and a practicing lexicographer to consider what exactly constitutes a word for Johnson, and how related words should be ordered in an alphabetical reference work. He notices a "striking mid-alphabet change in lexicographical method" for dealing with a class of words that has received little attention, hyphenated compounds. From the evidence of this small course-adjustment he derives an account of Johnson's increasing tendency toward descriptivism, calling this change in his treatment of hyphens "one small instance of how his desire to regulate the language gave way in the light of experience to the more modest aim of recording it."

For most scholars, "Johnson's *Dictionary*" refers to the large folio work published in two volumes in 1755, but the final four essays in this collection focus on the work's long and rich afterlife. Paul Luna, whose typographical expertise helped to shape the second edition of the *Oxford English Dictionary*, gives the most extended treatment to date of the typography of Johnson's work. He addresses not only the familiar first folio edition but also a series of folio, quarto, and octavo editions that have escaped the attention of most critics. He asks "how its visual presentation reflects the structure of the text, its usability, and perhaps even its compiler's intentions," and identifies several respects in which Johnson's *Dictionary* was both innovative and influential in the traditions of English lexicography.

Catherine Dille reminds us that the versions of the *Dictionary* familiar to most modern scholars are not in fact the ones that most eighteenth- and nineteenth-century readers knew. The folio editions were priced out of the reach of all but the wealthiest readers, and most of those who knew the *Dictionary* knew it in one of its abridged versions. Dille looks carefully at several of these "abstracted" editions, produces evidence that Johnson himself was involved in their production, and discusses the ways in which these shorter and more popular versions differed from their folio sources. "There is not one monolithic Johnson's *Dictionary of the English Language*," she argues, "but in a sense two parallel dictionaries, the abstracted edition deriving from the folio as its source, but each work evolving independently and developing its own textual history."

Allen Reddick, whose *Making of Johnson's Dictionary* broke new ground in its attention to the fourth edition of 1773, revisits some of his earlier conclusions in the light of little-known manuscript material Johnson used in preparing the revised text. The role of the six amanuenses has been a puzzle for more than two centuries: some have treated them as little more than unthinking copyists, while others have considered them almost co-authors with Johnson. Reddick's evidence suggests that their role was limited, at least in the preparation of the fourth edition, and that Johnson's *Dictionary* was not collaborative in any important way: Johnson never relinquishes "his own overarching authority as both author and compiler."

R. Carter Hailey demonstrates how analytical bibliography can illuminate a text's reception history. He begins with what seems to be a minor discovery – several "hidden" editions of what have usually been called the sixth and seventh editions – and goes on to argue that Johnson's authority was great enough in the decade after his death that publishers continued to introduce changes to the text in order to operate under the Johnson "brand name." He usefully reminds us that the story of Johnson's *Dictionary* does not end with the fourth edition in 1773, or even with Johnson's death in 1784. "Demand for the *Dictionary*," he points out, "clearly remained strong in the 1780s and 1790s, and such was the iconic status of Johnson's authority that the publishers saw fit not just to reprint their profitable product, but also to employ an unnamed editor who worked diligently to honor Johnson's legacy by increasing the accuracy of its text."

Readers will note many matters on which the contributors disagree: Weinbrot argues that the *Dictionary* has little to do with party politics, whereas Hudson insists that its apparent moderation is itself the product of the political situation of the 1740s; Barnbrook uses the methods of corpus linguistics to find Johnson's work prescriptive, while McDermott's approach reveals it to be descriptive; Lancashire's essay presents the *Dictionary* within the traditional collaborative framework for lexicographical works, whereas Reddick argues for the minimizing of any collaborative contribution, particularly from the amanuenses. It is perhaps inevitable that the diverse approaches have resulted in similarly diverse conclusions. We have not tried to reconcile or gloss over these disagreements. Rather than imposing a uniformity of opinion where no consensus exists, we have worked to highlight disagreements so as to encourage further research on these issues.

Encouraging further research is, after all, the most important aim of this volume. No collection of essays could give all of these neglected areas the coverage they deserve; this one makes no pretense of being the definitive word on the topics it covers. The purpose of the volume is, however, to bring together scholars working in the fields of literary scholarship, bibliography, historical lexicography and lexicology, and history of language. Historical lexicography has begun to move beyond the traditional lineal understanding of the development of monolingual English dictionaries by taking into account political, cutural, and textual considerations, as well as aspects of book history in general, which broaden the scope beyond the narrowly linguistic and Anglocentric. The work of scholars on the new *OED*, on the *Dictionary of Old English* and the *Middle English Dictionary* projects, and on numerous other lexicographical projects has brought renewed energy to the field of old dictionaries, and research on Johnson's *Dictionary* continues to benefit from this. The fruits of this research go far beyond the fields of historical lexicography or Johnson scholarship, since knowledge of the historical formation of the English language is a fundamental part of most English research. We hope that other scholars will pick up on and develop the ideas contained in these essays, that specialists in different fields will address one another and draw on each other's respective areas of expertise, and that the complexity and richness of Johnson's *Dictionary* will continue to inspire scholars to move beyond the isolation of their own distinct fields.

NOTES

1. James H. Sledd and Gwin J. Kolb, *Dr. Johnson's Dictionary: Essays in the Biography of a Book* (Chicago: University of Chicago Press, 1955), p. 2.
2. The most recent account of this kind is given by Janet Sorensen, "Vulgar Tongues: Canting Dictionaries and the Language of the People in Eighteenth-Century Britain," *Eighteenth-Century Studies* 37 (2003), 435–54.
3. Robert DeMaria, Jr., *Johnson's "Dictionary" and the Language of Learning* (Chapel Hill: University of North Carolina Press, 1986).
4. Allen Reddick, *The Making of Johnson's Dictionary, 1746–1773*, rev. ed. (Cambridge: Cambridge University Press, 1996).
5. Patrick Hanks, "Samuel Johnson and Modern Lexicography," unpublished lecture delivered to The Johnson Society, Lichfield, 2 March 1999.
6. Katie Zezima, "A Samuel Johnson Trove Goes to Harvard's Library," *New York Times*, 18 March 2004, p. E3.

CHAPTER I

The mythology of Johnson's Dictionary

Paul J. Korshin

Visitors to libraries will be familiar with the architectural concept of "the building as book." Libraries from Johannesburg to San Francisco embody this kind of engraving: the names of literary worthies from all ages, deeply engraved in Baskerville capitals, form an entablature that helps to identify the building as a house of books. The most ornate such building is the Chicago Public Library, the ground-breaking for which was one of the events of the city's Columbian Exposition of 1892–93. The architects – McKim, Meade, and White, Cass Gilbert, Carrère and Hastings, Sheply, Bulfinch, Richardson and Abbott – helped in this process of marmorealizing the classic past.[1] In the process of creating America's most ornate public building, they had a great many classics to commemorate, so many, indeed, that they arranged their names in genre-groupings. Thus there is a poets' grouping, "Wordsworth – Pope – Byron – Shelley"; a second poets' grouping (perhaps for narrative poets), "Scott – Burns – Tennyson – Gray"; and a historians' grouping, "Macaulay – Carlyle – Gibbon – Hume." Johnson is arranged with some curious associates in a tetrad of miscellaneous writers, "Swift – Johnson – Sheridan – Lamb," a literary fellowship of uncertain axis. There is no archival record about who arranged these tetrads or what taxonomy the framers (one naturally assumes that a committee was responsible for these catachreses) had in mind. We can see that by 1897, the year the city of Chicago dedicated this building, Johnson had already passed into the world of legend. The interpreters of the legend, however, still saw him as a writer, not as the subject of a famous biography: no names of Johnson's biographers appear on the Chicago library's walls or ceilings.

This legendary Johnson had long been available to the world by the time W. J. Bate published *The Achievement of Samuel Johnson*; we can even trace the beginnings of some of the legends to Johnson's own lifetime. Since the 1950s, Johnsonian scholars have not been reverent of these legends. James Clifford's *Young Sam Johnson* tried whenever possible to

undermine traditions for which there was no factual basis, and we can see
the genesis of Donald Greene's lifelong campaign to obliterate Boswellian
inventions from Johnsonian studies in the 1950s as well. Bate pointedly tells
us that the achievement he presents will be based mainly on Johnson's own
writings.[2]

The opening chapter of *The Achievement* is entitled "A Life of Allegory,"
a fractious term for the Johnson of legend, since his sentiments about
allegory, at least according to legend, are so negative: "Talking with some
persons about allegorical painting, he said, 'I had rather see the portrait
of a dog that I know, than all the allegorical paintings they can shew me
in the world.'" This comment surfaces for the first time in the notorious
miscellaneous volume, the eleventh, of what we call Hawkins's edition of
Johnson's *Works*, where it appears among twenty pages of "Apophthegms,
Sentiments, and Occasional Reflections."[3] Like all of these unattributed
anecdotes, this comment is second- or third-hand hearsay, lacking source,
location, or date, and it forms part of a minor constellation of unattributed
anecdotes that purport to show Johnson's hostility to painting. Johnson's
respect for allegory, as we know, is substantial, and many of his specific
descriptions are painterly, so we can directly confute this one-liner with
evidence from his own writings. Nevertheless, this *mot* appears regularly as
a boulder on the Johnsonian landscape. A close analysis of Bate's first chapter
reveals that he never actually uses the word "allegory" (the word "allegorical"
appears once), for he meant the term to refer to the old tradition of allegory
as *fabula*, the seventeenth-century iconographical tradition whereby a mere
figure in a painting could represent something much larger. So Bate, in
relating the major themes in Johnson's life in this chapter, shows that a life
of allegory is one which, in our minds, represents larger human themes of
physical and mental suffering, solitariness and loneliness, idleness and sloth
(and guilt at presumed idleness and sloth), and doubts about one's adequacy
for greatness, salvation, indeed, for anything. There was no need for Bate to
search Johnson's second- and third-hand apophthegms; he found abundant
primary evidence in Johnson's own diaries, prayers, annals, correspondence,
and essays. What Bate calls "the legendary Johnson," the Johnson of myth,
is a problem, but one which he believed we can dismiss: "Indeed, all the
stock characteristics associated with the legendary Johnson can easily be
matched by resolutions and efforts to overcome them," most of which
come from Johnson himself.[4]

Mythmakers are not evil, unless one thinks of lies, fictions, mendacities,
and inventions as a species of wickedness. Whom, then, do the stories of the

legendary Johnson not please? Nobody. Hence, as I set forth to discuss the early mythological Johnson, beginning with his first works and leading to the *Dictionary*, I am aware that many readers *want* Samuel Johnson to be the unreal buffoon, bully, and bigot which so many legends reveal him to be. And yet there is seldom any foundation to stories of the mythic Johnson. Here is one brief example. He was terribly nearsighted – almost blind, some sources insist – but, according to one myth, he adamantly refused to wear spectacles which, in their modern form, a London optometrist developed in 1726.[5] Careful readers of Johnson might come to a different conclusion: after all, in the *Life of Swift* he specifically criticizes Swift "for having, by some ridiculous resolution or mad vow, determined never to wear spectacles, [therefore] he could make little use of books in his later years."[6] There was no novelty to spectacles in Johnson's time, and it is reasonable to conclude that he got along fine without them. There are dozens of similar stories that, collectively, constitute the legendary Johnson; like rocks in a New England pasture, they crop up time and again in both popular and scholarly writings.

There are myths associated with almost every one of Johnson's works. Let me start with his translation of Father Jerome Lobo's *Voyage to Abyssinia*. Edmund Hector, writing in 1785, told Boswell how this work came about:

Johnson mentioned that he had read at Pembroke College Lobosts [*sic*] History of Abyssinia and thought an Abridgement and Translation of it might do well. How to get the book was the question. Hector borrowed it of the Library of Pembroke.

Johnson was very indolent. Osborn the Printer employed by [Thomas] Warren could not get other work till it was finished and Johnson furnished him with copy only progressively. Hector went to Johnson and told him how the poor Printer and his family suffered. He lay in bed – got the book before him and dictated while Hector wrote. Hector wrote it over almost the whole of it and carried it to the Press.[7]

Boswell, not satisfied with Hector's fifty-year-old reminiscence, embroiders a little: "Johnson upon this exerted the powers of his mind, though his body was relaxed. He lay in bed with the book, which was a quarto, before him, and dictated while Hector wrote" (*Life*, vol. 1, pp. 86–87). In the eighteenth century, heroic authors require large books, so Boswell decides that Johnson used the quarto version of Le Grand's French translation, but of course there was a duodecimo as well, and we do not know which one Johnson used – except that it did not come from the library of Pembroke College, which had no copy of Lobo.[8] Now, there are people who do a lot of their writing in bed;

indeed, there are even those who never get out of bed at all. Oblomov, the eponymous hero of Goncharov's novel, never leaves his bed. But a 416-page translation is rather a long book to dictate from one's bed; no matter how fast Edmund Hector could write, this task would have taken him a minimum of forty hours. Are we to imagine bedside sessions lasting several weeks? More troubling is the writing of Johnson's preface which, though short, shows distinct signs of research. Did Johnson likewise toss off this fine essay from a recumbent position?[9] It is clear, I think, that this story is part of the myth of the procrastinating author which surfaces repeatedly in accounts of his early writings.

Consider too his "Debates in the Senate of Magna Lilliputia," Johnson's reports in *The Gentleman's Magazine* which purport to represent proceedings in the Houses of Parliament from November 1740 to February 1743. The legends are well known: we are told that Johnson visited Parliament only once, he wrote the debates based on sketchy notes an amanuensis took for him, he stopped writing them as soon as he discovered that people believed they were genuine, and he "took care that the WHIG DOGS should not have the best of it."[10] But fictionalized parliamentary speeches were not exactly new by the 1740s; in fact imaginary speeches had been an integral part of Herodotus, Thucydides, Plutarch, Pliny, and other Greek and Roman writers, and the tradition lived on in the political writings of Jacques de Thou and Gilbert Burnet, whose *History of His Own Times* contains many invented speeches. Arthur Murphy's contribution to the folklore of the *Debates* consists of his felicitous statement about the Whig dogs, which surfaces for the first time in 1791 and found its way into Boswell's biography via footnotes and appendices. We have heard that Johnson preferred a portrait of a dog that he knew, but now he disdains dogs if they happen to be Whigs. Greene dismisses this anecdote by saying that it "was probably no more than a piece of ordinary jocularity."[11] It is much worse than casual hilarity: there is no basis for our believing such hearsay, especially since Whigs who opposed Walpole often emerge as successful disputants. Johnson's *Debates* are a major, unappreciated early work, a landmark in Swiftian imitation and irony; the Johnsonian myth, a species of the "Johnson-as-bigot" legend, reduces them to the product of a garret-dwelling journalist who was short on time.

The *Debates* exist only in humble octavo editions; no large quartos or enormous folios engage our attention here, but we do not need ponderous volumes when we have Whig dogs. Johnson's work on the Harleian Library, however, is different. The preface Johnson wrote and the five-volume catalogue he helped compile introduce a new legend. We have a real villain this time, the abusive Thomas Osborne, and we have the wonderful story of Johnson's beating him, striking him not with his fist but with a large book. The legendary Johnson needs a Hercules-like club, and a folio will do just fine. Hester Piozzi discusses the story twice. By the time she asked Johnson about it, this event had already entered the realm of fable. In 1786, she relates how "I made one day very minute enquiries about the tale of his knocking down the famous Tom Osborne with his own Dictionary in the man's own house."[12] In 1812 John Nichols corrected her – the book was indeed a folio, but neither Johnson's nor Osborne's; it was "Biblia Graeca Septuaginta, fol. 1594, Frankfort," and Nichols had himself seen the book at a booksellers in Cambridge.[13] The Harleian Library contained 530 bibles, according to the catalogue, and it is sad to report that there is no 1594 Frankfurt edition of the Septuagint among them.[14] Still, we are reluctant to yield this facet of the Johnson-as-bully legend; some exaggerated recountings of the story tell even that Johnson put his foot on the odious Osborne's neck and informed him that he planned next to kick him downstairs. In other accounts, Osborne becomes very large and threatening, a sort of Telamonian Ajax who has a sound thrashing coming to him. It is fair to say that, as Thomas Kaminski notes, "this event has received most of the attention given to Johnson's association with Osborne, while the catalogue that he labored on for at least fifteen months is virtually ignored."[15] Something else happens when anecdote calcifies into legend. When Sheridan's character Crabtree recounts the non-existent duel between Sir Peter Teazle and Charles Surface, he announces that Sir Peter's bullet missed, but "struck against a little Bronze Pliny that stood over the chimney piece – grazed out of the window at a right angle – and wounded the Postman who was just coming to the Door with a double letter from Northamptonshire." His nephew Sir Benjamin Backbite, who has related a mere duel with swords, concedes, "My Unkle's account is more circumstantial."[16] So anecdotes snowball as they roll along; the Johnsonian legend yields many classic examples.

There are three strands, then, to the legends of Johnson's writings. We have the dilatory, procrastinating genius; the Herculean figure with a tendency to trample people, or Johnson-the-bully; and the humble, impoverished scholar laboring alone under the weight of many handicaps. We find these strands interwoven in the 1750s, when Johnson was working on three enormous projects. *The Rambler* is supposed to typify the procrastinating genius, for the myths tell us that the essays were hasty efforts which he sometimes wrote even as the printer's devil waited for the copy and which he never bothered to revise. Piozzi actually introduces a Sheridan-style "circumstantial" story of how Johnson composed one issue in this manner in the drawing room of Sir Joshua Reynolds, and this anecdote has gathered force over two centuries.[17] Reynolds, however, had not yet met Johnson; he was living in Rome during the years of *The Rambler*'s composition, and thus had no drawing room – but no matter. The procrastinating author somehow managed to revise *The Rambler* twice during this decade. Moreover, without the help of a staff, he generated considerable copy for his edition of Shakespeare – the first 150 sheets of proof were in print by the beginning of January 1759 (see *Bibliography*, vol. II, p. 1089). This was quite a landmark month in the life of the dilatory genius, for in it he somehow also found a week with enough free evenings to compose the whole of *Rasselas* and the spare time to write four issues of *The Idler*. The procrastinating strand of the myth somehow lacks substance. Notwithstanding, we start to see a more relaxed Johnson after the publication of his edition of Shakespeare. "During the thirteen years after 1765 . . . he wrote very little," Bate himself tells us, except for *Journey to the Western Islands*, several political pamphlets, and some prefaces and dedications (*Achievement*, p. 48). Bate completely overlooks the thorough revision of the *Dictionary* for the fourth edition, which cost him eighteen months of labor between 1771 and 1773, but which somehow does not count as writing.

The legends sometimes provoke dithyrambs. Referring to this period of Johnson's literary career, Thomas Carlyle ejaculates as follows:

How he sits there, in his rough-hewn, amorphous bulk, in that upper-room at St. John's Gate, and trundles off sheet after sheet of those Senate-of-Lilliput Debates, to the clamourous Printer's Devils waiting for them, with insatiable throat, downstairs; himself perhaps *impransus* all this while! Admire also the greatness of Literature; how a grain of mustard-seed cast into its Nile-waters, shall settle in the teeming mould, and be found, one day, as a Tree, in whose branches all the fowls of Heaven may lodge.[18]

Hero-worship cannot take place unless its mythological figures are of gigantic stature and inhabit a vast, allegorical landscape of recognizably epic dimensions. Notwithstanding this epic rant, Carlyle is not the most extreme of the mythmakers; the publication of Beryl Bainbridge's novel, *According to Queeney* (2002), shows that Johnsonian mythmaking lives on.

The principal myths of the 1750s relate to Johnson's major project, and here many of the familiar themes come together. The *Dictionary* is a large book, and large books create bigger-than-life legends. Almost from the start, representers of the *Dictionary* have struggled with its size. Reynolds's first portrait of Johnson (1756) reduces the work to a single volume; what may be volume II appears on the very margin of the painting.[19] Goldsmith has the conductor of his Fame Machine (1759) refuse Johnson entry until he sets aside his "parcel of folios," and admits him solely on the basis of a little book in his pocket – thus the four-volume *Rambler* becomes a single duodecimo.[20] Becky Sharp even receives a single-volume octavo edition of the *Dictionary* (Thackeray memorably calls it "Johnson's Dixonary," a variant Fleeman does not record) as a farewell present from Miss Pinkerton, but she throws it from the coach window (Thackeray's illustrators seized upon this iconic scene).[21] Further iconography of the *Dictionary* includes the nineteenth-century history painting by E. M. Ward, which shows a youthful Johnson in Lord Chesterfield's outward rooms while a dandified fellow (presumably Colley Cibber) leaves his lordship's audience room. Ward entitled his work *Doctor Johnson in the Ante-Room of Lord Chesterfield, Waiting for an Audience, 1748.*[22] Ward's image of Johnson is puzzling for, while the Johnson figure is much younger in appearance than any of the existing portraits, he is supporting himself with a cane or walking stick, a fashion or disability which none of his contemporaries ever mentions. The Cibber story originates with Hawkins, who asserts that Johnson, waiting on Chesterfield, was told that he was "engaged with a gentleman . . . It was not till after an hour's waiting that Johnson discovered that this gentleman was Colley Cibber, which he had no sooner done, than he rushed out of the house with a resolution never to return."[23] Boswell repeats this story, much amplified with further details, but insists that Johnson had told him it never happened (*Life*, vol. I, pp. 255–56). As we have seen, the *Dictionary* is associated with Johnson, not with a date of publication, so in the legendary world the completed work has a timeless quality. Typical of these accounts is the one in which Boswell repeats Johnson's quip about Andrew Millar: "When the messenger who carried the last sheet to Millar returned, Johnson asked him, 'Well, what did he say?' – 'Sir, (answered the messenger) he said, thank GOD I have done with him.' 'I am glad (replied Johnson, with a smile,) that he thanks GOD for any thing.'"[24] So cutting a retort has been popular with scholars and biographers (Bate prints it *in toto*), but Boswell does not mention that he had lifted it from the author he least admired, Sir John Hawkins. Hawkins tells us that Millar was so pleased that Johnson had completed the copy that he sent "the following acknowledgment of the receipt of the last sheet of manuscript":

"Andrew Millar sends his compliments to Mr. Samuel Johnson, with the money for the last sheet of copy of the Dictionary, and thanks God he has done with him."

To which Johnson returned this good-humoured and brief answer:

"Samuel Johnson returns his compliments to Mr. Andrew Millar, and is very glad to find, as he does by this note, that Andrew Millar has the grace to thank God for any thing." (Hawkins, *Life*, pp. 340–41)

Hawkins gives no source for this account, and no editor of Johnson's letters thus far has traced this exchange.[25] Boswell presents an account of the myth of Cibber's visit to Chesterfield and then rejects it, yet he accepts without question Johnson's witty exchange with Millar, even though it comes from the same source. In the world of the legendary Johnson, writers have always been reluctant to relinquish his ripostes, especially when they are as clever as this one.

Boswell carefully noted a handful of definitions where Johnson was wrong; a folklore has arisen about some of these as well. The best known is Johnson's response to the woman who wanted to know why he had mis-defined *pastern*: "A lady once asked him how he came to define *Pastern* the *knee* of a horse: instead of making an elaborate defence, as she expected, he at once answered, 'Ignorance, Madam, pure ignorance'" (*Life*, vol. I, p. 293). This piece of third-hand hearsay comes from Frances Reynolds, who places the comment "at a gentleman's seat in Devonshire," and iden-tifies the questioner as "the lady of the House." Reynolds gives Johnson's blunt answer: "Ignorance, Madam, ignorance" (*Miscellanies*, vol. II, p. 278), so we can see how Boswell embellishes the account. Johnson's definition of *oats* ("A grain, which in England is generally given to horses, but in Scot-land supports the people") has been the object of much ridicule; despite its brevity, some people misquote it, while others claim it displays Johnson's habitual dislike of the Scots and Scotland.[26] The definition, however, is exactly accurate, since oats are widely employed in such (in)famous Scot-tish delicacies as oat cakes and haggis. Yet, while there is a folklore about Johnson's misleading or erroneous definitions, it is difficult to recall a sin-gle anecdote relating to the misdefinitions and embarrassing silences of Noah Webster or Sir James Murray and his staff on the *New English Dic-tionary*. We hear often about Johnson's solitary toil on his *magnum opus*, despite the evidence that he had a staff to assist him, despite our knowl-edge, thanks to Hawkins, of his large circle of associates in the early 1750s, notwithstanding the fact that *The Rambler*, underway simultaneously with the *Dictionary*, attracted both collaborators and a circle of admirers. John Wain even entitles one of his chapters on Johnson's *Dictionary* years "Alone," but in fact Johnson had more society and associates during the period from 1746 to 1755 than he had ever had since leaving university two decades earlier.[27]

The most persistent myth surrounding the *Dictionary* is the one relating to the encouragement, some even say the patronage, of Lord Chesterfield. There was a vast social difference between Johnson, the scholar of modest means, and Philip Dormer Stanhope, the polished aristocrat with an annual income reputed to be £30,000. The mythmakers, however, have not been content with the financial disparity between the two. Over the last two and a half centuries, the molders of the Johnsonian legend have needed to dramatize how dissimilar they are. Chesterfield, Alvin Kernan decides, "was a perfect image, perhaps the last, of the old polite letters and of the old oral culture," for his lordship was "a brilliant conversationalist" and "a notable public speaker" (*Printing Technology, Letters & Samuel Johnson*, p. 199).[28] We may have forgotten that Johnson's conversation, as his admirers have preserved or modified it, is the most widely quoted talk in the English language. It is further useful to remember that Johnson was indeed a superb orator; he even wrote a dozen of Chesterfield's "parliamentary" speeches. Chesterfield was eager to preserve "The King's English," "but Johnson [in the *Dictionary*] was about to make it 'The Author's English'" (Kernan, *Printing Technology, Letters & Samuel Johnson*, p. 202). Yet every one of the works Johnson cites as an authority will be found in the library of King George III, where Johnson himself was often a reader.

The letter to Chesterfield – the most famous personal letter in the literary history of any language – is part of this myth and, fittingly, we have no idea what became of Chesterfield's copy. Johnson must have dictated the letter to Giuseppi Baretti, for there is a undated copy in Baretti's autograph, which Johnson himself corrected. There is another copy in Boswell's handwriting which he tells us Johnson dictated to him in June 1781, with the date of "February 1755"; in the second edition of the *Life*, Boswell assigns it to a single day, "7 February 1755," although there is no evidence for this date.[29] The myth of the spurned offer to be the dedicatee has become part of the Johnsonian legend – Carlyle even has the letter sounding a "far-famed Blast of Doom . . . into the ear of Lord Chesterfield . . . that patronage should be no more!" (*Samuel Johnson*, p. 59). The development of this story is strange, for Chesterfield's essays in *The World* do not seek a dedication. Nor did Johnson suffer from want during the life of the project: his advance of £1,575 was one of the largest of the eighteenth century until that time, he received further advances from his publishers, and he profited from later revisions as well. Perhaps Johnson's somewhat melodramatic phrase, "without . . . one word of encouragement," has made his labors seem even more Herculean than they were, but his friends at Oxford evidently did not consult with Chesterfield when they arranged an honorary degree for him in time for the publishers to describe him as "Samuel Johnson, A. M." on the title page.[30]

The mythology of the *Dictionary* itself, of the work as a book and a contribution to English letters, is surprisingly enduring. From the beginning there was the notion that Johnson's achievement was superhuman, in the proportion of three Englishmen to sixteen hundred Frenchmen, a much greater accomplishment than the collaborative lexicons of the French and Italian learned societies. In fact, however, there is no comparative study about the making of the dictionaries of the Académie Française or the Accademia della Crusca or the single-scholar enterprises like the Hebrew lexicon of Johannes Buxtorf and the Greek dictionary of Henry Estienne. We study Johnson as a man of letters and the making of the *Dictionary* because it is among his major works; because few other lexicographers have major literary careers, we ignore the manner in which they generated their monumental works. Neither Noah Webster nor James A. H. Murray thought of himself as "a poet doomed to wake a lexicographer," although each was aware that Johnson was such a person, for each quotes or alludes to this famous comparison.[31] Indeed, according to one late twentieth-century argument, we now value literary texts of imaginative genius more greatly than we do mere research tools which, apparently, do not require insight or imagination:

Created by genius, filled with mysterious presence, imaginative works like *Hamlet*, *Paradise Lost*, and *The Waste Land* now rise far above the normal range of writing.
 Few of Johnson's writings – perhaps by the strictest tests none finally – belong to these masterworks of the imagination. An imperfect edition of Shakespeare, a dictionary, a set of uneven poetic biographies, a number of occasional essays, a few imitative poems, an oriental moral tale, and various prefaces and critical writings – this is not, for all the skill, honesty, and intelligence with which it was done, a great romantic literary *oeuvre*. (Kernan, *Printing Technology*, p. 203)

Alvin Kernan is not deliberately discrediting Johnson here; rather, he proposes him as an early, perhaps even the first, professional writer whose works reflect what the common reader (a term which Johnson himself invented) was eager to read and for whose production the publishing industry would therefore pay. According to this view, we should compare Johnson favorably to miscellaneous writers like Coleridge, Carlyle, and Arnold, whose multivalent literary output covers many genres and who responded constantly to the shifting demands of the literary marketplace.

Every act of demythologizing is also a remythologizing, and the process which Kernan outlines, as a result of which none of Johnson's writings now deserves to be ranked as a work of imaginative genius, is not a new one. The first biographer who had not known him personally or who had not been part of the circle surrounding him, Robert Anderson, is also the first person to place the reputation of the *Dictionary* in a strictly non-heroic context. Anderson ignores most of the *Dictionary* myths; instead, he praises Johnson for the variety of his literary output, his miscellaneity: "As an author, Johnson is to be considered in the multifarious characters which he assumed, of a *philologist*, a *biographer*, a *critic*, an *essayist*, a *bibliographer*, a *commentator*, a *novelist*, a *journalist of travels*, a *political writer*, an *epistolary writer*, a *theologian*, and a *poet*."[32] With the rise of the first commentators on Johnson outside his literary circle, we see with Anderson the beginning of the concept of his multifarious genius. The *Dictionary* is no longer a Herculean labor, but one of a variety of works that qualify Johnson as a philologist. We see that Johnson did not regard himself as a philologist, but his scientifically minded contemporaries (Anderson was a physician) did. Both Webster and Murray saw their dictionaries as philological works; the *OED* was actually sponsored by a learned group called the Philological Society. Yet the mythic Johnson has a long reach because, as I said earlier, we *want* the figure of Johnson-the-bully, master of the rapier one-liner. More than forty years after his death, Henry Digby Best, a zealous collector of anecdotes, told of how his wife and sister-in-law "were every now and then honoured by the visits of Dr. Johnson":

He called on them one day soon after the publication of his immortal dictionary. The two ladies paid him due compliments on the occasion. Amongst other topics of praise they very much commended the omission of all *naughty* words. "What, my dears! then you have been looking for them?" asked the moralist. The ladies, confused at being thus caught, dropped the subject of the dictionary.[33]

Third-hand hearsay, especially third-hand hearsay that appears more than forty years after a person's death and nearly eighty years after the events it purports to represent, has no historical value, but many biographers of Johnson have come across this story and love to include it as if it really happened.[34] H. D. Best is known for other bits of charming anecdote that we love to quote.[35] Whom do these harmless stories of the legendary Johnson not please?

The allegorical life of Johnson, as Bate first proposed it, is a brilliant invention that he derived from a legion of stories about the legendary Johnson which emerge mainly in the forty years after his death, and which editors of Boswell have embalmed and treasured up on purpose to a life beyond life. The Johnsonian scholars of the 1950s inaugurated a process which is still underway of disinterring the real Johnson from these sediments of anecdote, an archaeological feat akin to that of Heinrich Schliemann's excavating the lost city of Troy. Along the way Schliemann found many artifacts, shards and gleanings of what he considered to be the Homeric past, greatly valuable in tracing ancient civilizations, but not the real Troy. The mythology of Johnson's *Dictionary*, these layers of anecdote that surround the history of his book, do not merit the serious treatment archaeologists have given to the artifacts Schliemann and others have excavated at the site of ancient Ilium. Yet an understanding of the legendary Johnson, as I have tried to outline it here, must precede broader intellectual theory that allows us to understand the magnitude of his achievement.

NOTES

1. *The People's Palace: The Story of the Chicago Cultural Center* (Chicago: Chicago Cultural Center, 1999), unpaged, describes the architecture and literary inscriptions.
2. Walter Jackson Bate, *The Achievement of Samuel Johnson* (New York: Oxford University Press, 1955), p. v: "The emphasis in this book has been on Johnson's own writings."
3. *The Works of Samuel Johnson, LL.D.*, 11 vols. (London, 1787), vol. XI, pp. 195–216. G. B. Hill reprints the "Apophthegms" in *Johnsonian Miscellanies*, ed. G. B. Hill, 2 vols. (Oxford: Clarendon Press, 1897), vol. II, pp. 1–20, with speculations about the sources.
4. *The Achievement of Samuel Johnson*, p. 51; cf. pp. 42, 44.
5. "Questions Answered," *The Times*, 13 March 2003. Commentators often enlarge Johnson's disabilities to suit themselves. Lennard J. Davis, for instance, discussing Johnson's "multiple disabilities," confidently assures us that "His face was . . . ravaged extensively by smallpox"; see "Dr. Johnson, Amelia, and the Discourse of Disability in the Eighteenth Century," in *"Defects": Engendering the Modern Body*, ed. Helen Deutsch and Felicity Nussbaum (Ann Arbor: University of Michigan Press, 2000), pp. 54–74, on p. 54. There is no basis for this assertion; Johnson only once mentioned that he had had smallpox as a child, but no contemporary ever speaks of how visible or extensive were the scars, if any.
6. *Lives of the English Poets*, ed. G. B. Hill, 3 vols. (Oxford: Clarendon Press, 1905), vol. III, p. 47.
7. *The Correspondence . . . of James Boswell Relating to the Making of the "Life of Johnson,"* ed. Marshall Waingrow (New York: McGraw-Hill, 1969), pp. 87–88.
8. See *ibid.*, p. 87 n. 15; cf. *Life*, vol. I, p. 528.
9. See *A Voyage to Abyssinia*, in Yale *Works*, vol. XV, pp. 3–6. If Johnson wrote this preface, too, in bed, then he must have had some reference books with him.

10. See Arthur Murphy, *An Essay on the Life and Genius of Samuel Johnson, LL.D.*, in 1825 *Works*, vol. I, p. xxi.

11. *The Politics of Samuel Johnson* (New Haven: Yale University Press, 1960), p. 122. Greene adds in a note, "If the remark were to be taken seriously, it would be a very puzzling one. After all, most of the opponents of Walpole were Whigs, too" (pp. 311–12).

12. *Anecdotes of the Late Samuel Johnson, LL.D.*, ed. S. C. Roberts (Cambridge: Cambridge University Press, 1925), p. 150. In *Thraliana*, ed. Katharine C. Balderston, 2 vols. (Oxford: Clarendon Press, 1942), vol. I, p. 195, Piozzi remembers asking Johnson about the assault in December 1777; no folio enters the picture there, either.

13. John Nichols, *Literary Anecdotes*, 9 vols. (London, 1812–15), vol. VIII, p. 446. See *Miscellanies*, vol. I, p. 304. Nichols says he saw an annotation in the book attesting to its rare provenance.

14. See *Catalogus Bibliothecae Harleianae*, 5 vols. (London, 1743–45), vol. I, pp. 1–30 (the preface has a separate pagination).

15. Thomas Kaminski, *The Early Career of Samuel Johnson* (New York: Oxford University Press, 1987), p. 182.

16. *The School for Scandal*, in *The Dramatic Works of Richard Brinsley Sheridan*, ed. Cecil Price, 2 vols. (Oxford: Clarendon Press, 1973), vol. I, p. 429 (act 5, scene 2).

17. *Rambler* 134. Bate appears to accept this anecdote (*Achievement*, p. 28); the Yale editors observe that Johnson had not met Reynolds at this time (Yale *Works*, vol. IV, p. 345).

18. Thomas Carlyle, *Samuel Johnson* (London, 1853), p. 74.

19. The original of this painting is in the National Portrait Gallery. See also Irma S. Lustig, "Facts and Deductions: The Curious History of Reynolds's First Portrait of Johnson, 1756," *The Age of Johnson: A Scholarly Annual* 1 (1987), 161–80.

20. See *The Collected Works of Oliver Goldsmith*, ed. Arthur Friedman, 5 vols. (Oxford: Clarendon Press, 1966), vol. I, pp. 447–48.

21. William Makepeace Thackeray, *Vanity Fair*, ed. Peter L. Shillingsburg (New York and London: Garland, 1989), p. 8. Thackeray claims that Miss Pinkerton owes her eminence to having met Johnson decades earlier, part of his arch ridicule of the *Dictionary*. In chapter 54, however, Rawdon Crawley uses a copy of the *Dictionary* to write his challenge to Lord Steyne (p. 487). There is a counterpoint here between the social climber Rebecca, who spurns her copy of Johnson, and her husband, who needs it to transact the affairs of gallantry.

22. Edward Matthew Ward (1816–79) specialized in history paintings of scenes from English literature (this scene derives from Boswell); the original of this painting is in the Tate Gallery.

23. John Hawkins, *The Life of Samuel Johnson, LL.D.* (London, 1787), p. 189.

24. *Life*, vol. I, p. 287. Alvin Kernan, *Printing Technology, Letters & Samuel Johnson* (Princeton: Princeton University Press, 1987), has Johnson "somewhat deflated" by Millar's comment and coming up with his retort as a concession (p. 183).

25. Bruce Redford, in his appendix of "Letters Substantiated by Mention" in *Letters*, vol. v, pp. 37–48, does not include this exchange, whose existence is highly dubious.
26. See *Samuel Johnson's Dictionary: Selections . . .*, ed. Jack Lynch (Delray Beach, Fla.: Levenger Press, 2002; New York: Walker & Co., 2003), p. 590. For one of the misquotations see James Trager, *The Food Chronology* (New York: Henry Holt, 1995): "a cereal grass of the genus *avena* (*avoin* in France), the best-known species being Scots oats, a grain they fed [*sic*] to horses, fine live-stock, and to men in Scotland" (pp. 162–63).
27. See John Wain, *Samuel Johnson: A Biography* (New York: Viking Press, 1974), pp. 162–70. Kernan is not content with the death of Elizabeth Johnson, and asserts that the *Dictionary* was "Written . . . by a living man whose wife *and mother* . . . died while he was working on [it]" (*Printing Technology, Letters & Samuel Johnson*, p. 185; my italics).
28. Johnson, however, according to Kernan (who overlooks Johnson's legal orations for the benefit of Boswell), was not a gifted speaker.
29. Redford notes that Boswell supplies the date of 7 February in the second edition of the *Life*, but does not surmise how he decided on it (*Letters*, vol. i, p. 94).
30. For a lengthy discussion of Johnson's quest for an academic degree before the publication of the *Dictionary*, see Chris P. Pearce, "Johnson's Proud Folio: The Material and Rhetorical Contexts of Johnson's Preface to the *Dictionary*," *The Age of Johnson: A Scholarly Annual* 15 (2004), 1–35.
31. Webster, *An American Dictionary of the English Language*, 2 vols. (New York, 1828), vol. i, sig. A2^{v}, quotes Johnson's preface and alludes to it elsewhere (vol. i, sig. A3^{r}), mentioning his own "frigid indifference." Murray quotes Johnson's Preface in *A New English Dictionary*, 13 vols. (Oxford: Clarendon Press, 1888–1933), vol. i, p. xi.
32. *The Life of Samuel Johnson, LL.D., with Critical Observations on His Works* (Edinburgh, 1815), p. 491.
33. *Personal and Literary Memorials* (London, 1829), p. 11; cf. *Miscellanies*, vol. ii, p. 390.
34. Joseph Wood Krutch, *Samuel Johnson* (New York: Henry Holt, 1944), p. 127, treats this story as received truth; Lynch cites the story as deriving from "an early biography" (*Samuel Johnson's Dictionary*, p. 9).
35. Best's most widely known anecdote, which Hill included in the *Life*, although it has nothing whatsoever to do with Johnson, is the comment of William Henry Duke of Gloucester to Gibbon on receiving the second volume of his *History of the Decline and Fall of the Roman Empire*: "Another d—mned thick, square book! Always scribble, scribble, scribble! Eh! Mr. Gibbon?" See Boswell's *Life*, vol. ii, p. 2.

CHAPTER 2

Dictionaries and power from Palsgrave to Johnson

Ian Lancashire

The early modern English dictionary had three makers: the lexicographer, the printer-publisher, and the patron. The first wrote it, the second financed it, and the third ensured that it would be bought by others. Why some patrons also gave funds to the first two, Johnson professed not to understand: "I considered," he wrote in his *Plan*, "such acts of beneficence as prodigies, recorded rather to raise wonder than expectation" (1825 *Works*, vol. v, p. 2). Atypically, the "English Dictionary" which Johnson created and a consortium of printers led by Robert Dodsley funded and published, had, to all appearances, no patron.[1] Why it did not has been a subject of speculation for decades. I will argue that sixteenth- and seventeenth-century patrons of dictionaries published in England had two things in mind: they hoped to fix English as a peer among European languages, and they believed that by flooding the language with foreign-language terms, particularly from French, they could succeed. For English royalty and nobility, language capacity was a measure of national power. To *preserve* the English of his country's best authors (1825 *Works*, vol. v, p. 3) and to stall the demand for lexical imitation and copiousness, Johnson had to reject his would-be patron. Men like Chesterfield had for over two centuries led English into an identity crisis by preferring calques – what Elizabeth Hedrick has called "words without a past . . . a mob of rebellious bastards."[2]

Despite publishing a *Plan* addressed to Philip Dormer Stanhope, fourth Earl of Chesterfield, in 1747, Johnson explained in his Preface that his *Dictionary* "was written . . . without any patronage of the great" (1825 *Works*, vol. v, p. 51). Strictly speaking that was untrue. Chesterfield had met Johnson to discuss the *Plan* and had given Johnson a small sum, £10, for expenses. Paul J. Korshin has shown that "small gift patronage" was common.[3] Johnson revised the text of the *Plan* to include the earl's advice and agreed to act as his "delegate" in purifying English usage. Chesterfield's willingness to accept Johnson's addressing the *Plan* to him also strengthened Dodsley's position with the consortium of publishers who backed the project with funds to pay Johnson. Just as important, Robert Dodsley had already acknowledged Chesterfield to be his own patron.[4] Because Johnson regarded Dodsley as his "patron" for having negotiated a contract of £1,575 to undertake the lexicographical work, as well as for ensuring that Johnson got £100 more than that as his needs mounted,[5] Johnson would have had to be obtuse not to recognize an indirect obligation to Chesterfield, his patron's patron. And in November and December 1754, Chesterfield did Dodsley and the *Dictionary* another favor: he published in Dodsley's own weekly, *The World*, two complimentary articles about Johnson's work as lexicographer.[6] The earl issued this imprimatur five months before the printer, William Strahan, delivered the finished work, and helped guarantee a sale to those of means, for only they could afford the book at £4 10s. per copy.

Despite these favors, Johnson went out of his way to write Chesterfield an acerbic letter in February 1755, rejecting his articles in *The World* and any implication in them that the earl was patron to the *Dictionary*. Johnson accused Chesterfield of having refused to see him when he called at his place. Later he retracted that charge, and told Boswell that his bitterness was occasioned not by a specific incident, but by "continued neglect" (Reddick, *The Making of Johnson's Dictionary*, p. 23). It was in the *Dictionary* that he most clearly registered contempt for Chesterfield's patronage. Johnson met most traditional expectations for the contents of a sizable lexicon – by the mid-seventeenth century these included a preface, a history of the language, the citation of previous dictionaries, notes on etymology, and even sample quotations – but he left out one thing everyone expected to find: testimonies of advice and assent, that is, a dedication to someone in authority, and complimentary poems by the author's friends.[7] Even Johnson's main competitor, Nathan Bailey's very commercial *Universal Etymological English Dictionary* (1749), had a dedication – to the entire royal family.[8]

Johnson said that he expected Chesterfield to give him money. Yet "By what right," as Jacob Leed asked, "did Johnson blame Chesterfield for not coming to his aid?"[9] The printer normally bore all the expenses of dictionary-making. From the early Renaissance, the printer was often the lexicographer himself. The first English lexicon printed in London, an explication of law-words in the statutes, saw light in 1523 only because John Rastell was both its compiler and its publisher.[10] Peter Treveris published another lexical encyclopedia, the so-called *Grete Herball*, in 1526, but the name of the lexicographer is not even mentioned.[11] Treveris paid the bill, and this herbal is now known by his name. Henry VIII encouraged John

Palsgrave, one of Thomas Wolsey's servants and a tutor for the Princess Mary, to undertake his English–French *Lesclarcissement* (1530), the first great bilingual dictionary of the sixteenth century. Accordingly, Palsgrave dedicated the work to the King. Yet Palsgrave had paid for the printing of his own dictionary and received from Henry only a crown-protected copyright for seven years.[12] This control enabled Palsgrave to hand-pick those to whom the publisher could sell the book,[13] and that permission was infrequent. Later Thomas Thomas – whose Latin–English dictionary partly supplanted Thomas Cooper's *Thesaurus* and who dedicated it to none other than William Cecil, Lord Burghley – was himself printer to the University of Cambridge.[14] John Minsheu, whom Johnson regularly cites, had no alternative but to print and distribute, "at his own risk," his own *Ductor in linguas* (1617).[15] The Tudors and Stuarts were enthusiasts for languages, but they made no financial investment. Yet lexicographer-printers did not moan about lack of patronage, and Palsgrave, Elyot, Cooper, and Minsheu did not attack the Crown because it had not bankrolled their work.

What we know about the early modern English lexicon suggests that a two-tiered patronage system commonly produced dictionaries. The printer patronized the lexicographer (unless the two were the same) by paying him a fee; the influence of a noble patron enabled the printer to sell enough copies in order to recoup monies that went out to pay for the lexicographer's time and expenses, and for printing costs, and to make a profit. Against this background, Chesterfield's behavior is not atypical. It is curious, however, that Johnson kept silent on the money he obtained from the contract with the printers. It goes thankless in his Preface. In 1580, Henry Bynneman obtained a monopoly for printing the Lily–Colet grammar, and – at the urging of the Earl of Leicester and Sir Christopher Hatton – another for printing Thomas Cooper's *Thesaurus* and all dictionaries in all languages. This action shows that lexicons had become, for printers, as lucrative as the Bible and the statutes.[16] John Barnes (son of the printer who owned John Rider's great English–Latin dictionary of 1588) launched a lawsuit against a syndicate of stationers for copyright infringement, in the documents about which we learn that they spent more than one hundred marks in paying Francis Holyoake to do the revision.[17] Nothing had changed by the beginning of the eighteenth century, when the most valuable copyrights continued to hold for dictionaries and religious works. Johnson, of course, did not hold the copyright to his great work: his publishers did, and even the King's Printer, Strahan, bought shares in it by 1760.[18] Johnson's objections must have worried Dodsley; his employee was biting the hands that fed him. Johnson did not have the excuse of Sir Thomas Urquhart – utter neglect – when he dedicated his *Logopandecteision* in 1653 to "No-body," "My non supponent Lord."[19] Johnson deleted a patron from his *Dictionary*.

Under the new conditions that Johnson dictated, the lexicographer did not inherit the printer's obligations to his patron. The old compact of dictionary-makers fell apart under Johnson. A closer look at why patrons accepted dedications in the preceding two centuries will show how.

At the opening of his Preface, Johnson describes the "writer of dictionaries" as occupying one of the "lower employments of life," as a "humble drudge."[20] He defines *drudge* as "One employed in mean labour; a slave; one doomed to servile occupation" and supplies, among several illustrative quotations, a sentence from Tillotson's "Sermon 4": "The hard master makes men serve him for nought, who rewards his *drudges*, and slaves with nothing but shame and sorrow, and misery." Johnson's readers have been amused for two and a half centuries by this admission, but he was serious, and his anger went beyond Chesterfield, whom Reddick termed his "faithless patron" (*The Making of Johnson's Dictionary*, p. 2), to his true masters, the consortium of printers to whom he had failed to deliver a finished dictionary in 1749. Much has been made of Johnson's words against Chesterfield and patrons in general, but little of the silence in his Preface about his contract with the printers, and especially about his friend Dodsley. Johnson closes the Preface by explaining that the delay in finishing the *Dictionary* meant that all those he had hoped to please by its publication were dead. Johnson, in 1755, therefore did not hope to please either Chesterfield or the printers.

Hired lexicographers had for several centuries been in low esteem, particularly when making English monolingual glossaries. When schoolmaster Richard Mulcaster urged his countrymen to prepare a monolingual English dictionary for the 8,000 words he listed in his *Elementarie* (1582),[21] no one rushed into the breach. Patronless, Edmund Coote produced the first general English hard-word list in his *English Schoole-Maister* (1596), but he got no honor from the book or from the fifty-four editions it received to 1737.[22] In fact, he lost his job as a schoolmaster at Bury St. Edmunds about the time that his textbook appeared. Robert Cawdrey's *Table Alphabeticall* (1604), a small quarto with but four editions to 1617, and his successor John Bullokar's *English Expositor* (1616), another small quarto with nineteen editions to 1775, took themselves out of the market for significant lexicons by aiming at an uneducated population and by dedicating their glossaries to ladies.[23] Henry Cockeram's *English Dictionarie* (1623), with twelve editions to 1670, doubled the size of Cawdrey and Bullokar largely by supplying the same glossary twice, once with hard words as headwords, and once with the corresponding easy words as headwords.[24] Thomas Blount's *Glossographia* (1656), a remarkable antiquarian dictionary of several decades' effort with more than ten thousand word-entries, has quotations and etymologies, but it disappeared after only five editions, partly because his successor, Edward Phillips, plagiarized almost the entire work in *The New World of Words* (1658), which enjoyed two more editions than Blount and lasted until 1720.[25] Elisha Coles's *English Dictionary* (1676), lacking a patron, had eleven editions to 1732, and his successors, John Kersey (1702) and Nathan Bailey (1721), expanded the hard-word glossary into full English dictionaries.[26] Collectively, their monolingual lexicons went through many editions, plagiarizing from one another freely and silently, surviving on sales, their targeted readership being uneducated craftsmen and merchants, children preparing for grammar school, and ladies.

Johnson showed little admiration for most of these, the English lexicographers who preceded him. Of the 342 lexicons Johnson catalogued in the Harley library, not one English monolingual dictionary received an annotation. As Korshin shows, Johnson's lexicographical tastes ran to major polyglot dictionaries, almost uniformly by Continental authors.[27] Johnson's own library, when catalogued after his death, had no general monolingual English lexicon, as far as we can tell. A single bundle of three dictionaries in lot 532, otherwise unnamed, might have held a Bailey, of course, but the only English lexicons Johnson possessed at his death were John Gerard's herbal (a lexical encyclopedia from 1633), three bilingual dictionaries (a Latin–English dictionary by Holyoake and Dutch–English lexicons by Henry Hexham and William Sewel), John Ray's proverbs, and Minsheu's etymological dictionary of eleven languages, *Ductor in linguas*.[28] Johnson bought books by those who showed knowledge that he lacked, especially in the sciences of language, law, and plants.

Johnson regarded two of these, among about a dozen early modern English dictionary-writers, highly enough to acknowledge the definitions he took from them in 1755. His Preface mentions Edward Phillips (Milton's nephew) and Nathan Bailey, as well as Robert Ainsworth (for his Latin–English lexicon, evidently the second edition of 1746). Quotations also come from the "Doctor of Languages" in London, John Minsheu, and John Gerard, for his great herbal as revised and published by Thomas Johnson in 1633. Johnson also cites John Cowell's legal lexicon, *The Interpreter* (1607); Richard Rowland's *Restitution* (1605); lawyer Thomas Blount's legal *Nomo-Lexikon* (1670), though not his *Glossographia* (1656); Stephen Skinner's Latin work of English etymology, *Etymologicon linguae anglicanae* (1671); Joseph Moxon's *Mechanick Exercises* (1677–83); Abel Boyer's *Royal Dictionary* (1699; French and English); Francis Junius's *Etymologicum Anglicanum* (edited by Edward Lye in 1743); and Thomas Wallis's farrier's dictionary (1726).[29]

Several of them may have appealed to Johnson for more than their erudition: Cowell, Minsheu, and even Blount were, like him, aggrieved authors. James I suppressed Cowell's legal lexicon by proclamation in 1610 after an outcry about his interpretation of the King's authority over Parliament. Publicly humiliated as John "cow-heel," forced to resign from his position as Regius Professor of Civil Law at Cambridge, copies of his work confiscated and burned by the public hangman, this Oxford scholar died a year after his disgrace. Only in 1637 was his learned book republished, and only much later did John Manley edit and expand it with a defense of its author. Minsheu's case was almost as bad. No printer-publisher would take on his etymology, and the stationers would not contract to buy it. Minsheu had to solicit subscribers personally in order to escape debt; he even prepared individual dedication pages as an incentive. The title of a sheet that lists these subscribers shows his indignation.[30] Minsheu was forced to sell the book personally to subscribers after he had already committed the funds to pay for its publication and had discovered that the stationers had no intention of bailing him out of his predicament. This indignation rings a little hollow; he was as great a thief as any dictionary-writer in the period, having inserted most of Cowell's entries into the *Ductor* without acknowledgment.

Blount enjoyed scarcely two years of profit from the publication of his *Glossographia* before Edward Phillips silently plagiarized the bulk of it. The lesson from this "Theft," Blount argued, was "That such a Dictionary cannot be hudled up in Eight or ten Moneths, nor without much industry and care, though the Author be never so learned."[31] Blount also had reason to be unhappy with Thomas Manley, who at least acknowledged the copying. Based on Cowell's book, Manley's *Nomothetes* (1672) was supplemented with many entries from Blount's *Nomo-Lexikon, A Law-Dictionary*. In 1673 Blount took some satisfaction by publishing *A World of Errors Discovered in the New World of Words, or General English Dictionary, and in Nomothetes, or the Interpreter of Law-Words and Terms*. Manley had in fact observed the letter of the copyright law of 1662–63, which forbade only verbatim copying: unauthorized re-use of an author's work was permitted if minor additions, deletions, and changes in word-order and phrasing were introduced on every page. Blount still called him a "Land-Pirate," though it is worth noting that Blount himself plagiarized liberally from the work of his predecessors.

Johnson generally ignores lexicons with undistinguished dedicatees, or with none at all, like those by Coote, Cawdrey, Bullokar, Cockeram, Coles, and Kersey. All the lexicographers he favors had important patrons. John Gerard chose Sir William Cecil, Lord Treasurer of England, Elizabeth's favorite counselor; Richard Bancroft, Archbishop of Canterbury, made John Cowell his vicar-general after receiving the dedication of his *Interpretor*; Minsheu dedicated *Ductor in linguas* to James I. Blount dedicated *Nomo-Lexikon* to three eminent legal minds: Sir Orlando Bridgeman, Lord Keeper of the Great Seal, and two Lord Chief Justices, Sir John Kelynge (Court of King's Bench) and Sir John Vaughan (Court of Common Pleas). Ainsworth's English–Latin lexicon, licensed by George II, was dedicated to the king's physician, Richard Mead. The history of English lexicography from 1500 shows that major dictionaries or lexical encyclopedias seldom went forward without a patron who, in Johnson's terms, was likely guilty of "continued neglect."

The most powerful patron of early modern English was Henry VIII, a master of neglect. He encouraged John Palsgrave to produce his English–French *Lesclarcissement* to strengthen English, and the reputation of its language experts, against French. At the Field of the Cloth of Gold in 1521 Henry celebrated his sovereignty over French territory and his power in Europe. Palsgrave offered the King another opportunity to subjugate an old rival. In his Introduction Palsgrave says, "If any one of vs all [Alexander Barclay, Petrus Vallensys, and Palsgrave himself] . . . haue by our diligent labours nowe at the laste/brought the frenche tong vnder any rules certayn & preceptes grammaticall . . . we haue nat onely done the thyng whiche by our noble graces progenitours/of all antiquite so moche hath ben desyred," because the French "tong for the most generall is corrupted for want of rules and preceptes grammaticall" (*Lesclarcissement*, sig. A3ᵛ). The *Lesclarcissement* made English terms the headwords, as if asserting the relative importance of the two languages, and in so doing reduced a "corrupted" Gallic tongue to "rules certayn." Palsgrave mapped English words to French and supplied potential neologisms in English wherever equivalents for French words were lacking. English benefited, although it would take more than French terms to strengthen an anemic early Tudor English vocabulary. Yet Henry VIII gave Palsgrave no money. Sir Thomas Elyot's Latin–English *Dictionary* (1538), also dedicated to Henry VIII, was finished only at the King's instance.[32] Elyot's conversion of material from Continental polyglot lexicons into English significantly expanded the English vocabulary. Most word-entries showed which Latin forms were suitable for calquing; and there was no English dictionary or authoritative census of its vocabulary to prevent anyone from inventing words. Again, the King did not spend any of his money on a favored lexicographer's effort.[33]

The law was a good friend to the Renaissance English lexicon from the time of John Rastell's *Exposition* (1523). How powerful an incentive it was to the language can be seen in William Salesbury's *Dictionary in Englyshe and Welshe*, published in 1547 to encourage the Welsh to learn English. Salesbury's effort grew from a statute in 1535–36 (27 Henry VIII) that all proceedings in the Courts of Wales must be kept in English: "fromehensforth no personne or personnes that use the Welsshe speche or langage shall have or enjoy any maneroffice or fees within the Realme of Englond Wales or other the Kinges Dominions, upon peyn of forfaiting the same offices or fees, onles he or they use and exercise the speche or langage of Englisshe."[34] Under the early Tudors, what superficially appears to be another bilingual dictionary turns out to have been published to strengthen the English tongue. Inevitably, Salesbury dedicated his work to Henry VIII.

Under Elizabeth, royal patronage for dictionaries declined. Although she permitted Henry Lyte to dedicate his herbal to her in 1578, crown policy did not, openly at least, support the engorgement of English with foreign words. Her trusted partners in negotiating the Elizabethan compromise in religious dogma, William Cecil and Archbishop Matthew Parker, stimulated interest in reviving ancient native Saxon words by lending their patronage to two men who founded Old English scholarship in the 1560s and 1570s.[35] Laurence Nowell devised his bilingual Old English lexicon, dating from about 1567, while living at Cecil's own house. At Nowell's death, his lexicon must have been passed by William Lambarde, a friend, to John Joscelyn, who worked with Archbishop Parker's own son to produce the "Dictionarium Saxonico-Latinum."[36] The Elizabethan Society of Antiquaries was founded in 1572 on scholarship of Nowell, Joscelyn, and Lambarde. The Queen's indirect stimulation of their work may have stemmed from concern that English was being overwhelmed by what the logician Thomas Wilson called "ink-horn terms" imported from languages whose peoples were often hostile to the English.[37]

Elizabethan lexicographers dedicated dictionaries to members of the nobility, not in payment for past financial backing but in hope of business to come. The reward might take many forms. Cooper dedicated his great *Thesaurus linguae romanae* to Robert Dudley, Earl of Leicester, and got bishoprics from the Queen afterwards. In 1591, three years after the defeat of the Spanish fleet, Richard Percevall dedicated his Spanish–English dictionary to Robert, Earl of Essex, Ewe, Viscount Hereford, and Bourghchier, Lord Ferrers of Chartley. Essex's failure in Ireland in 1599 forced

John Minsheu to resort to lesser nobility in his revision of Percivall that same year: Sir John Scot, Sir Henry Bromley, Sir Edward Grevel, and Master William Fortescue. John Florio also dedicated his Italian–English *Worlde of Words* (1598) to three noblemen, the Earls of Southampton, Bedford, and Rutland, but Florio made his living as much from teaching Italian to the nobility as from his books.[38]

The Stuarts exerted more direct control of dictionary-makers. Francis Holyoake in 1606 dedicated his revision of John Rider's English–Latin dictionary (1588) to Henry, Prince of Wales. Florio, the prince's tutor in Italian, not only dedicated his second edition of the Italian–English lexicon (1611) to Queen Anna but also named the book after her.[39] Lord Burghley gave his patronage to Randle Cotgrave's great French–English dictionary in the same year. James repressed Cowell's law lexicon four years later for its championing of divine right but accepted Minsheu's dedication of the troubled *Ductor* to him in 1617. The mind of James worked as did that of Henry VIII, the namesake of his older son. Bilingual dictionaries served not the foreign tongue but English, by enhancing its copiousness.

An amusingly entrepreneurial lexicographer at this time was Sir Henry Mainwaring, whose "Nomenclator Navalis," the first sea dictionary, was remarkable for existing in sixteen manuscripts before it reached print. For five years, until Captain John Smith's *Sea Grammar* appeared in 1627, Mainwaring cornered the market in sea language. He dedicated the "Nomenclator" first to Edward, Lord Zouch, Lord Warden of the Cinque Ports, his patron, in February 1623. Mainwaring then produced other single copies dedicated to the Duke of Buckingham, George Abbot, Archbishop of Canterbury, and Algernon Percy, Earl of Northumberland. Sea-words had a dollar value for members of the English nobility who, though they had never gone to sea, were transported by royal favor into positions where they would have to command ships. Mainwaring's manuscript got into print only in 1644, on the verge of the Civil War, at a time when the nobility were more concerned with land enterprises than with ones by sea. Mainwaring's practice of dedicating his lexicon afresh to every purchaser recalls John Minsheu's desperate measures in 1617.[40]

Under Charles I, the Civil War curtailed the ambitions of patrons to influence the growth of English, although the King permitted John Parkinson to dedicate a herbal to him in 1640. With the Restoration, King and Court once more turned their lexical eyes to French models. Charles Hoole dedicated his *Lexicon tetraglotton*, an English–French–Italian–Spanish dictionary, to Charles II in May 1660, Adam Littleton his

Linguae latinae to the King in 1678, and Abel Boyer his French lexicon to His Royal Highness, William, Duke of Gloucester, in 1694. It was the English gentry, nobility, and royals, according to researchers in diachronic English linguistics, who introduced new French forms into conversation. Tertu Nevalainen points out that the number of unassimilated French loan-words from 1651 to 1700 more than doubles those from 1550 to 1650.[41] Under the Stuarts, polyglot and bilingual lexicographers, the predecessors Johnson admired, commonly dedicated work to a royal or noble patron. These patrons increased the cosmopolitan reputation of English culture and encouraged the wealthy to create lucrative ties with the Continent.

In retrospect, then, the Crown and the Court patronized dictionaries in the early modern period so as to swell English with new words from other European tongues. Although lexical engorgement served patriotic ends, a backlash was to be expected. Edmund Bolton tried but failed to get Parliament, from 1617 to 1624, to charter a language academy.[42] In 1649 George Snell unsuccessfully proposed that English be controlled by law (see Jones, *The Triumph of the English Language*, pp. 295–96), but with the founding of the Royal Society, which set up a committee in 1664 to improve English for philosophical purposes, a new patron seemed to have stepped up for English, one determined to stabilize, regulate, and define its vocabulary scientifically. The first English thesaurus-lexicon by Bishop Wilkins and William Lloyd (1668), dedicated to the president of the Royal Society, and the first universal English dictionary, by Elisha Coles (1676), did so, but by then the Society's committee had long since disbanded.[43] The friends of linguistic entrenchment and isolationism retreated into the literary world, nurtured by authors like John Evelyn, Thomas Sprat, John Dryden, Thomas Addison, Jonathan Swift, and Alexander Pope. Johnson was their standard-bearer, not in fixing the tongue but in reining in those who would gallicize it.[44]

Johnson's rejection of Chesterfield as patron should be understood against this historical background. Crown and Court traditionally exercised their power over English by awarding patronage to printers of dictionaries and grammars, usually expressed as copyright protection and public approval. For more than two hundred years, this informal policy had been to expand the vocabulary of English by importing words from European languages. Bilingual dictionaries by Palsgrave, John Baret, Cotgrave, Boyer, and others served to frenchify English diction, as indeed the Stuart and Restoration Courts favored Gallic culture generally. Translation of French works into English, as Johnson recognized, brought many new calques into the language. Johnson's antipathy to words carelessly introduced by translators from French has a history. In the Preface to his *New English Dictionary* (1702), more than fifty years before Johnson, John Kersey promised to purge all "obsolete, barbarous, foreign" words, "an innumerable multitude of *Greek, Latin, French, Italian, Spanish, British, Saxon*, and old *English* Words . . . which are never used in *English*."[45] His Preface objected to the frenchifying of English through the introduction of Gallicisms in bad translations. From this perspective, Johnson's francophobic sentiments are inherited and reformist. Moved by the same Teutonic patriotism we find in Richard Rowlands's *Restitution of Decayed Intelligence* (1605, and one of Johnson's sources), Johnson used a dictionary to *preserve* a by-then decreasingly vital stream of English, what had been written and spoken by literary people from 1580 to 1660. Restoration English, and the language of Johnson's own time, introduced change and revitalized the tongue. The mechanism for that innovation, foreign idioms, was anathema to Johnson because it left English "copious without order" (1825 *Works*, vol. v, p. 23).

Chesterfield approved of Johnson's *Plan* in 1747, but it had no anti-Gallic sentiments. Johnson's Preface introduced them in 1755, and Chesterfield may have read it because in his articles in *The World*, for 28 November and 5 December 1754, he condemns mere "WORD-BOOKS" of the English language for their indiscriminate mixture of "good and bad" terms, allowing English to "be overwhelmed and crushed by unnecessary foreign ornaments."[46] Although not singling out French, Chesterfield contrasts it, spread by means of the military victories of Louis IV "over most parts of Europe, to the degree of making it almost a universal" language, with English, which spreads under its "own weight and merit" (*The World* 100, p. 602). The time has come, the Earl writes, for someone to put linguistic "anarchy" to "Good order" and discriminate between good borrowings and bad. Chesterfield at first seems reconciled to Johnson's censures for frenchifying because he nominates Johnson as a dictator of English usage and, in this, reveals a sympathy for the notion of a controlling academy.[47]

Yet Chesterfield makes a conditional "total surrender" of his "rights and privileges in the English language" to Johnson only "during the term of his dictatorship." In conceding to him papal infallibility "while in the chair; but no longer," does Chesterfield, with Dodsley's tacit approval, hint that Johnson might never enjoy a second edition? Like any new dictionary, Johnson's tome could be quickly dispatched by plagiarist competitors. Only months after it appeared, rival printers put out Joseph Nicol Scott's revision of Nathan Bailey in *The New Universal English Dictionary*, which plagiarized from Johnson's work, offered 25,000 more headwords, and went at half the price. Only by bringing out a dictionary repeatedly, in successively larger and larger editions over several decades, in which each edition swallowed the innovations of lesser lexicographers, could a printer prosper in the competitive dictionary industry, and could a lexicographer maintain his "dictatorship." Chesterfield also complains about a potentially tyrannical "act of power" (*The World* 100, p. 605) in Johnson's rule: the banishment of the vocabulary and the grammar of "the BEAU MONDE" (p. 610). Chesterfield urges Johnson, at first with tongue in cheek, to add a supplemental dictionary of predominantly Gallic terms used by "The fashionable world, 'society'" (as the *OED* defines that phrase). The Earl gallantly attributes this power to the speech of ladies of fashion. In return for Johnson's acquiescence, Chesterfield evenhandedly insists that those same ladies should use Johnson's spelling rules and avoid their unsystematized "auricular orthography" or spelling by sound (p. 608). This banter makes occasion for two amusing stories about the lapses of women taking lovers, and we might conclude that the Earl is having some fun, had he not, in his last paragraph, "seriously" advised Johnson to undertake this supplement in order to bring its neologisms "within the pale of the English language" and to make customers of his "countrywomen, the enrichers, the patronesses, and the harmonizers" of English (p. 610).

Coming from the hand of Dodsley's patron, in a journal published by Dodsley, this request calls Johnson's principles of exclusion into question and asks him to reconsider. Dodsley might have been alarmed that Johnson had just two-thirds the number of word-entries of the leading English lexicographer, Nathan Bailey,[48] that he chose headwords sanctioned by writers mainly living between 1580 and 1660, and that he pretended to exclude neologisms favored by those sufficiently well off to buy the book. Did Dodsley have that concern in mind when he mentioned the imminent publication of Johnson's *Dictionary* to Chesterfield, whose fluency in French was well known, and whose life was largely spent in the *beau monde* and overseas in European capitals? Having ceded to Bailey the claim of most compendious English dictionary, serving all arts and sciences, Johnson would have to appeal to the upper classes, those not directly earning their livelihood by trade. Chesterfield's proposal for a supplement has been thought "rather silly, trivial, and ill informed" (Reddick, *The Making of Johnson's Dictionary*, p. 78), but the former secretary of state was no fool.

Chesterfield begins his first article in *The World* with news that Dodsley advised him that Johnson's work would be published "this winter." The *Dictionary* came out four months later, on 15 April 1755, just six weeks after

Dodsley had taken the unusual step of freely releasing 1,500 copies of the *Plan*, with its dedicatory address to Chesterfield intact. Dodsley gave away these copies barely three weeks after Johnson's acerbic letter to the Earl, which Johnson begins: "I have been lately informed by the Proprietor of The World that two Papers in which my Dictionary is recommended to the Public were written by your Lordship." That Proprietor was Dodsley, who paid Johnson's bills. Johnson significantly characterizes Chesterfield with a French quotation from Scudéry's *Alaric*, "Le Vainqueur du Vainqueur de la Terre" (*Letters*, vol. 1, p. 95), a pointed allusion to his Gallic sympathies for the *beau monde*.

These events applied pressure on Johnson to rethink his absolute "power." Chesterfield behaved like two centuries of noble predecessors in advancing the interests of the *beau monde*. English society as late as the mid eighteenth century had inherited Henry VIII's love for expanding native vocabulary from other European languages, especially French and Italian. Dodsley, as publisher, was also flexing his muscles in a way typical of his trade, which regarded most English monolingual lexicographers as paid servants rather than authors. The two men together upheld the traditional partnership between rich printer and his influential patron. The publisher wanted to appeal to those who had money to buy the *Dictionary*, and the patron represented that group. On 28 November 1754, Chesterfield pointedly reminded his readers – and Johnson – that those "who intend to buy the dictionary" are "those who can afford it" (*The World* 100, p. 600).

Early modern English lexicographers do not prepare us for Johnson. Never having had a patron before (as he admitted in the letter to Chesterfield), Johnson may not have known that patrons did not normally supplement the income he could expect from his syndicate of printers. (Should the patron do so, the legal ownership of the dictionary might even be muddied.) Nicholas Hudson argues that not just resentment over financial neglect but an "intellectual division" created Johnson's falling out with Chesterfield.[49] Hedrick thinks that Johnson's skepticism about fixing English (a conventional aristocratic notion) precipitated this division. Following H. A. Baker, who showed how deep a francophile the Earl was, Hudson thought the Earl's lobbying for inclusion of the frenchified neologisms of the *beau monde* was the breaking point.[50] I agree with this interpretation. Chesterfield's "neglect," by itself, should not have precipitated Johnson's anger. Dictionary patrons had behaved like Chesterfield from the times of Henry VIII and the Earl of Southampton.

Johnson may not have excluded as many Gallic idioms in practice as his Preface promised,[51] but more than indignation over money moved him to betray the trust of his patron-printer and his printer's patron. Dodsley in 1747 had stated that Chesterfield's "authority" made the English "language as a national cause" (Reddick, *The Making of Johnson's Dictionary*, p. 22), and Chesterfield in *The World* defined that cause with respect to men and women of the contemporary *beau monde*. Johnson, equally patriotic, rejected that definition, and Chesterfield fell, a casualty to a love of the Gallic. For Johnson, what Anne McDermott aptly calls a "canon," determines the English language.[52] He tried to halt two and a half centuries of expanding English vocabulary by drawing on French. Before him, lexicographers happily forced novelties on English. They did not think to preserve what was in need of change. Johnson's "undefiled" English had elements of an archaic literary register scarcely heard outside playhouses. It goes hard against the grain of any scientific lexicographer today to smile at a principled rejection of real speech for any reason.

If Chesterfield lost the authority to make Johnson's work "a national cause," whose authority took the place of his? As humble lexicographer, Johnson pointed gladly to the authors of his quotations, those writers and poets from Sidney to Milton, who, he asserts, give the *Dictionary* its authority. For this reason, Johnson minimizes the importance of most English monolingual lexicographers who preceded him.[53] In the last paragraph of the Preface, however, he gently points to himself, "the author," as that authority. With that single epithet, Johnson takes from his patrons, his authors, and his printers what his own dictionary explains to be the synonym of the term *authority*, that is, *power*, and the drudge becomes a dictator *malgré lui-même*.[54]

NOTES

1. Allen Reddick suggests that Johnson might have thought of Oxford University, which had granted him his M.A. degree early in 1755, as his authority or patron, but Johnson explains that he had "little assistance of the learned," and the degree is not attributed on the title page. See *The Making of Johnson's Dictionary, 1746–1773*, rev. ed. (Cambridge: Cambridge University Press, 1996), pp. 79, 81.
2. Elizabeth Hedrick, "Fixing the Language: Johnson, Chesterfield, and the Plan of a Dictionary," *ELH* 55, no. 2 (1988), 421–42, on p. 426.
3. See Paul J. Korshin, "Types of Eighteenth-Century Literary Patronage," *Eighteenth-Century Studies* 7 (1973), 453–73.
4. *The Correspondence of Robert Dodsley, 1733–1764*, ed. James E. Tierney (Cambridge: Cambridge University Press, 1988), pp. xiv, 18.
5. See Reddick, *The Making of Johnson's Dictionary*, p. 82, and Korshin, "Johnson and Literary Patronage: A Comment on Jacob Leed's Article," *Studies in Burke and His Time* 12 (1970–71), 1804–11, on p. 1808.

6. See "Adam Fitz-Adam" (pseudonym of Philip Dormer Stanhope, fourth Earl of Chesterfield), *The World* 100–1 (28 Nov. and 5 Dec. 1754).

7. Johnson's famous definition of *patron* as "One who countenances, supports, or protects. Commonly a wretch who supports with insolence, and is paid with flattery" carried this bitterness to an extreme.

8. Nathan Bailey, *An Universal Etymological English Dictionary*, 13th ed. (London, 1749), sig. a2ʳ.

9. Jacob Leed, "Johnson and Chesterfield: 1746–47," *Studies in Burke and His Time* 12 (1970), 1677–90, on p. 1684.

10. John Rastell, *Exposiciones terminorum legum anglorum* (London, 1523).

11. Peter Treveris, *The Grete Herball* (Southwark, 1526).

12. John Palsgrave, *Lesclarcissement de la langue francoyse* (London, 1530; repr. Menston: Scolar Press, 1969), sig. A4ʳ. The first printed medical glossary, published in 1543 by Bartholomew Traheron, served an English translation of Jean de Vigo (1460–1525), surgeon to Pope Julius II. Whytchurch, the printer of this huge tome, enjoyed the same copyright privilege of seven years from Henry VIII as Palsgrave did in 1547.

13. See Gabriele Stein, *John Palsgrave as Renaissance Linguist* (Oxford: Clarendon Press, 1997), p. 40.

14. Thomas Thomas, *Dictionarium linguae latinae et anglicanae* (Cambridge, 1587; repr. Menston: Scolar Press, 1972), sig. ¶1ʳ.

15. John Minsheu, *Ductor in linguas (Guide into the Tongues) and Vocabularium hispanicolatinum (1617)*, ed. Jürgen Schäfer (Delmar, N.Y.: Scholars' Facsimiles & Reprints, 1978), p. vii.

16. Henry R. Plomer, "Henry Bynneman, Printer, 1566–83," *The Library* n.s. 35 (July 1908), 225–44, on pp. 242–43; and *A Companion to Arber*, ed. W. W. Greg (Oxford: Clarendon Press, 1967), p. 44.

17. See C. J. Sisson, "The Laws of Elizabethan Copyright: The Stationers' View," *The Library*, 5th series, 15, no. 1 (March 1960), 8–20, on p. 10.

18. See Reddick, *The Making of Johnson's Dictionary*, pp. 198 n. 25, 87.

19. Thomas Urquhart, *Logopandecteision* (London, 1653; repr. Menston: Scolar Press, 1970), sig. A2ʳ.

20. 1825 *Works*, vol. v, p. 23. Johnson repeats himself from the *Plan*, where he describes lexicography as "drudgery for the blind" (vol. v, p. 1).

21. Richard Mulcaster, *The First Part of the Elementarie* (London, 1582), p. 166.

22. Edmund Coote, *The English Schoole-Maister* (London, 1596; repr. Menston: Scolar Press, 1968). See also the edition by Ian Lancashire, Linda Hutjens, Brent Nelson, Robert Whalen, and Tanya Wood (Toronto: Renaissance Electronic Texts, 1997), http://www.library.utoronto.ca/utel/ret/coote/ret2.html.

23. Robert Cawdrey, *A Table Alphabeticall* (London, 1604; repr. Amsterdam: Theatrum Orbis Terrarum, 1970); John Bullokar, *An English Expositor* (London, 1616; repr. Menston: Scolar Press, 1967). Cawdrey's was not the first stand-alone monolingual glossary; it in fact followed Rastell's *Exposiciones* by eighty years.

24. Henry Cockeram, *English Dictionarie; or, An Interpreter of Hard English Words* (London, 1623).

25. Thomas Blount, *Glossographia* (London, 1656; repr. Menston: Scolar Press, 1969); Edward Phillips, *The New World of English Words* (London, 1658; repr. Menston: Scolar Press, 1969).

26. Elisha Coles, *An English Dictionary* (London, 1676); John Kersey, *Dictionarium Anglo-Britannicum* (London, 1708; repr. Menston: Scolar Press, 1969); Nathan Bailey, *An Universal Etymological English Dictionary* (London, 1721).

27. Korshin, "Johnson and the Renaissance Dictionary," *Journal of the History of Ideas* 35 (1974), 300–12, on p. 302 n. 8.

28. See J. D. Fleeman, ed., *The Sale Catalogue of Samuel Johnson's Library: A Facsimile Edition* (Victoria: University of Victoria, 1975), and Donald Greene, *Samuel Johnson's Library: An Annotated Guide* (Victoria: University of Victoria, 1975). Holyoake is probably Francis Holyoake's son, Thomas.

29. Cowell, *The Interpreter, 1607* (Menston: Scolar Press, 1972). Catharina Maria de Vries finds Johnson indebted to Ainsworth (584 entries), Bailey (197), Phillips (39), and unspecified "Dict." (for "Dictionaries," 1,144). She lists the following other pre-seventeenth-century lexicographers from whom Johnson borrowed: Blount, Cowell, Skinner, Junius, and F. Gouldman. See *In the Tracks of a Lexicographer: Secondary Documentation in Samuel Johnson's "Dictionary of the English Language" (1755)* (Leiden: LEd, 1994), p. 225 n. 22.

30. A CATALOGUE and true note of the *Names* of such *Persons* which *(vpon good liking they haue to the worke being a great helpe to memorie)* haue receaued the DICTIONARIE of XI. *Languages* viz. *English, Brutish or Welsh, French, Italian, Spanish, Portuguese, High-Dutch, Low-Dutch, Latine, Greeke, Hebrew*: with the Reasons and Deriuations of *Words* in all these *Tongues*, with the *exposition* of the *Tearmes* of the *Lawes* of this *Land*, and the *description* of *Offices*, and *Titles* of *Dignities*, from the handes of Maister MINSHEV *the Author*, and *Publisher* of the *same in Print*; in consideration they finde, *that by compiling and printing the same*, at his owne charge, *for the publicke good*, and the *aduancement of Learning and Knowledge* hee hath not onely *exhausted and spent thereon all his stocke and substance*, but also runne himselfe into many and greate debtes, *vnpossible for him euer to pay*, without the assistance of like *Receauers of the said Bookes from his hands*: In regard the *Company of Stationers of London*, vtterly refusing to buy them from him, *He is forced to tender them himselfe*, to such like worthie persons as are heere in this *Catalogue* truly set downe. (London, 1617; STC 17944a)
    Cf. Sarah L. C. Clapp, "The Beginnings of Subscription Publication in the Seventeenth Century," *Modern Philology* 29 (1931), 199–224, on pp. 209–16.

31. Thomas Blount, *A World of Errors Discovered in The New World of Words* (London, 1673), sig. A2ʳ.

32. Thomas Elyot, *The Dictionary of Syr Thomas Eliot* (London, 1538).

33. Elyot's successor, Thomas Cooper, dedicated the 1548 edition of Elyot's lexicon to Edward VI. See *Bibliotheca Eliotae (1548) Augmented by Thomas Cooper*, intro. Lillian Gottesman (Delmar, N.J.: Scholars' Facsimiles & Reprints, 1975), sig. A1ʳ.

34. William Salesbury, *A Dictionary in English and Welsh, 1547* (Menston: Scolar Press, 1969), sig. A1ʳ; Richard W. Bailey, *Images of English: A Cultural History of the Language* (Ann Arbor: University of Michigan Press, 1991), p. 27; and *The Statutes of the Realm* (London, 1810–28), chapter 26, section XVII, p. 567.

35. See David C. Douglas, *English Scholars, 1660–1730*, 2nd ed. (London: Eyre and Spottiswoode, 1951), pp. 52–53.

36. See Albert H. Marckwardt, *Laurence Nowell's Vocabularium Saxonicum* (Ann Arbor: University of Michigan Press, 1952). Nowell's lexicon is now Bodleian MS Selden Supra 63; the "Dictionarium" is British Library Cotton Titus MSS A.15–16.

37. Thomas Wilson, *Art of Rhetorique* (London, 1553), cited in Richard Foster Jones, *The Triumph of the English Language* (Stanford: Stanford University Press, 1953), pp. 101–2.

38. Thomas Cooper, *Thesaurus linguae Romanae et Britannicae, 1565* (Menston: Scolar Press, 1969); John Minsheu, *A Dictionarie in Spanish and English* (London, 1599), sig. A2^r; John Florio, *A Worlde of Wordes, or Most Copious, Dictionarie in Italian and English* (London, 1598), sig. A3^r.

39. Francis Holyoake, *Riders Dictionarie Corrected and Augmented* (London, 1606); John Florio, *Queen Anna's New World of Words* (London, 1611).

40. See *The Life and Works of Sir Henry Mainwaring*, ed. G. E. Mainwaring and W. G. Perrin, Navy Records Society, 54 (1920), 85–303; 56 (1922), 67–210.

41. Tertu Nevalainen, "Early Modern English Lexis and Semantics," in *The Cambridge History of the English Language, vol. III: 1476–1776*, ed. Roger Lass (Cambridge: Cambridge University Press, 1999), 5.4.3.2.

42. See Alexander Brede, "The Idea of an English Language Academy," *English Journal* 26, no. 7 (1973), 560–68, on p. 561.

43. On Wilkins and Lloyd, see Fredric Dolezal, *Forgotten but Important Lexicographers, John Wilkins and William Lloyd: A Modern Approach to Lexicography before Johnson* (Tübingen: Max Niemeyer, 1985).

44. See E. Freeman, "A Proposal for an English Academy in 1660," *Modern Language Review* 19 (1924), 291–300; O. F. Emerson, "John Dryden and a British Academy," *Proceedings of the British Academy* 10 (1921–23), 45–58.

45. John Kersey, *A New English Dictionary; or, A Compleat Collection of the Most Proper and Significant Words, Commonly Used in the Language* (London, 1702), sig. a3^r.

46. *The World* 100 (28 November 1754), 601.

47. In a letter to his son on 24 November 1749, Chesterfield writes approvingly of "the Italians and the French; witness their respective academies and dictionaries, for improving and fixing their languages" in regard to "diction" (*The Letters of Philip Dormer Stanhope, 4th Earl of Chesterfield*, ed. Bonamy Dobrée, 6 vols. [London: Eyre & Spottiswoode, 1932], vol. IV, p. 1455).

48. Bailey's *Dictionarium Britannicum* (1736) has about 60,000 word-entries, and Johnson's only two-thirds of that (see Reddick, p. 198 n. 21). In his Preface, Johnson explains that he is leaving out proper names, compounded and double words, verbal nouns in *-ing*, participles, obsolete terms, "words now no longer understood" (current only before Sidney), and "many terms of art and manufacture" (1825 *Works*, vol. V, pp. 40, 44).

49. Nicholas Hudson, "Johnson's *Dictionary* and the Politics of 'Standard English,'" *Yearbook of English Studies* 28 (1998), 77–93, on p. 88.

50. See H. Arthur Baker, "Chesterfield and Johnson," *The Contemporary Review* 137 (1930), 353–60.

51. Thomas B. Gilmore, Jr., presents persuasive evidence that Johnson's responsibilities as a lexicographer to record outweighed the francophobic statements he made in the Preface. See Gilmore, "Johnson's Attitudes toward French Influence on the English Language," *Modern Philology* 78, no. 3 (February 1981), 243–60.

52. Anne McDermott, "Johnson's *Dictionary* and the Canon: Authors and Authority," *Yearbook of English Studies* 28 (1998), 44–65, on p. 63.

53. Johnson uses Skinner and Junius so often, he explains, that he gives "one general acknowledgment" in the Preface rather than citations in individual word-entries (1825 *Works*, vol. v, p. 29). The frequent collective citation, "*Dict.*," also may show a diminished respect.

54. Johnson's third sense for *authority* is "Power; rule"; his first sense for *power* is "Command; authority; dominion; influence."

CHAPTER 3

What Johnson's illustrative quotations illustrate: language and viewpoint in the Dictionary

Howard D. Weinbrot

Much recent scholarship on Johnson's *Dictionary of the English Language* has included three at once overlapping and divergent points of view. The Right see it as a principled Tory political and theological document. It urges a High Church and Jacobite concept of British culture, for which it should be praised. The Left comparably see it as a Tory political and theological document that privileges written over spoken, gentleman's over plebeian's, and English over Scottish language and culture. It is an imperialist document for which it should be blamed. Some scholars presumably in the Center also regard the *Dictionary*, but especially its fourth edition of 1773, as a source of illustrative quotations that are politically and theologically agenda-driven.[1]

There are two shared assumptions behind these views. One is that in the Preface, definitions, and illustrations, the *Dictionary* is a dictionary of Johnson's language, not of the English language prominent on the title page. Johnson himself, however, says in his Preface that he does "not form, but register the language"; he does "not teach men how they should think, but relate how they have hitherto expressed their thoughts" (1825 *Works*, vol. v, p. 44). The other, related, assumption is that Johnson's own words regarding his mode of proceeding are largely irrelevant to his mode of proceeding. In the *Plan of an English Dictionary* (1747) Johnson says that he will select his authorities for their "elegance of language, or some precept of prudence, or piety" (vol. v, p. 20) – that is, generalized secular or spiritual counsel. The Preface itself makes plain that his illustrations came from "fortuitous and unguided excursions into books" and were subject to "industry . . . or chance," not design (vol. v, p. 31). When he was more focused, he sought "from divines striking exhortations" again presumably pious rather than polemical. Those exhortations are within "mutilated" quotations and "are no longer to be considered as conveying the sentiments or doctrine of their authors" (vol. v, pp. 38–39). For many ideological critics of the Left, Right, and Center, then, Johnson must have either been uninformed regarding his own intention or said the Thing That Was Not. I propose to examine whether such proponents listen with credulity to the whispers of fancy.

THE CASE ON EITHER SIDE

The ideological assumption indeed has eighteenth-century precedent. In 1755 Matthew Maty scolded Johnson for not inculcating virtues presumably exemplified in Maty's patron Lord Chesterfield. Johnson too feebly acquaints readers with proper "principes de politique & de religion." Thomas Edwards was scarcely so oblique. As "a vehicle for Jacobite and High-flying tenets," he insisted, the *Dictionary* is filled with "many examples from the party pamphlets of Swift, from South's Sermons and other authors in that way of thinking."[2]

This approach is not wholly wrong. Johnson excluded the morally odious Hobbes, the theologically heterodox Samuel Clarke and, so far as I can tell and Milton obviously excepted, any friend to the civil wars and interregnum. Johnson also initially designed the illustrations as moral exemplars, however much his design when practiced wanted modification. Such a concept of language and its organizers is also consistent with a general and a particular Johnsonian given. He regularly regards the world as divinely made: "Infinite goodness is the source of created existence."[3] As the agent of that goodness Johnson uses his talent to teach religious and moral knowledge through letters. A particular example begins the Preface to the *Dictionary* in which Johnson images himself as the humble pioneer ahead of a civilizing army in a wilderness. Organization must proceed in some way, and Johnson's "pioneering" way of course is broadly moral, Anglican Christian, literary, and English. As he again says in the Preface, he hopes to make his own and other nations aware of the glories of Hooker, Bacon, Newton, and Boyle and certainly of the often-cited Shakespeare, Milton, Dryden, and Pope (vol. v, p. 50). He enlivens these and many other ancestral voices for their conversations with posterity.

That much being said, however, it scarcely follows that from 1747 to 1755, or especially for the fourth edition revised from 1771 to 1773, Johnson ordered some 116,000 quotations or their supplements along polemically political or theological lines. He initially compiled his *Dictionary* during about eight years, with the help of his own and borrowed books, and with the human help of one English and five Scottish amanuenses. Much of the illustrative venture surely was a function of random accident perhaps aided by those amanuenses rather than coherent design. The consortium of booksellers who wanted Chesterfield as their patron, and who paid Johnson at least £1,575 for the job, would not have tolerated an audience-limiting venture. Johnson himself always was sympathetic to booksellers' concerns. On 20 July 1763 he thus criticizes Edinburgh's Alexander Donaldson for undercutting the price of English books. Johnson "uniformly professed much regard" for London booksellers and lamented that they had too little profit (see *Life*, vol. I, p. 438). It would be a peculiar strategy to filter judgments into his lexicon that were anathema to then-dominant political concepts and to the deserved profit for booksellers' risk. His Preface often mentions the purchaser as an object of his attention. That commercial sensitivity respected a politically broad audience willing to spend a substantial £4 10s. for a benign rather than malign text. Apparently the Hanoverian government recognized his lexicon as politically acceptable and worth publicizing. On 12 June 1755 the British chargé des affaires presented a copy of the *Dictionary* to the Académie Française. It gratefully acknowledged receipt, promised its own dictionary in return, and recognized the international importance of Johnson's national achievement.[4]

There were indeed genuine differences between religious sects and political groups, perhaps especially so during the years from the late 1670s through 1714; but there was also essential overlap among them. Gordon Rupp argues that we should not "forget the coherent body of convictions which for Church of England men cut across the labels 'Whig,' 'Tory,' or even 'high church' and 'low church.'"[5] As Johnson told Boswell in 1781, "A wise Tory and a wise Whig . . . will agree. Their principles are the same, though their modes of thinking are different" (*Life*, vol. IV, p. 117). Johnson also thought Anglicans and Catholics more divided by political – that is national and international competition – than by religious differences.[6] When in *Rambler* 185 (1751) Johnson asks us to exercise "a continual reference of every action to the divine will" (Yale *Works*, vol. V, p. 209), he speaks of the general human need for general adherence to a general Western European view of general Christian theology. Some others indeed occasionally claimed to perceive a putative ideological agenda in the illustrative quotations; but on commercially prudent and intellectually communal grounds, Johnson avoided rather than courted such controversy.

We see some of this theological pacifism in 1755 in his use of divines together with, though very different from, Robert South in his often-quoted second volume of *Twelve Sermons Preached on Several Occasions* (1694). Here is Tory high-flying South as quoted in part under *independent* adj. 1: "Creation must needs infer providence, and God's making the world irrefragably proves that he governs it too." Here is Richard Bentley, the

Great Satan Modern Whig favorite enemy of Swift and the Christ Church Wits.[7] "Bentley's Sermons" illustrate the adverb *accurately*: "That all these distances, motions, and quantities of matter, should be so *accurately* and harmoniously adjusted in this great variety of our system, is above the fortuitous hits of blind material causes, and must certainly flow from that eternal fountain of wisdom." Here is John Tillotson, William III's Latitudinarian Archbishop of Canterbury on *frame* n.s. 1: "We see this vast *frame* of the world, and an innumerable multitude of creatures in it; all which we, who believe a God, attribute to him as the author." All three draw upon physico-theology confirmed by the divinely ordered Newtonian universe.

I offer one more group of easily multiplied instances of general Christian belief in the *Dictionary*: the further friendly yoking of apparent enemies, as in South and Tillotson. Johnson uses nearly the same number of quotations from each man – about 1,100 in each case. He can do so because of "the coherent body of convictions which for Church of England men cut across the labels 'Whig,' 'Tory,' or even 'high church' and 'low church'" – as on the afterlife. For *promiscuous*, Tillotson says, "No man, that considers the *promiscuous* dispensations of God's providence in this world, can think it unreasonable to conclude, that after this life good men shall be rewarded, and sinners punished." South shares that view with *remorseless*: "O the inexpressible horrour that will seize upon a sinner, when he stands arraigned at the bar of divine justice! when he shall see his accuser, his judge, the witnesses, all his *remorseless* adversaries." In each case, shared belief dominates differences of tone, nuance, and context. Johnson often thus includes apparent theological and political enemies in one illustrative mosaic. *To advance* v.a. cites both Tillotson and South; *to affect* v.a., *atheist* n.s., and *beyond* prep. cite both South and Bentley; and *argument* n.s. cites both Tillotson and Atterbury.

If we examine South alone, we again see how Johnson moves toward consensus rather than confrontation. As Thomas Edwards's remark makes plain, even in 1755 South was known as a high-flying Tory. That judgment was consistent with aspects of South's *Twelve Sermons*, but not consistent with Johnson's use of them.

ANGRY SOUTH, AMIABLE JOHNSON

Johnson heavily annotated that second volume of abrasive sermons against Latitudinarians and various Dissenters. The Latitudinarians, for example, insisted that "*Little Things*" in worship and doctrine should be abandoned for the sake of Church unity.[8] For South the "*Little*" is merely the wedge with which the *"Innovating Spirit"* seeks to attack and destroy Anglican doctrine and discipline. South's sermons here are less exposition of faith than aggressive defenses against "the *Hand* which is lifted against us." Such an enemy is as dangerous "in *Ninety-three* . . . [as] in *Forty-one*" (*Twelve Sermons*, vol. II, sig. A3^{r-v}). South thus writes against threats of "a Total Abolition" of religion by the same crew of earlier rebels, regicides, and enemies to episcopy. Those motives "in Religion and Religious Matters are generally fatal and pernicious" (vol. II, sig. A4^{r-v}).

South's sermons reflect the mingled fear and hostility of his Epistle Dedicatory. In his sermons upon Proverbs 10:9 he excoriates drunken wits "magisterially censuring the Wisdom of all Antiquity, scoffing at all Piety, and (as it were) new modelling the whole World" (vol. II, p. 48). "They are enough to make the Nation like *Sodom* and *Gommorha* in their Punishment, as they have already made it too like them in their Sins." In a remark that surely alludes to the Royal Society, South recognizes "a kind of *Diabolical society* for the finding out *new experiments* in Vice" (vol. II, pp. 49–50). Dissenters and Latitudinarian churches, we hear in his sermon on Ecclesiastes 5:2, are "Mints of Treason and Rebellion" at which congregants learn "a *Spirit* of Pride, Faction, and Sedition" (vol. II, p. 160).

The sermon on Romans 1:32 further exemplifies South's rhetoric consistent with other High Church pamphlets and sermons that savage perceived threats to Church and State. These enemies, we now hear, preach doctrines "to be lookt upon as the Devil's Prophets and Apostles." They induce sin in others and one day will be punished as if they "had actually and personally committed it themselves" (vol. II, p. 286). Such modern casuists are "like the Devil's *Amanuenses*, and Secretaries to the Prince of Darkness." They have taken evil notions from the Devil's cabinet and propagated them through "Magazines and Store-houses of all Immorality and Baseness" (vol. II, p. 287). When the time comes, they will cut our throats, seize our estates, and let "the Rabble . . . loose upon the Government once again" (vol. II, p. 298). In South's tenuous world and fear of repeated disorder, an "*Ocean of Vice* . . . now *swells*, and *roars*, and *lifts up it self* above all Banks and Bands of humane Laws" (vol. II, p. 319). That militant voice recalled 1641 and did everything it could to deny innovation that even hinted at challenges to Anglican episcopacy.

Johnson recognized South's severity. On 7 April 1778 he answered Sir John Pringle's question regarding "what were the best English sermons for style." South "is one of the best, if you except his peculiarities, and his violence, and sometimes coarseness of language" (*Life*, vol. III, p. 248).[9] Johnson often quoted South in the *Dictionary*, but he also acted on those "exceptions." The quotations overwhelmingly expel South's violence and exclusionary tactics. Instead, they concentrate upon his shared Christian religious values. Many illustrative quotations from South in fact could serve as introductory mottoes to the *Rambler's* Christian moralism. Under *appellation* we see that "Good and evil commonly operate upon the mind of man, by respective names or *appellations*, by which they are notified and conveyed to the mind." Under *ardour* 2 we see that "Joy, like a ray of the sun, reflects with a greater *ardour* and quickness, when it rebounds upon a man from the breast of his friend." Under *avenue* 1 we see that "Truth is a strong-hold, and diligence is laying siege to it: so that it must observe all the *avenues* and passes to it." These are what Johnson meant by "striking exhortations."

We recall that Johnson often truncated and thereby changed the quotations' meaning. Here is one instance of how in 1755 he mingles his own temperament, concern with general truths, and accommodation for space through an illustration from South's sermon on John 3:21: "I am sure, no other *Alteration* will satisfie *Dissenting Consciences*; no, nor this neither, very long, without an utter Abolition of all that looks like Order or Government in the Church" (*Twelve Sermons*, vol. II, pp. 615–16). Johnson uses and abbreviates the sentence to illustrate *alteration* 2: "No other *alteration* will satisfy; nor this neither, very long, without an utter abolition of all order." As printed, this lacks polemic and neutralizes South's take-no-prisoners anger. Johnson drops the attack upon Dissenters, the specific threat to the Anglican Church, and the consequent particularity. Instead, he moves the remark toward richly human rather than defensively English conduct. In the same sermon South scolds the Catholic Church as vain, proud, putrefied, and "a Church which allows *Salvation* to none without it, nor awards *Damnation* to almost any within it" (*Twelve Sermons*, vol. II, pp. 545–46; 1 John 3:21). Johnson's verb *to award* 1 again mutes hostility by refusing to name a target: "A church which allows salvation to none without it, nor *awards* damnation to almost any within it."

Such irenic generalizing indeed characterizes Johnson's typical mode of proceeding in his illustrative quotations from South, which generally are not theologically oriented. As a sample by the Canon John E. Wallis long ago demonstrated, only 5.8 percent of the words Johnson quoted from South's sermons "are specifically theological."[10] Most of the quotations, indeed, also are based on broad Christian belief. Under *all-wise*, for example, we see that "There is an infinite, eternal, *all-wise* Mind governing the affairs of the world." *Ascendant* adj. 1 tells us that "Christ outdoes Moses, before he displaces him; and shews an *ascendant* spirit above him." This is the orthodox belief that the New Testament supersedes the Old Testament, as Mercy supersedes Justice.

The generalizing and softening mode of proceeding is extensive but not uniform; there surely are exceptions among the illustrations, as with those hostile to atheists, schismatics, and other apparent enemies to the Church. The illustration from South for *atheistical* thus reads: "Men are *atheistical*, because they are first vicious; and question the truth of christianity, because they hate the practice." Under *bane* 2 South says that "False religion is, in its nature, the greatest *bane* and destruction to government in the world." Even such occasional forays provide further evidence that Johnson sought agreement available in the received and commonplace dicta of Christian wisdom rather than polemic and confrontation. Robert DeMaria, Jr., observes that the "overwhelming majority of theological material in the *Dictionary* is made up of unsophisticated reminders of religious fundamentals." Indeed, "an unwillingness to take sides in intramural religious disputes is characteristic of all of Johnson's religious pronouncements, but he seems to have taken special care to avoid such presumption in the *Dictionary*."[11]

THE REVISED VERSION

Thus far I have been dealing with illustrative quotations in the first edition of the *Dictionary*. One of the *Dictionary*'s most distinguished students tells us that Johnson's fourth, revised, text of 1773 is more polemical: Johnson adds quotations from Stuart, Non-Juring, and sometimes Jacobite theologians and others who urge Anglican values against the skeptical tides as, for example, exemplified in the movement to eliminate subscription to the Thirty-nine Articles for university admission. Failure to recognize such change limits one to the first edition's less politically engaged approach.[12] Examination of that hypothesis, however, offers results comparable to those for the 1755 text. After all, Johnson's respect for and gratitude to his booksellers was at least as strong in 1773 as it was in 1755. The vast number of illustrative quotations was but slightly enlarged in the revised version. Immigrants were both swamped by lexical natives and were not singled out as a coherent ideological body. Johnson would oddly overestimate the power of a harmless drudge to think that many readers might notice or be moved by his additions on a fleeting topic, about which even fewer were likely to consult a dictionary.

Moreover, when Johnson discusses agitation against the Thirty-nine Articles he is more dismissive than threatened. He was in the midst of revising the *Dictionary* when on 21 March 1772 Boswell mentioned "the petition

to Parliament for removing the subscription to the Thirty-nine Articles."
Johnson immediately says: "It was soon thrown out." With Edmund Burke
among the leaders, on 6 February 1772 the Petition was defeated by the
wide margin of 217–71 and denied the right to be raised again (*Life*,
vol. II, pp. 150–51 and n. 7). On 4 March 1773 Johnson wrote to the Rev.
Dr. William White informing him about relevant political and theological
matters: "Opposition seems to despond; and the dissenters, though they
have taken advantage of unsettled times, and a government much enfee-
bled, seem not likely to gain any immunities" (*Life*, vol. II, p. 208).[13] As
Johnson thus well knew, attempts to loosen Church authority were defeated
and Dissenters thwarted. There is no reason for Johnson to add polemical
quotations after the Petition "was soon thrown out," and then to respond
ideologically and "surreptitiously to the public and parliamentary debates"
in order to buttress "symbols of orthodox belief . . . as a reaction to the
topical debate."[14] So far as he could tell, even in unsettled times, those
orthodoxies were well protected.

Johnson's Advertisement to the fourth edition alerts readers to the
changes he made in the *Dictionary*. He discusses the difficulty and fatigue
of his job, the inevitable errors that creep in and that he hopes at least
partially to correct, and the nature and quantity of his revisions:

Many faults I have corrected, some superfluities I have taken away, and some
deficiencies I have supplied. I have methodised some parts that were disordered,
and illuminated some that were obscure. Yet the changes or additions bear a very
small proportion to the whole. The critick will now have less to object, but the
student who has bought any of the former copies needs not repent; he will not,
without nice collation, perceive how they differ; and usefulness seldom depends
upon little things . . . I have left that inaccurate which never was made exact, and
that imperfect which never was completed. (*1773*, vol. I, sig. [C]1ʳ)

According to Johnson, then, the new illustrative quotations essentially are
imperceptible. The putatively polemical additions must also be a small
proportion of a very small proportion. Whether he was wrong about his
own practice in 1773 remains now to be considered.

As the Advertisement suggests, focus on one group of entries distorts the
breadth of revision in the fourth edition. As some "nice collation" shows,
Johnson or someone else corrected typographical errors and changed many
etymologies.[15] A quotation from South that began with "Thou such men"
becomes "Though such men" in *1773*, s.v. *yet* conj. Johnson continued to
edit and often condense non-judgmental quotations, as in *advantage* n.s. 2,
in "Superiority gained by stratagem, or unlawful means." I have italicized

the words Johnson eliminates: "*It is a noble and a sure defiance of a* great malice, backed with a great interest; *which* yet can have no advantage of a man . . ." He also slightly enhances some definitions or comments (*to baffle* 1; *gird* n.s.), adds other definitions (*arrest* n.s. 3), adds illustrative quotations (*avocation* n.s. 2; *accommodation* adj. from Tillotson; *widely* adv. 2 from South), and drops some words (*hence*). When Johnson adds a quotation from South in the fourth edition he also is humanly general. Under *aching* n.s. as "Pain; uneasiness," we see that "When old age comes to wait upon a great and worshipful sinner, it comes attended with many painful girds and *achings*, called the gout." For the most part, the other nominal High Church Tory additions are unrecognizable as such and, as Johnson makes plain, are too few to be noticed "without nice collation" that no common reader is likely to endure.

At least as important, though, is Johnson's concept of normally competing nuances within definitions. Johnson's mosaic of quotations is designed to show the several paths to truth that "diversities of signification" encourage (1825 *Works*, vol. v, p. 41).

This hypothesis gains support when we examine the illustrative quotations in the apparently key term *unity*. That concept long had been the cry of the higher Church of England men. Like South, they regularly accused Dissenters, Latitudinarians, and many Whigs of being agents of darkness. Schism is a sin; unity of Protestants is necessary for protection against the unholy trinity of the Devil, Rome, and France. Nonetheless, the dominant example of actual schism was the Altitudinarian Non-Jurors who both alienated their colleagues and attempted to found their own line of Non-Juring bishops.[16] Moreover, Lower churchmen also regularly argued on unity. For them, the High Church wrongly excluded their brethren for small matters indifferent, like crossing, the priest's surplice, and genuflection, all of which should be abandoned in the cause of unity among Protestants who overwhelmingly shared belief. The plea for unity thus was not peculiar to one side and is not a necessary ideological marker. Low-Church Benjamin Hoadly so spoke to Dissenters in 1704 in the cause of Protestant concord:

There is no one thing, in which all *Protestants* amongst us, as well as *Dissenters* as *Conformists* do more agree, than in this plain Proposition, *That all causeless and unnecessary Divisions and Distinctions, are most carefully and conscientiously to be avoided by Christians*. In a deep sense of this Truth, the best *Writers* on all sides, have, with one Consent, and with one common Zeal and Concern, pressed upon the Consciences of Men, the Duty and Importance of *Peace* and *Concord*, and the Guilt and Mischief of *needless distinctions and Divisions*.[17]

A call for unity among Christians is demonstrably ecumenical, as indeed was much even of the earlier eighteenth-century Anglican Church. For example, the *Spectator's* country Tory Sir Roger de Coverly installed an amiable clergyman, to whom he presented a collection of the best English sermons to be read on various Sunday services. Upon being asked whose sermon he would read next, the clergyman answers that in the morning it is the Whig William Fleetwood, Bishop of St. Asaph, and in the afternoon Tory Robert South. The list of preachers for the year included Latitudinarian Tillotson, Tory Robert Sanderson, Latitudinarian Isaac Barrow, and (probably) the higher churchman Benjamin Calamy.[18] Here indeed is a benevolent theological and social *concordia discors* that increased rather than decreased later in the eighteenth century. In Fielding's *Amelia* (1752), for example, Captain Booth reforms when he reads Isaac Barrow's sermons; but South also was one of Fielding's favorite and admired divines, whom he often quoted and often complimented.[19]

The *Dictionary* quotations themselves under *unity* generally follow the pattern of general Christian or secular knowledge generally received within general literate culture. As one example, definition 4 is "Principles of dramatick writing, by which the tenour of the story, and propriety of representation is preserved." Johnson there includes a presumably normative illustration from Dryden saying that *All for Love* exactly observes the unities. Immediately thereafter he provides a condensed version of lines from Addison's *Spectator* 409: the unities should be "thoroughly understood, but there is still something more essential, that elevates and astonishes the fancy."[20] Whatever Johnson's own beliefs, he presents both sides because both sides have eminent authorities for a legitimate alternative regarding what men have thought.

The fourth edition's slightly enlarged discussion of *unity* includes twelve illustrative quotations from twelve authors for five shades of meaning. There are three changes from the first edition. Johnson adds one quotation from Barten Holyday and one from John Pearson. Neither is recognizably polemic or ideological. Holyday (1593–1661) was Archdeacon of Oxford and indeed a supporter of the Stuart Church and dispensation. By 1773, however, his largely irenic sermons and his deservedly ignored poem *A Survey of the World in Ten Books* (1661) would almost surely have been forgotten.[21] Those who knew the name in 1773 probably would have recalled his posthumously published translation of Juvenal and Persius in 1673, to which Dryden referred and which was familiar to interested readers. Moreover, the illustrative quotation Johnson cites is based on commonplace physics and physico-theology: "Take unity then out of the world, and it dissolves into chaos." True enough.

The citation from John Pearson (1613–88), Bishop of Chester, is comparably pacific. Pearson's well-regarded *Exposition of the Creed* (1659) is a centrist Church document that draws upon the Church fathers. It cites three variously mainstream targets of variously mainstream divines: atheists, Photinians – Arians and Socinians who denied the divinity of Christ – and Jews. Socinians, for example, were unprotected by William III's Toleration Act of 1689.[22] By the late 1760s Socinianism had indeed returned to theological argument, but the illustrative quotation from Pearson is innocent of such squabbles. Johnson quotes from "Article IX. The holy Catholick Church, the Communion of Saints." He omits the italics, the biblical citation, and the opening eight words up to "nature." These make plain that Pearson is speaking of Christian charity, not dissent: "Charity is of a fastning, and uniting nature, [Johnson begins here] nor can we call those many, who *endeavour to keep the unity of the Spirit in the bond of peace. By this,* said our Saviour, *shall all men know that ye are my disciples, if ye have love one to another.* And this is the Unity of charity."[23] Pearson's marginal note identifies the respective italicized sections as from Ephesians 4:3 and John 13:35. He goes outside of his book towards the ultimate religious authority and emphasizes Christian love, not anger.

The passage is framed in positive rather than negative terms. In its context it exalts the unity of Christians worldwide as congregants of "one Church. And this under the name of *Church* expressed in this Article, I understand a body, or collection of humane persons professing faith in *Christ*, gathered together in several places of the world for the worship of the same God, and united into the same corporation" (Pearson, *An Exposition of the Creed*, p. 341). Johnson is not likely to have found or encouraged polemic regarding dissent in the Church of England if Pearson is talking about worldwide rather than insular Christian unity.[24]

There is another sign of the essential coherence of the illustrative quotations regarding *unity* from the first to the fourth edition. The third change is small: the removal of the identifying "*b.* iv" from "*Hooker*" (*unity* n.s. 3, "Agreement; uniformity"), whose words from *The Laws of Ecclesiastical Polity* (1594–1613) remain the same: "To the avoiding of dissension, it availeth much, that there be amongst them an *unity*, as well in ceremonies as in doctrine." That is from 4.13.2, in a book devoted to the reconciliation of the reformed Church of England with the Church of Rome. By the earlier eighteenth century Hooker had been adopted by at least some

Latitudinarian divines as the paternal ecclesiastical voice of contract theory –
as in the eighth book of the *Laws* among other places: every society has "full
dominion over it self . . . God creating mankinde did indue it naturally
with full power to guide it self in whatever kinds of societies soever it should
choose to live."[25]

Benjamin Hoadly noticed such remarks and used them to support
the concept of limited constitutional monarchy behind the Williamite
anti-Stuart revolution. *The Original and Institution of Civil Government,
Discuss'd* (1710) characterizes Hooker as overtly founding "*Civil Government*
upon the *Voluntary Agreement, Composition,* or *Compact* of the Members
of the *Govern'd Society*; from whom *originally* comes all the *Authority* of
Governours." The people have "a reserve of *Right* to change" a government they perceive to be intolerable and of which "they were not at first
apprehensive."[26] Like *unity,* Hooker's presence in Johnson's quotations signals broad agreement rather than isolated polemic. The father of conservative Anglican order also advocated what would become the Lockean theory
of a revocable "*Voluntary Agreement*" of people and rulers.

Indeed, according to Hawkins, Johnson filtered Hooker on the obedience
of subject to crown "as explained by Hoadly." Johnson thus "condemned the
conduct of James the second" during his reign and embraced a position that
"leads to whiggism."[27] In this respect, Johnson was the ancestral paradigm
of Tory man and Whig measures. Accordingly, within the meaning of
"unity" Johnson encourages us to read illustrative quotations that combine
Hooker (via Hoadly) and Milton, Dryden and Addison, the secular and
theological, Tory and Whig. As Carey McIntosh well observes, Johnson
typically "implies that no one person or book has all the knowledge his
reader needs even from a single field."[28]

JOHNSON AND BEATTIE

One of those fields, though, has been called part of the polemic of the
fourth edition. Namely, Johnson included quotations from James Beattie's
*Essay on the Nature and Immutability of Truth, in Opposition to Sophistry and
Scepticism* (1770) in his campaign to support "orthodox Anglicanism and
its establishment."[29] Johnson's illustrations for *skeptick* and other words
suggest otherwise.

For Johnson's culture, *skepticism,* like the Pyrrhonism from which it
stems, is "universal doubt." The *skeptick* n.s. is "One who doubts, or pre-
tends to doubt of every thing." Under *skeptical* Johnson includes words

from Bentley in hopes that such painful doubt can be alleviated by divine certainties: "May the Father of mercies confirm the *sceptical* and wavering minds."³⁰ Under *skeptick* Johnson's citations include Anglican Whig Blackmore, Catholic Pope, and Nonconformist Isaac Watts, whom, Johnson said, "every Christian Church would rejoice to have adopted" (*Lives*, vol. III, p. 303). The illustration from Watts's *Logick*, for example, observes that "The dogmatist is sure of every thing, and the *sceptick* believes nothing." In all cases Johnson generalizes on to human conduct and to the peace that belief may bring. Johnson returns to the conflict between skepticism and mercy by means of the broadly popular *Essay* by that Scottish professor of moral theology.

Johnson and James Beattie were mutually admiring and sympathetic allies when they met at the end of July 1772. On 3 August 1772 Johnson wrote to Boswell saying that "Beattie's book is . . . every day more liked; at least I like it more as I look upon it" (*Letters*, vol. II, p. 391). The chief skeptic Beattie's *Essay* lashes is David Hume. On 4 October 1771 Beattie gave Johnson the second edition of his book with its long postscript. Beattie there defends himself from charges of excess severity, a defense Johnson found convincing and that Burke called "one of the most masterful pieces of eloquence he has ever seen."³¹ The Postscript includes a remark that becomes an illustrative quotation for *to violate* v.a. 2, "To infringe": "Those reasonings which, by *violating* common sense, tend to subvert every principle of rational belief, to sap the foundations of truth and science, and to leave the mind exposed to all the horrors of scepticism."

Johnson of course rejects skepticism as an acceptable conclusion to rational thought. He just as clearly selects his illustration from an attack upon Hume, who deserves every condemnation appropriate for someone whose values, Beattie argued and Johnson agreed, "are totally subversive of science, morality, and religion both natural and revealed."³² Beattie does not consider Church of England unity and grants the power of "natural" religion. The bigger fish he hopes to fry is David Hume's apparent attack upon revelation and Christianity. Johnson himself is concerned with human spiritual peace. Anglican theology is a smaller part of something on which all Christians should agree in the face of threats to belief.

CONCLUSION

Johnson indeed occasionally deviates from the straight and narrow of neutral illustration. He also regularly views his job as one of encouraging moral education through broadly Christian values consistent with his Protestant Anglicanism. When he deploys higher churchmen like South or Latitudinarian churchmen like Tillotson, he normally either quotes or modifies quotations so that they embody received and broadly acceptable Christian commonplaces. Though the fourth edition adds several putatively even more "conservative" Church of England men, they often are included with several other illustrations and they too generally utter commonplaces. Moreover, they are merely a part and not the whole of the *Dictionary's* revisions that include many merely cosmetic corrections as well. The safest and most persuasive way to regard the illustrative quotations is to start by accepting Johnson's stated title. It is *A Dictionary of the English Language* in which he registers rather than forms the language. He does "not teach men how they should think, but relate how they have hitherto expressed their thoughts" (1825 *Works*, vol. v, p. 44), whether in 1755 or 1773. It is reasonable to assume that Johnson knew what Johnson had done.

NOTES

1. For a study on the Right see J. C. D. Clark, *Samuel Johnson: Literature, Religion, and English Cultural Politics from the Restoration to Romanticism* (Cambridge: Cambridge University Press, 1994), pp. 74–75, 125, 130–31, 134, 137, 184–87, 211–12, 237. For some studies on the Left see John Barrell, *English Literature in History, 1730–80: An Equal, Wide Survey* (London: Hutchinson, 1983), pp. 144–61, and Tony Crowley, *Language in History: Theories and Texts* (London and New York: Routledge, 1996), pp. 56–57, 60, 81–83. For the Center, see Allen Reddick, *The Making of Johnson's Dictionary, 1746–1773*, rev. ed. (Cambridge: Cambridge University Press, 1996), pp. 90–91, 94, 121–22, 141–45, 151–69.

2. Matthew Maty, *Journal Britannique* 17 (July–August 1755), 227; Thomas Edwards, quoted in James H. Sledd and Gwin J. Kolb, *Dr. Johnson's Dictionary: Essays in the Biography of a Book* (Chicago: University of Chicago Press, 1955), p. 135. In contrast, others found the *Dictionary* vulgarly accommodating to inappropriately low speech. See James Thomson Callender, *Deformities of Dr. Samuel Johnson: Selected from His Works*, 2nd ed. (London, 1782), pp. 53, 60, 68, 71, 74. On p. 74, for example, Callender reminds the reader of "what a profusion of low, and even blackguard expressions are to be met with in the Doctor's celebrated work." See also Callender, *A Critical Review of the Works of Dr. Samuel Johnson*, 2nd ed. (London, 1783), p. v. Donald T. Siebert has discussed such words in "*Bubbled, Bamboozled*, and *Bit*: 'Low Bad' Words in Johnson's Dictionary," *Studies in English Literature* 26 (1986), 485–96. Jack Lynch has conveniently included relevant lists as well as "Ludicrous Words" in his "Index of Piquant Terms" in *Samuel Johnson's Dictionary: Selections . . .* (Delray Beach,

Fla.: Levenger Press, 2002; New York: Walker & Co., 2003), p. 642. There are
numerous "low" words scattered throughout other categories.

3. Yale *Works*, vol. III, p. 239 (*Rambler* 44). Religion is the speaker.
4. Aujourd'hui Mr de Cosne, chargé des affaires du Roi de la Grand Bretagne, a remis à
   M^r le Secretaire, un Dictionnaire anglois en deux volumes in folio, dont Mr Johnson,
   auteur de cet ouvrage fait présent à l'Académie. M^r le Secretaire l'a prié d'assurer M^r
   Johnson que la Compagnie étoit fort sensible à cette marque d'attention qu'elle reçevoit
   de sa part, et qu'elle lui en donneroit un preuve en lui en voyant la nouvelle édition de
   son Dictionnaire, aussitôt qu'elle paroitroit.

   See Institut de France, *Les Registres de l'Académie françoise, 1672–1793*, ed.
   Charles Camille Doucet, 4 vols. (Paris, 1895), vol. III, p. 67. The minutes
   record "Mrs Mirabaud, Dulivet, Alary, DeBernis, Duclos, Marivaux, De Bissy,
   Chateaubrun" present at the time. Presentation of the *Dictionary* by the British
   chargé des affaires also suggests that the British government thought Johnson sufficiently loyal to act as his agent on an international matter of national
   pride. One supposes that these eminent men of letters at the Académie also
   discussed Johnson's *Dictionary* with others. Claude de Thyrad, Comte de
   Bissy, was admitted to the Académie on 29 December 1750 and was especially interested in British literature. He translated and commented on the
   first of Edward Young's *Night Thoughts* in Jean-Baptiste-Antoine Suard and
   François Arnaud's *Variétés littéraires*, 4 vols. (Paris, 1768–69), vol. II, pp. 38–
   62.
5. Gordon Rupp, *Religion in England, 1688–1791* (Oxford: Clarendon Press, 1986),
   p. 74. For arguments on later accommodation within the Church of England, see
   William Gibson, *The Church of England, 1688–1832: Unity and Accord* (London
   and New York: Routledge, 2001).
6. See *Life*, vol. I, p. 405. On 2 March 1772 Johnson says that "all denominations of
   Christians have really little difference in point of doctrine." Forms of worship
   in Presbyterian and Italian Catholic churches are different, "yet the doctrine
   taught is essentially the same" (*Life*, vol. II, p. 150). That clearly is even more
   true of lower and higher Church Anglicans. See also two other sources. One is
   the *Life of Boerhave* (1756): however much "Men may differ . . . in many religious
   opinions . . . all may retain the essentials of Christianity" (1825 *Works*, vol. VI,
   p. 502). The other source is Sir John Hawkins, *The Life of Samuel Johnson, LL.D.*
   (Dublin, 1787), where Hawkins quotes Johnson quoting Howells: the "complete
   Christian" should "have the works of a Papist, the words of a Puritan, and the
   faith of a Protestant" (p. 479).
7. All quotations are from *1755*. For some of the bitter "orthodox" hostility to
   Bentley, see my "'He Will Kill Me Over and Over Again': Intellectual Contexts
   of the Battle of the Books," in *Reading Swift: Papers from the Fourth Münster
   Symposium on Jonathan Swift*, ed. Hermann J. Real and Helgard Stöver (Munich:
   Wilhelm Fink Verlag, 2003), pp. 225–48.
8. Robert South, *Twelve Sermons Preached on Several Occasions*, 2 vols. (London,
   1694), Epistle Dedicatory, to the University of Oxford, vol. I, sig. A2^r, with
   italics reversed.

9. Compare the use of South here discussed and in Robert DeMaria, Jr., *Johnson's "Dictionary" and the Language of Learning* (Chapel Hill: University of North Carolina Press, 1986), pp. 155–56, 223, 239, with Thomas Edwards's remark, as in Sledd and Kolb, *Dr. Johnson's Dictionary.*

10. John E. Wallis, "Doctor Johnson and His English Dictionary," *The Johnson Society* [of Lichfield] *Addresses and Transactions* 4 (1939–53), 18. Canon Wallis, however, does not define what he means by "specifically theological." If one includes references to God, Jesus, or the Church Fathers the proportion is higher.

11. DeMaria, *Johnson's "Dictionary" and the Language of Learning*, pp. 222, 223.

12. Allen Reddick, "Johnson Beyond Jacobitism," *ELH* 64, no. 4 (1997), 983–1005, on pp. 985, 992–93. Reddick had considered and rejected the notion of ideological organization in the first edition: "Critical emphasis on the content of the quotations rather than context reflects a misunderstanding of what the *Dictionary* represents and indeed how one encounters it. The vehicle of the text, as arranged by Johnson, is inadequate to the preservation of a consistent didactic programme." See Reddick, "Johnson's *Dictionary of the English Language* and Its Texts: Quotation, Context, Anti-Thematics," *Yearbook of English Studies* 28 (1998), 67. As I shall argue, this seems to me accurate for the fourth edition as well.

   It also seems possible that the addition of older authors was a function of books Johnson acquired from the leavings of his father's bookshop. These may well have included the sort of Non-Juring texts that Michael Johnson found attractive, but for which the commercial market no longer was friendly. By the early 1770s Johnson's friends were reluctant to lend him books they knew would be ravaged. He thus would have called on whatever was available from earlier slips, and from other books on hand, including inherited stock. I am indebted to Anne McDermott for this suggestion.

13. See also the *Journal of a Tour*, in *Life*, vol. v, pp. 64–65, on the need for university students to subscribe to the Thirty-nine Articles. For the letter in its modern edition, see *Letters*, vol. ii, pp. 12–14.

14. See Reddick, "Johnson beyond Jacobitism," p. 988. Reddick offers an excellent brief summary of the Petition and its parliamentary fate: see pp. 986–88, and 1004 n. 10.

15. For changes in etymology, see Daisuke Nagashima, "Johnson's Revisions of His Etymologies," *Yearbook of English Studies* 28 (1998), 94–105. Robert DeMaria, Jr. and Gwin J. Kolb speculate that many of the added illustrative quotations in *1773* were made by amanuenses. See "Johnson's *Dictionary* and Dictionary Johnson," *Yearbook of English Studies* 28 (1998), 33–35, based in part on a suggestion from Robert Burchfield, who edited the Supplement to the *OED*. This of course remains conjectural.

16. See Gibson, *Church of England*, p. 54. Johnson himself said that he never knew a Non-Juror who could reason, and described Elijah Fenton's "perverseness of integrity" in refusing the oaths. See, respectively, Boswell's *Life*, vol. iv, p. 286; and *Lives of the English Poets*, ed. George Birkbeck Hill, 3 vols. (Oxford:

Clarendon Press, 1905), vol. II, p. 257. Johnson admired the rabid Charles Leslie's energetic reasoning and faith; but he must have disapproved of Leslie's self-alienation from the Church of England. This contrasts with Johnson's admiration for Fenton's refusal to accept such zealous enthusiasm.

17. Benjamin Hoadly, *A Persuasive to Lay-Conformity; or, The Reasonableness of Constant Communion with the Church of England; Represented to the Dissenting Laity* (Dublin, 1704), sig. A2ᵛ. Whig and Latitudinarian arguments on unity were especially powerful during the controversial attempt to repeal the Test Act. See David Nokes, *Jonathan Swift, A Hypocrite Reversed: A Critical Biography* (Oxford: Oxford University Press, 1985), pp. 76, 89, 103.

18. *The Spectator*, ed. Donald F. Bond, 5 vols. (Oxford: Clarendon Press, 1965), vol. I, pp. 441–42 (no. 106). For further discussion of the breadth of unity in the eighteenth-century Anglican church, see Gibson, *Church of England*, and the introduction and several articles in *The Church of England, 1689– 1833: From Toleration to Tractarianism*, ed. John Walsh, Colin Haydon, and Stephen Taylor (Cambridge: Cambridge University Press, 1994). Gibson makes plain that Sir Roger's clergyman was characteristic of country parishes that discouraged division and dispute (p. 56).

19. Henry Fielding, *Amelia*, ed. Martin C. Battestin (Oxford: Clarendon Press, 1983), book 12, chap. 5, p. 511 and n. 1 for Booth. For South, see pp. 364 n. 1 and 391 n. 3. I owe this reference to Eric Rothstein.

20. Johnson in fact makes Dryden's remark more normative than did Dryden himself. See *The Works of John Dryden*, 20 vols. (Berkeley and Los Angeles: University of California Press, 1956–2000), vol. XIII, p. 10: "the Unities of Time, Place and Action, [are] more exactly observed, than, perhaps, the *English* Theater requires." For Addison, see *The Spectator*, vol. III, p. 530. I have italicized the lines Johnson alters or omits exclusive of capitalization and punctuation, at least as based upon the Bond edition. The passage begins with Addison's hopes that authors went beyond "the Mechanical Rules" and "would enter into the very Spirit and Soul of fine Writing." Shortly thereafter he says:

> *Thus altho'* in Poetry it be absolutely necessary that the Unities of Time, Place and Action, *with other Points of the same Nature* should be thoroughly *explained and* understood; there is still something more essential, *to the Art, something* that elevates and astonishes the Fancy, *and gives a Greatness of Mind to the Reader, which few of the Criticks besides Longinus have consider'd.*

21. Barten Holyday's *Motives to a Good Life in Ten Sermons* (Oxford, 1657) are not likely to have offended anyone not looking to be offended by conventional trinitarian orthodoxies.

22. J. C. D. Clark, *English Society, 1689–1832* (Cambridge: Cambridge University Press, 1985), p. 283, and Gibson, *Church of England*, p. 15.

23. John Pearson, *An Exposition of the Creed: By John Pearson D. D. and Margaret Professor in Cambridge, and Chaplain to His Majestie*, 3rd ed. (London, 1669), p. 341.

24. The career of Thomas Sprat (1635–1713) suggests the danger of labeling someone a "Tory" and then assigning both a political position and public awareness of it. By 1773, Sprat was better known as the historian of the Royal Society than as the Bishop of Rochester. Though a nominal High-Church Tory, he also "assisted at the coronation of William and Mary. It was his hand that added to the service of 5 Nov. the sentences of the church's gratitude for her second great deliverance on that day" (*DNB*).

25. Richard Hooker, *Of the Laws of Ecclesiastical Polity*, ed. Georges Edelen (Cambridge, Mass.: The Belknap Press, 1977), in *The Folger Library Edition of the Works of Richard Hooker*, ed. W. Speed Hill *et al.*, vol. I, p. 328. For "full dominion," see *Laws* 8.2.5–10 (vol. III, p. 334). Mark Goldie notes the Whigs' post-Revolution use of Hooker on contract theory: see "The Revolution of 1689 and the Structure of Political Argument: An Essay and an Annotated Bibliography of Pamphlets and the Allegiance Controversy," *Bulletin of Research in the Humanities* 83 (1980), 486.

26. The full title is helpful: *The Original and Institution of Civil Government, Discuss'd. Viz. I. An Examination of the Patriarchal Scheme of Government. II. A Defense of Mr. Hooker's Judgment, &c. against the Objections of several late Writers. To which is added, A Large Answer to Dr. F. Atterbury's Charge of Rebellion: In which the Substance of his late Latin Sermon is produced, and fully examined. By Benjamin Hoadly, M. A. Rector of St. Peter's Poor* (London, 1710), pp. 137–38. Hoadly extensively discusses Hooker.

27. Hawkins, *Life of Johnson*, pp. 446–47. If Hawkins was correct, Johnson was more Erastian as well as more Whiggish than is commonly assumed.

28. Carey McIntosh, "English Dictionaries and the Enlightenment," *Yearbook of English Studies* 28 (1998), 16.

29. Reddick, *Making of Johnson's Dictionary*, p. 164.

30. I am pleased to acknowledge the help of Amanda Kenny with my use of Anne McDermott's splendid Cambridge CD-ROM of the first and fourth editions of the *Dictionary*. It helped me quickly to find the fourth edition's use of Beattie, below. For further such discussion, see also Reddick, *Making of Johnson's Dictionary*, pp. 122, 160, 165–66, and "Johnson Beyond Jacobitism," pp. 983–1005.

31. Burke said this when Beattie visited him on 14 May 1773. See *James Beattie's London Diary, 1773*, ed. Ralph S. Walker (Aberdeen: Aberdeen University Press, 1946), p. 33. The diary includes several instances of Beattie's pleasant and approving visits with Johnson and his friends. See also Everard H. King, *James Beattie* (Boston: Twayne Publishers, 1971), p. 22. Beattie's presentation copy, with Johnson's handwritten note on the inner flyleaf, is in the British Library.

32. See the second edition of Beattie's *Essay* (1771), p. 539. See also *Life*, vol. III, p. 11: "Those only who believed in Revelation have been angry at having their faith called in question; because they only had something upon which they could rest as matter of fact." For brief discussion and an illustration of Sir Joshua Reynolds's portrait of Beattie and *The Triumph of Truth* (1774) see

Nicholas Penny, ed., *Reynolds* (New York: Harry N. Abrams, 1986), pp. 257–59, and Richard Wendorf, *Sir Joshua Reynolds: The Painter in Society* (London: National Portrait Gallery, 1996), pp. 116–17. Frances Reynolds, Sir Joshua's sister, also painted Beattie's portrait. Johnson was part of a larger European movement against skepticism in general and Hume in particular. See John Christian Laursen, "Swiss Anti-Skeptics in Berlin," in *Schweizer im Berlin des 18. Jahrhunderts*, ed. Martin Fontius and Helmut Holzhey (Berlin: Akademie Verlag, 1996), pp. 261–81. Laursen demonstrates that Hume was translated to be refuted.

CHAPTER 4

Reassessing the political context of the Dictionary: Johnson and the "Broad-bottom" opposition

Nicholas Hudson

From its publication to the present day, Johnson's *Dictionary* has been a battlefield of conflicting political interpretations. Johnson's contemporary enemies rained abuse on what they chose to regard as the effusion of a "high-flying Tory," as the Whig Thomas Edwards put it.[1] In the course of history, this Whig reading of the *Dictionary* has ramified rather than transformed in significant ways. On the one hand, the epigones of Edwards's Whiggish hostility have portrayed the *Dictionary* as a Trojan horse launched by the rich and titled into the unsuspecting citadel of English culture. "Johnson's notion of language, as of government," writes John Barrell, "is quite openly and frankly one in which the majority should be idle and helpless spectators, while the customs of the polite are converted into law."[2] On the other side of the Atlantic, this line has been repeated, but in the strange form of transmogrifying the *Dictionary* into the manifesto of a liberty-loving liberal. The political orientation of this work, concludes Robert DeMaria, turns out to be the promotion of "freedom."[3] These permutations on Whig history have not gone entirely unchallenged. Still others, such as Allen Reddick and J. C. D. Clark, have reaffirmed Johnson's reputation as "a high-flying Tory," though without the implication that we should think less of him as the result.[4]

That the political predilections of "Dictionary Johnson" should have spawned such a range of interpretations seems itself worthy of investigation. These differences have arisen in part from the intentions of the particular commentator or historian: the narratives of modern Whig or Marxist history, for instance, often need Johnson to be either a villain or a hero, and his *Dictionary* seems to take on a different ideological hue as illuminated by political lights of different colors. On the other hand, evidence for quite opposite conclusions about the politics of the *Dictionary* can be readily marshaled. Those who interpret the *Dictionary* as promoting a Tory agenda can point to definitions of terms such as *abdication* or *non-juror* which seem deliberately to flaunt Johnson's reputation as a not-so-crypto-Jacobite, or to his frequent quoting of authors such as Charles I, Robert South, Francis Atterbury, or William Law, widely associated with high Tory or even Jacobite sentiments. But those who wish to fumigate the *Dictionary* of the musty odor of High-Church orthodoxy can point with equal validity to Johnson's diligent recourse to the great philosopher of Whig thought, John Locke, whose *Essay concerning Human Understanding* he seems to have known virtually by heart, and to numerous definitions of controversial terms that seem neutral and even liberal.

Yet is it possible that all sides in this discussion have adopted an oversimplified account of political debate during the time when Johnson wrote and then revised the *Dictionary?* It is the purpose of the following essay to broach this question and to reconsider the highly complex and amorphous political context of the time during which Johnson was offered and then undertook this project. My argument pivots on an observation just implied – that the *Dictionary* seems so politically bisexual, swinging both ways, right and left. For the political group which had contracted the brilliant but impoverished Johnson to write this work championed, precisely, the elimination of party difference and the creation of a nonpartisan and patriotic system founded on the promotion of beleaguered men of "merit" rather than political favorites, the latter being the infamous habit of Sir Robert Walpole. After the professed "Patriots" Carteret and Pulteney agreed to keep silent in exchange for places in the House of Lords after Walpole's resignation in February 1742, this group spent time in continued and furiously resentful opposition, calling themselves, through their journal *Old England* (edited by "Jeffrey Broad-bottom"), the "Broad-bottom" coalition. Predictably, jokes about the wide breeches of the aristocratic leaders of this alignment followed from the title "Broad-bottom." But its intention was to suggest the absorption of previously proscribed Tories into a movement devoted patriotically to the promotion of national interest over party interest. Hence a shadow opposition formed that included well-known Tories such as Gower, Cotton, and Wynn alongside an array of people whose names should be suggestive to anyone who has studied Johnson's early career and the making of the *Dictionary* – Robert Dodsley, Lord Chesterfield, Alexander Pope, Henry Fielding, George Lyttelton, William Warburton, Richard Savage, and others. Studying the views of this group of politicians and literary men, I will maintain, provides the appropriate context for understanding the evident ambiguity of Johnson's political orientation in the *Dictionary*.

A key figure who links Johnson to this group is Robert Dodsley. As is well known, Dodsley first suggested the dictionary project to Johnson and headed the consortium of booksellers which drew up the contract. But Dodsley had long played the footman – a metaphor that I will take up in a moment – who brought Johnson's name and worth to the ear of powerful literary and political figures in the English establishment. Dodsley had already published Johnson's first literary success, *London*, drawing it to the admiring attention of his friend and patron Alexander Pope, whose Opposition poem, "One Thousand Seven Hundred and Thirty-Eight," apparently appeared the very same day. Pope's famous comment that the author of *London* would soon be "déterré" likely represents something more than a literary judgment, for it had indeed long been the project of Pope and his circle to unearth meritorious though obscure writers, particularly if they might be made *politically* useful. And here we return to Dodsley as "footman": when Pope first came across Dodsley, he was indeed employed as a mere footman, albeit one inclined to scribbling pathetic laments for his own unearthed talent. Dodsley's first success, *A Muse in Livery; or, The Footman's Miscellany* (1732), can hardly be called accomplished, yet it struck just the right chord with Opposition figures disgusted with Walpole's practice of preferring cronies and lackeys before men of genuine value. This work bears the frontispiece of a figure chained by "poverty" and unable to ascend to "Happiness, Virtue, Knowledge." The obvious message is driven home in a poem: "In vain, in vain, I stretch my CHAIN; / In vain I strive to rise."[5] Later in the same miscellany, Dodsley includes an essay on a theme close to Johnson's heart, "The Contempt which Poverty brings Men into" (Dodsley, *A Muse in Livery*, p. 138). Dodsley's lament reached the ears of just the right people. Pope set him up as a bookseller who specialized in retailing the literary wares of the Opposition, and was willing to run the attendant risks. In 1738 Dodsley printed a political poem entitled "Manners; A Satire" by another obscure author, Paul Whitehead, ending up on the wrong side of a prosecution for publishing seditious libel.

At this point we cross paths with another powerful figure who would become a significant character in the story of Johnson's *Dictionary*, Lord Chesterfield. We tend to recall Chesterfield as the wealthy and meretricious socialite whose letters to his illegitimate son displayed, as Johnson quipped disdainfully, "the morals of a whore, and the manners of a dancing master" (*Life*, vol. 1, p. 266). Until his retirement in 1748, however, Chesterfield was among the most influential politicians in England, a proselyte of his fellow nobleman, the mercurial political philosopher Tory Lord Bolingbroke, and the unchallenged parliamentary leader of the Broad-bottom Opposition between Walpole's resignation in 1742 and his own appointment in 1744 to the administration. Unlike Carteret and Pulteney, Chesterfield faced very little recrimination for joining the Pelham ministry. On the contrary, his wide circle of admirers and friends – including Dodsley, Fielding, Thomson, and Lyttelton – applauded his appointment as a great Opposition victory, for Chesterfield had the reputation, not entirely undeserved, for unshakable integrity and profuse generosity. In 1737, he had led the drive against Walpole's Theatrical Licensing Act, speaking forcefully against it in the House of Lords. He loyally supported Dodsley during the bookseller's trial for distributing seditious writing, even lending him his carriage for transportation around town.[6] In this support of less privileged acquaintances, Chesterfield came to embody the ideal that only "merit" should be rewarded. As Dodsley asserted in his puff for Johnson's *Plan of an English Dictionary* in the *Museum*, Chesterfield was "incapable of giving Countenance to anything but Merit."[7] Two different poems entitled "Merit," the first in 1746 and the second published by Dodsley in 1753, celebrated the peer as the "Mycenæus" of the age, an exemplar of aristocratic virtue able to discern worth even when disguised beneath the humble lineaments of poverty or low estate.[8]

Johnson's personal links with Chesterfield, while hardly close, preceded Dodsley's proposal that he be solicited as patron for the *Dictionary* – a proposal that Johnson, perhaps not entirely frankly, later claimed that he accepted only to buy time in producing his *Plan* (see *Life*, vol. 1, p. 183). Chesterfield had close friends in the circle of genteel men and women at Ashbourne, Derbyshire, where Johnson loved to visit as a young man. A major political figure in the Broad-bottom, George Lyttelton, sparred intellectually with Johnson and seems even to have been something of a sexual competitor for the attention of Hill Boothby.[9] Cornelius Ford, who later showed a willingness to help his nephew Sam Johnson afford university, served as Chesterfield's chaplain. During the time that Johnson was composing his coded version of the parliamentary debates for *The Gentleman's Magazine*, many esteemed Chesterfield as the best speaker of all. Johnson's versions of Chesterfield's speeches captured enough of this eloquence that two of them were reprinted, along with admiring commentary, in Chesterfield's posthumous *Complete Works*, much to the older Johnson's amusement (see *Life*, vol. III, p. 351 and n. 2). Another story places Chesterfield's early patronage of Johnson in the context of the Broad-bottom project to unearth unjustly scorned men of merit. One evening Walter Harte, the tutor to Chesterfield's son, was dining at the house of Edward Cave, and took the opportunity to praise Johnson's recently published *Life of Savage*. A few days later, Cave told a perplexed Harte that these comments "made a man very happy": Johnson had in fact been eating in the same room behind a screen, too ashamed of his ragged clothes to emerge (*Life*, vol. I, p. 163 n).

There are shades here of Dodsley's rise from footman to favored literary agent of a specific and close-knit group of Opposition writers and politicians. The choice of Johnson as author of a new English dictionary, that is, along with Chesterfield's intervention as its patron, followed a clear pattern and had important political implications. Could Johnson even have dangled for just such a momentous break, in his own proud and grudging way? The climactic lament of *London*, "Slow rises worth, by poverty depress'd," closely echoed the sentiments of the poem's publisher, Robert Dodsley, in *A Muse in Livery*. Johnson contributed to the Opposition attack on the Theatrical Licensing Act, led by Chesterfield, in *A Compleat Vindication of the Licensers of the Stage* (1739), an ironic "defence" of the government's suppression of Henry Brooke's *Gustavas Vasa*. Donald Greene insists that the *Vindication* "cannot legitimately be [the work] of a Tory; it must be opposition Whig, and 'left-wing' opposition at that."[10] Yet the subscription list to Brooke's play represents a virtual cross-section of what would emerge as the joint Tory–Whig Opposition of the 1740s, including Chesterfield, Lyttelton, Bolingbroke, Wyndham, Cotton, and – in this significant company – Johnson himself. Johnson's technique in this satire, moreover, was very similar to that of another parody of Walpole's sycophantic followers only a month before in *Common-Sense*, a journal closely associated with the Opposition wing represented by Chesterfield and dependents like Henry Fielding.[11] In other words, Johnson appears to have enlisted himself eagerly in the group that would eventually emerge as the "Broad-bottom" Opposition. He also seems to have embraced the mantra of this circle that Walpole's major crime had been the neglect of obscure or impoverished merit. According to Sir John Hawkins, the bond between young Johnson and Savage had been sealed by their mutual sense of being unjustly neglected:

They seemed both to agree in the vulgar opinion, that the world is divided into two classes, of men of merit without riches, and men of wealth without merit; never considering the possibility that both might concenter in the same person, just as when, in the comparison of women, we say, that virtue is of more value than beauty, we forget that many are possessed of both.[12]

It is indeed likely that Johnson's feelings were more complicated than Hawkins gives him credit for, even at this early stage. By the time he wrote the *Life of Savage*, we can detect Johnson's discomfort with the whole ideology of unrewarded merit. Savage, after all, had in fact founded his claims to recognition not on his own literary merit, but on his supposed relations with a family of patently worthless aristocrats. Yet there is every evidence that Johnson had seized the opportunity presented by association with a group of powerful figures who believed in the principle of recognizing real talent, even in the character of an unconnected and struggling Tory.

Central to the Broad-bottom ideology was, indeed, the idea that the very distinction between Whig and Tory had become a Pandora's box of national evils and should be obliterated. This was the position articulated most influentially by the famous former Tory and erstwhile Jacobite, Lord Bolingbroke. Bolingbroke's insistence on the evils of party became one of the fashionable opinions of the Opposition era, "a Kind of Methodism in Politics," as one writer quipped in 1741.[13] "Sure it is high time," wrote another pamphleteer in 1739, "for us to throw aside all Party Names. Let us banish them [from] our Language, and expunge them from our Dictionaries, and for ever forget the injurious Thoughts of one another that have accompanied them."[14] And indeed the Broad-bottom pursued this destruction of party distinctions with energy, not only embracing Tories and alleged crypto-Jacobites in their midst, but brazenly criticizing the whole Hanoverian regime in ways that waved a red flag in the direction of snorting Walpolean bulls. Provoking this challenge was the coincidence in 1742 of Walpole's resignation, the defection of vaunted "Patriot" leaders, and the opening of the War of Austrian Succession in accordance with a treaty that, while signed with Hanover rather than Britain, consigned British treasure and troops to a nationally profitless war on the Continent. Between 1742 and 1744, when Chesterfield entered the administration on the public promise to end this war, berating the Hanoverian direction of foreign policy became a mainstay of Broad-bottom propaganda. *Old England*, the Opposition paper run by the Broad-bottom, reacted with dramatic indignation when George II rode into the Battle of Dettingen wearing a yellow sash announcing his identity as the Elector of Hanover rather than as the red-sashed sovereign of British troops under his command. As protested by "Jeffrey Broadbottom," "the tawdry, worthless YELLOW was prefer'd to, and triumphed over the, till then, victorious RED."[15] The paper followed a week later with what might seem the amazing assertion that the coronation oath, like marriage vows, could lead in extreme cases to "a Divorce."[16]

Determined to portray Johnson as a Jacobite, some recent scholars have insisted that his famous hostility to George II signaled rebellion against the Hanovers' dynastic claims. This assumption should surely be regarded as a pervasive mistake in the recent spate of neo-revisionist accounts of eighteenth-century politics. As we have just noted, openly criticizing and even despising the second George became the general disposition of Broad-bottom politicians, at least between 1742 and 1744. Yet men such as Chesterfield, Fielding, and Lyttelton seemed so invulnerable to suspicions of Jacobitism that even their most flamboyant attacks on the King's links to Hanover apparently provoked no serious rumors of sedition. Johnson's credentials, to be sure, were not so secure. Tories of this time were fighting an uphill battle to convince the public that most of them had renounced the maligned tenets of Tories in the previous generation – *jure divino*, non-resistance, absolute intolerance of religious dissent – and had accepted the legitimacy of both the 1669 Act of Succession and the Hanoverian succession. The anonymous author of *The Loyal, or, Revolutionary Tory* (1733) claimed that only "degrees" divided the mainstream of contemporary Tories and Whigs, whatever their prospective extremes of Jacobitism and republicanism. "Loyal" in this new Tory nomenclature meant a commitment to the alliance of Church and State. Only "a *National Establish'd Church*," this author declared, "will ever be the grand Safeguard of our Liberty and Property."[17] Modern Tories, wrote the author of *The Sentiments of a Tory* (1741), "are for the Church, that they may secure Peace hereafter, and for the Constitution that they may enjoy it here" (p. 6). During a slightly later era, notorious Tories such as John Shebbeare insisted that the connection between his party and Jacobitism had been absurdly exaggerated for political reasons, for Tories stood above all for a nation committed to Christian principles (imagined in the deep purple of conservative Anglicanism), and political anger against the drainage of English blood and money towards Hanover.[18]

Such protestations failed, naturally, to sway those who had a political interest in stigmatizing Tories as covert Jacobites who played Whigs on the political stage while pursuing sinister objectives in the wings. For those who had thrown their chips in the pot with supporters of Walpole and the Pelhams, there were good strategic reasons to declare that Tories really were crypto-Jacobites. When prominent Tories teamed up with the Whigs who stayed in Opposition, alleged turncoats such as John Perceval, Earl of Egmont, saw the opportunity to turn the tables on his former allies. In his widely read pamphlet *Faction Detected by the Evidence of Facts* (1743), Egmont protested that those with "*no Principle*" were not recusant "Patriots" such as himself but dastardly Broad-bottom Whigs who had cozied up to Tories. As for the Tories, they had principles, but of the most detested sort. They only masqueraded as men loyal to the Hanoverian succession: "the most inveterate Jacobite Faction, to carry its View, will profess to act upon Whig Principle, when that becomes the favourite Principle, as it is at this time."[19] Supporters of the Pelhamite dynasty re-echoed these charges throughout the 1740s and 1750s, claiming that the Tory party "is generally composed of secret *Papists, Jacobites, Non-jurors*, and such *bigoted Churchmen*,"[20] and unwittingly providing evidence, however shaky, for claims in our time concerning all Tories' covert loyalty to the Stuarts.

Such was the political atmosphere that surrounded Johnson as he set to work on the *Dictionary*. How should this background influence our understanding of Johnson's lexicography? In answering this question, we need to understand the complexities of the political situation and his place within it. On the one hand, for reasons that seem partly self-interested and partly principled, Johnson doubtless threw his hat in with the people who associated with the Broad-bottom coalition, a decision, or perhaps only an acquiescence, that helped to secure the opportunity he embraced, the chance to write the first great *Dictionary of the English Language*. On the other hand, we should observe from the outset that the proud and high-minded Johnson harbored mixed feelings about this movement, structured as it was as a group of generally sycophantic underlings singing the praises of an aristocratic cadre whose intellectual caliber, particularly when compared with Johnson's, was modest at best. As a self-proclaimed "Tory" in this movement, young Sam Johnson must be regarded as both marginal and transitional. He was marginal because even prominent Tories were clearly meant to feel beholden to the elite Whigs who, for generally political reasons, had built rickety and provisional bridges toward these erstwhile enemies, now fellow members of the Opposition. Yet he was also transitional in attempting to transform Toryism, I think as a matter of heartfelt commitment, from a dynastically obsessed rump into a party committed to Anglicanism and moral principle.

One does not have to look far to find affirmations of identifiably "Broad-bottomed" principles in Johnson's *Dictionary*. At least on an ideological (if not emotional) level, Johnson had absorbed the fashionable lesson that devotion to "party" is inherently evil. He defines *party* as "A number of persons confederated by similarity of design or opinions in opposition to others; a faction."[21] This definition he illustrates with quotations drawn from the work of Locke and Swift, both deeply distrustful of the motives of *party*. "When any of these combatants strips his terms of ambiguity," Locke is cited as observing, "I shall think him a champion of truth, and not the slave of *party*." The citation from Swift evinces even greater hostility to party: "The most violent *party* men are such, as, in the conduct of their lives, have discovered least sense of religion or morality." Similarly, Swift denounces the extremes of both Toryism and Whiggism in a passage cited under the definition of *Whig*: "Whoever has a true value for church and state, should avoid the extremes of *whig* for the sake of the former, and the extremes of tory on the account of the latter." An irenic program to defuse party-spirit also inspired the following lines from Pope's "First Satire of the Second Book of Horace Imitated," used by Johnson as an illustration for *moderation*: "In *Moderation* placing all my Glory, / While Tories call me Whig, and Whigs a Tory."[22] The same lines would be echoed in Pope's "One Thousand Seven Hundred and Thirty-Eight."[23]

These definitions and quotations represent clear signals that Johnson distrusted extreme party spirit even among Tories. He even seemed willing to endorse a version of Bolingbroke's "Patriot King," the ideal of a monarch who, unlike George II, favored no party but spoke instead for the "spirit" of the whole nation. In *The False Alarm* (1770), he scolded fellow Tories for continuing to behave as if they were proscribed from the King's councils despite George III's attempt to emulate Bolingbroke's model of kingly disdain for party: "they have at last a king who knows not the name of party, and who wishes to be the common father of all his people" (Yale *Works*, vol. x, p. 344). Yet there can be little doubt that Johnson considered himself a Tory. While he evidently found himself able, if only for a relatively brief time, to cooperate with open-minded but professed Whigs in the Broad-bottom coalition, he called himself a Tory and gave provocative indications of this identity at many points in the *Dictionary*. Does not this willingness to associate himself with Toryism contradict his supposed support for Broad-bottom hostility to party?

A clue as to how to answer this question can be found in Johnson's well-known definition of *Tory*: "One who adheres to the antient constitution of the state, and the apostolical hierarchy of the church of England." This definition closely echoes the description of Tory principles previously cited from *The Sentiments of a Tory*. Tories, wrote this anonymous author, "are for the Church, that they may secure Peace hereafter, and for the Constitution that they may enjoy it here" (p. 6). We know for a fact that Johnson had both read and agreed with this pamphlet, for he cites it approvingly in his dramatization for *The Gentleman's Magazine* of a momentous parliamentary debate that occurred in February 1741. This was the debate over the Patriot resolution to banish Sir Robert Walpole from the King's councils forever,

a measure that the Patriots' colleagues in Opposition, the Tories, refused
to support because they regarded it as underhanded and unconstitutional.
Led by Edward Harley, the third Earl of Oxford, the Tories even walked
out of the chamber, pursued by Whig catcalls that they were "Sneakers."
The Sentiments of a Tory, published shortly afterwards, set out to rebut this
allegation of cowardice or duplicity, maintaining that the very action of
refusing to persecute George II's favorite minister demonstrated that the
Tories followed deeper principles than a blind hatred of the Hanoverians
or a determination to restore the House of Stuart. In fact, the Tories had
become the true upholders of the nation's constitutional principles and
popular interests. They had previously opposed such government measures
such as the Riot Act and the Black Act, becoming the true champions of the
nation's rights and freedoms; now they opposed the cynical Whig procedure
to deny Walpole every Englishman's right to defend himself in the face of
his accusers. At the conclusion of his version of this confrontation between
the Opposition Whigs and Harley's Tories (which did not appear until
1743, well after some of these same Patriots proved their lack of principle
by joining the administration), Johnson recounted the arguments of *The
Sentiments of a Tory*, proclaiming triumphantly that "To this defence of the
High-heel'd Party, no Reply was attempted."[24]

Importantly, Johnson's praise for *The Sentiments of a Tory*, as well as his
support for Harley's Tories in this debate (which well might have encouraged his agreement to catalogue Edward, the second Earl of Oxford's great
library after his death in 1741), corroborates evidence for his allegiance to the
ideology of so-called "loyal" or "revolution" Tories. As we have indicated,
this ideology upheld the legitimacy of the Glorious Revolution and the
Hanoverian succession while also claiming that the Tories, not the Whigs,
had recently stood by principle over self-interest, and that they ultimately
represented the mainstream of England's religious and constitutional heritage, being the true defenders of its traditional "liberties." As Linda Colley
has correctly argued, Tories wrapped themselves in a populist, nationalistic,
and anti-establishment flag before the succession of George III in 1760.[25]
John Shebbeare, Johnson's most notorious cohort as a Tory benefactor of
George III's "Broad-bottomed" patronage, spent the 1750s building a reputation that reflects Johnson's own, except in more dangerously radical colors.
Shebbeare twice spent time in the stocks, first for ridiculing, in true-blue
Anglican terms, the ministry's infamous Marriage Act in 1753, and again
in 1758 for writing a series of six *Letters to the People of England*. The latter
work epitomizes the loosely democratic impulses that Greene, DeMaria,

and others have confused with a full-fledged commitment to liberal American values: while renouncing Jacobitism, Shebbeare called on the people to rise up and oppose the King's supposed preference for Hanoverian over English interests, a position that made Shebbeare a great people's hero of the late 1750s. (To great applause, Shebbeare was allowed merely to lean against the stocks during his second trip there.) The essence of this form of modern Toryism lay in the belief that only Tories had risen above the base and unprincipled opportunism of the administration's Whig supporters, creating a political front that was *not* "factional" nor truly party-oriented, but rather coherent with the religious, moral, and constitutional heritage of England. Contrary to what recent scholars have wanted us to believe, such an adjustment of Tory ideology during the Walpole era certainly did *not* imply a commitment to a Stuart succession. Indeed, James II's aggressively Roman Catholic orientation during his brief reign ran directly against the constitutionalism and proudly Anglican grain of eighteenth-century Tory conservatism.

At this point, we might recall Johnson's famous definition of *Whig* – "A faction." Johnson seems to have had in mind the kind of sentiments voiced in Egmont's *Faction Detected*, which, as cited earlier, charged the Broad-bottom Whigs with being a "Faction" possessed of *"no Principle,"* willing to appease even Jacobites for personal interest. In response, Johnson accused Whigs in general – pro-government and administration – of being an unprincipled "faction," a blustery challenge to his political opponents that he re-echoed throughout the Boswell years.[26] The force of this challenge lay in a quite historic debate concerning the nature of political disagreement and political groupings. Despite his proclaimed hatred of "party," which he equated with "faction," Johnson could remain a professed Tory because Tories stood both for "principle" and for what he considered mainstream English cultural traditions – "the antient constitution of the state, and the apostolical hierarchy of the church of England." Clearly rehearsing the arguments of Tory pamphlets in the 1730s and 1740s, Johnson was trying to reconfigure this ideology as a movement that remained true to the whole history of England. Of that history, he certainly possessed a greater knowledge and wider range of reference than some scholars have given him credit for. He knew well that England's record of dynastic succession was profoundly discontinuous – indigenous Britons had been replaced with a jagged line of Romans, Saxons, Normans, Welsh, Scots, and Germans. Against this background, the *jure divino* idea of monarchy could not possibly be regarded as indigenous. Consider again the supposedly

"Jacobite" *Marmor Norfolciense*: in this work, a professed "Saxon" interpreter comments hysterically on an inscription by an ancient "Briton"
that, set in its appropriate historical context, should probably be taken as
an ominous prediction of the *Saxon* conquest and its aftermath, and only
secondarily of that more recent German incursion, the Hanoverian succession. Before taking on the *Dictionary* project, Johnson seriously considered
writing the life of one of his heroes, Alfred the Great. Alfred, an Opposition hero and protagonist of the 1740 masque by Thomson and Mallet
that gave us the words to "Rule Britannia," had established a tradition of
balanced powers between King and Parliament – at least according to the
Vinerian law lectures that Johnson would help to write with his friend Sir
Robert Chambers.[27] In other words, even the young Johnson, before the
redirection of English politics that J. C. D. Clark and others locate at about
1760, held an essentially rationalistic and pragmatic commitment to this
balance of power, believing that the monarch legitimately checked rather
than prescribed to Parliament. This orientation is suggested by his citations from the writing of the Stuart monarch whose entirely constitutional
reign had been destroyed by "factions." Under *faction*, Johnson quotes
Charles I, insisting that "By the weight of reason I should counterpoise the
overbalancing of any *factions*." Under *factious*, as if to drive the point home,
Johnson again quotes Charles I, in a spirit of defending limited and constitutional monarchy: "*Factious* tumults overbore the freedom and honour
of the two houses."

All this evidence indicates that Johnson produced, politically speaking, the kind of dictionary anticipated by the Broad-bottom ideology
that coalesced during Johnson's first decade in London, the period that
gave this unlikely recipient, the son of an obscure provincial bookseller,
such a prestigious and expensive project. In considering this event we
should take into account that Johnson represented precisely the kind of
neglected man of "merit" the Opposition liked to champion during this
era of notorious patronage. He also seems to have been the "right kind"
of Tory – angry at George II like many prominent Whigs, but essentially
interested in cooperating on the project of building a new, Hanoverian
England founded on the promotion of merit rather than self-interest, of
the "constitution" rather than party or dynastic loyalties. Yet Johnson's association with the Broad-bottom Opposition, probably always rather uncomfortable, ground to the bitter halt memorialized by his indignant letter to
Lord Chesterfield in February 1755. What motivated this acrimonious split
from the political alignment that had helped to lift Johnson to his literary
pedestal?

This famous letter can be fruitfully read in the context that we have just drawn. As we have considered, Chesterfield had inspired a minor genre of mid-century encomia devoted to celebrating his selfless and principled promotion of "merit," his ability to perceive ability and virtue even beneath the livery of a footman. To this little genre, Johnson's letter represents, in effect, the anti-genre. In contrast to the standard glorification of Chesterfield as the exemplar of high-minded and impartial nobility, Johnson implicitly portrays his vaunted "patron" as haughty, vain, and neglectful, unable to discern merit beneath the rough manners of a unpolished though worthy man: "When I had once addressed your Lordship in public," he wrote, "I had exhausted all the Art of pleasing which a retired and uncourtly Scholar can possess. I had done all I could, and no Man is well pleased to have his all neglected, be it ever so little" (*Letters*, vol. 1, p. 95). The note of wronged virtue so palpable in this letter can also be found in the Preface to the *Dictionary*, where Johnson depicts himself in purple hues as a "humble drudge" toiling in the mines of the English language: "It is the fate of those who toil in the lower employments of life . . . to be exposed to censure, without hope of praise; to be disgraced by miscarriage, or punished for neglect, where success would have been without applause, and diligence without reward" (1825 *Works*, vol. v, p. 23). Here is Dodsley's *Muse in Livery*, but with a cynical twist. Dodsley was still to be "unearthed" when he wrote a very similar lament. But Johnson has created the role (surely integral also to his view of himself during this period) of a man of merit, diligence, and exploited humility who had been shunted aside by the same men who rescued Dodsley, expected to spread a glow over undeserving patrons who pretended to stand up for obscured merit but who had signally failed to support the most meritorious man of them all.

Johnson's narrative performance as the wronged and beleaguered man of merit seems inspired as much by problems of social class as politics. Indeed, Johnson of the *Dictionary* period found himself caught precisely on the horns of these two forces. The political thrust of the Broad-bottom coalition had been to challenge the Walpolean hegemony by charging the administration with valuing self-interest and status over virtue and merit. Yet, whatever the benefits of this rhetoric in terms of political strategy, it obscured the extent to which Broad-bottom culture remained essentially elitist, a condescending project of rich and powerful men wrapped in the ermine of their own beneficence. The young Johnson found himself able to encourage, even enthusiastically, the notions that "party" equaled "faction" and that England's essential tragedy lay in the failure of worthy people of whatever background to be promoted. Especially in its harsh definitions of *party* and related terms, Johnson's *Dictionary* remains a product of Broad-bottom ideology. But all evidence suggests that Johnson also despised the sacrifice of his dignity in being obliged to rich and vain men like Chesterfield and his entourage of effete gentlemen such as Lyttelton and that "block-head" Fielding. He even came to distrust the practical possibility, however desirable, of a social hierarchy grounded systematically on "merit." *The Rambler*, written in the winter of his discontent with Chesterfield's sup-posed "patronage," repeatedly returns to the theme that popularity and favor are founded on superficial qualities of manners, *not* genuine worth or virtue, a bitter reprise of the Machiavellian theme that runs through Chesterfield's *Letters to his Son*.[28]

So let us return to our opening question. Is Johnson's *Dictionary* the product of an authoritarian and Jacobite Tory or a freedom-loving liberal? My answer is, of course, neither. The ambiguity of the *Dictionary*, the source of current scholarship's ambivalent response to this question, derives from both the fluidity of the political environment in which Johnson com-posed this work and the controversial situation of party politics in general during this period. Dictionary Johnson lived during a time when tradi-tional Toryism was undergoing a gradual process of redefinition and when proclaimed "Tories" identified themselves with the "people" in a manner that might seem "liberal" from a modern perspective. Whigs of a certain "unprincipled" breed had become as suspect as Tories who claimed to have turned a new leaf. The need to do away with party distinctions altogether had become a kind of political mantra. By the fourth edition of 1773 Johnson may have felt the need to strengthen scattered indications of his Toryism, as argued by Allen Reddick.[29] But he also knew that in 1773 doctrines of *jure divino* seemed about as relevant to readers of dictionaries as the existence of witches and Ptolemaic cosmology. In large part, the *Dictionary of the English Language* never lost its political shape – a baggy shape, to be sure, but one that testifies to the amorphous quality of party divisions during this time, and the jagged trajectory of Johnson's own development as a political thinker.

NOTES

1. Thomas Edwards to Daniel Wray, 23 May 1755, Bodleian Library, Oxford, Bodleian MS 1012, fol. 208.
2. John Barrell, *English Literature in History, 1730–80: An Equal, Wide Survey* (London: Hutchinson, 1983), p. 148.
3. Robert DeMaria, Jr., "The Politics of Johnson's *Dictionary*," *PMLA* 104 (1989), 64–74.

4. See Allen Reddick, *The Making of Johnson's Dictionary*, rev. ed. (Cambridge: Cambridge University Press, 1996), p. 153; J. C. D. Clark, *Samuel Johnson: Literature, Religion and English Politics from the Restoration to Romanticism* (Cambridge: Cambridge University Press, 1994), pp. 130–31.

5. Robert Dodsley, *A Muse in Livery; or, The Footman's Miscellany* (London, 1732), p. 1.

6. See Harry M. Solomon, *The Rise of Robert Dodsley: Creating the New Age of Print* (Carbondale and Edwardsville: Southern Illinois University Press, 1996), p. 121.

7. *The Museum*, 1 August 1747, 389.

8. See *Merit: A Satire, Humbly Addressed to His Excellency the Earl of Chesterfield* (Dublin, 1746); Henry Jones, *Merit, a Poem: Inscribed to the Right Honourable Philip Earl of Chesterfield* (London, 1753).

9. See James L. Clifford, *Young Sam Johnson* (New York: McGraw-Hill, 1955), p. 227.

10. Donald J. Greene, *The Politics of Samuel Johnson* (New Haven: Yale University Press, 1960), p. 105.

11. See *Common-Sense* 116 (21 April 1739). According to Greene's preface to the *Vindication*, Johnson's piece was first advertised on 25 May 1739 (Yale *Works*, vol. x, p. 54).

12. Sir John Hawkins, *The Life of Samuel Johnson* (London, 1787), p. 53.

13. Anon., *The Sentiments of a Tory, in Respect to a Late Important Transaction* (London, 1741), p. 5.

14. Anon., *Observations on the Conduct of the Tories, Whigs, and the Dissenters* (London, 1739), p. 39.

15. *Old England* (7 January 1744).

16. *Ibid.* (28 January 1744).

17. Anon., *The Loyal, or, Revolutionary Tory* (London, 1733), p. 18.

18. For example, in Shebbeare's comic novel *Lydia; or, Filial Piety*, 2 vols. (London, 1755), a government minister worries to his colleagues about the need to keep the myth of Tory Jacobitism alive in order to keep the Tory Opposition in the political wilderness: "The *Jacobites* are already expired, and the very Name cannot be kept long alive, if this young Man [the Pretender] be destroyed" (vol. 1, p. 75).

19. John Perceval, Earl of Egmont, *Faction Detected by the Evidence of Facts* (London, 1743), pp. 5–6.

20. Anon., *The Balance; or, The Merits of Whig and Tory Exactly Weigh'd and Fairly Determin'd* (London, 1753), p. 3.

21. All quotations of the *Dictionary* come from *1755*.

22. "First Satire of the Second Book of Horace Imitated," lines 67–68, in *The Poems of Alexander Pope*, ed. John Butt (New Haven: Yale University Press, 1963).

23. This poem is also known as "Epilogue to the Satires," its title in Butt's edition. See Dialogue 1, line 8.

24. *The Gentleman's Magazine* 13 (1743), 181.

25. See Linda Colley, *In Defiance of Oligarchy* (Cambridge: Cambridge University Press, 1982), pp. 146–47.
26. Whiggism, as he told Boswell, was "*the negation of all principle*" (*Life*, vol. 1, p. 141).
27. See Sir Robert Chambers and Samuel Johnson, *A Course of Lectures on the English Law*, ed. Thomas M. Curley, 2 vols. (Madison: University of Wisconsin Press, 1986), vol. 1, p. 100.
28. See, e.g., *Rambler*s 56, 72, and 188.
29. See Reddick, *The Making of Johnson's Dictionary*, p. 153.

CHAPTER 5

Johnson's extempore History and Grammar of the English language

Robert DeMaria, Jr.

As I argued in *Johnson's "Dictionary" and the Language of Learning* (1986) and in *Samuel Johnson: A Critical Biography* (1993) and as I still believe, Johnson's *Dictionary*, like much of his writing, expresses his affinities with European humanism – a deep and varied tradition that valued learning above everything but piety. At key moments in his great book of learning Johnson seems to sum up his message, as, for example, when he defines *crossrow*: "Alphabet; so named because a cross is placed at the beginning, to shew that the end of learning is piety." Surely this is the meaning of the *Dictionary* – and yet, I must confess, Johnson is also simply defining the word *crossrow*. His book, after all, is a dictionary. It is a dictionary; and yet, the selection of texts – all those works of physico-theology, for example – and the occasional direct comment lead one to believe that a moral and intellectual design governs the whole. If he were only composing a dictionary, why, for example, would Johnson feel compelled to add after his definition of *caitiff* the Greek epigram about the moral evil of slavery ('Ημισυ τῆς ἀρετῆς ἀποαίνυται δούλιον ἦμαρ, "the day of slavery decimates virtue")?

As this little dialogue with myself suggests, the question in much of my work on the *Dictionary* has been about its mixture of philological exposition and moral or educational design. Lately, however, I have been considering the extent to which parts of the *Dictionary* belong neither to philological nor to moral designs but simply occur, as the result of Johnson's more spontaneous responses to the tasks before him: these spontaneous, unplanned parts of the book may be informed by Johnson's deep humanism, but they may also be expressions of more immediate interests and experiences. The phrasing of the definition of *crossrow*, for example, may reflect Johnson's recent work on *The Preceptor*, particularly his concluding allegory "The Hermit of Teneriffe." Johnson was commissioned to do this work by Robert Dodsley, whom he called his "patron," and who was most responsible for landing him the job as national lexicographer. Perhaps he defined *crossrow* as he did to flatter Dodsley and to keep the *Dictionary* in line with Dodsley's other projects, such as *The Preceptor* and *The Economy of Human Life*. The epigram after *caitiff*, though part of a deep tradition, might reflect Johnson's recent thoughtfulness on the contemporary issue of slavery. He must have been thinking about the topic as he composed the early parts of the *Dictionary* around 1750; his black servant, Francis Barber, had recently been placed in his "care" by his friend Richard Bathurst, who brought him to London from his family plantation in Barbados. Perhaps Johnson was eager to broadcast a protest against slavery because he was feeling uncomfortably close to slave-holding himself. Perhaps that feeling is a more immediate cause of his outburst under *caitiff* than deeper convictions. It could be a combination of the two. One cannot be sure.

It is difficult to make the case for immediacy in any particular instance, but overall there seems to be a spontaneous, extempore quality to the *Dictionary* as well as a design. The famous gems in the *Dictionary* – the definition of *lexicographer* as "a harmless drudge" or the Homeric paean appended to the word *Grubstreet*, for example – are traditional evidence of "personality" in the *Dictionary*. The spontaneous element in the *Dictionary*, however, is broader than the so-called personal element or the expressions of personality, though they overlap. The immediate, spontaneous, or extempore comprise responses to contemporary situations, whether they are strictly personal or not. Johnson's wish to please Dodsley and his expression of anger at slavery, if indeed active in the *Dictionary*, are not personal in the same way as the famous gems. The gems construct a personality rather than show one in the process of acting on contemporary concerns.

In tracing the sources of quotations in the *Dictionary* one can see how spontaneous Johnson was at times when he was not necessarily expressing personality at all: he sometimes picked up a recently published book (such as Jane Collier's *Essay on the Art of Ingeniously Tormenting* or Pitt's *Vergil*), took a word or two from it, and put it aside. He read parts of books while neglecting other parts (e.g., in Burton's *Anatomy*); he rejected authors not only by design (because they were morally unacceptable, for instance, in the cases of Hobbes and Bolingbroke), but also because he did not want to read them or because they did not fall into his hands. It is no surprise that a lover of "desultory reading" should indulge the practice even in the midst of a lot of methodical reading for a great project. I have in recent years, however, become more aware of Johnson's generally desultory ways in composing the *Dictionary*, and the great book itself seems in some ways more immethodical to me than it did twenty years ago. That is to say that the force of spontaneous reactions to the challenges of the book, rather than planned strategies, seems stronger; Johnson's present impulses and present concerns, rather than timeless humanistic topics, seem stronger; and accident seems stronger than it once did in relation to design.[1] This is especially true with respect to Johnson's History of the English Language and his Grammar of the English Tongue. These parts of the *Dictionary* may not be representative of the whole – they probably are not – but examining them sensitizes one to features of the book that are surprisingly prominent in the whole work.

The preliminary parts of the *Dictionary* – Preface, History, and Grammar – were the last parts that Johnson wrote. In view of the fact that the latter parts of the *Dictionary* proper were composed more hastily than the first parts (the contrast between the work in A, B, C and the work in X, Y, Z is most striking), it is not surprising that the preliminaries appear the most hastily composed of all. (The Preface is the exception, but it rests on the *Plan*, itself the culmination of at least two earlier drafts.) Admittedly, Johnson had a plan for writing the History and Grammar, but he did not keep to it.[2] On 16 July 1754 he wrote to Thomas Warton, praising him for his *Observations on the Faerie Queene of Spenser* (1754). He especially approved of Warton's historical method – his use of Spenser's contemporaries and forerunners to explain his language – and he found affinities between Warton's work and his own great project:

The Reason why the authours which are yet read of the sixteenth Century are so little understood is that they are read alone, and no help is borrowed from those who lived with them or before them. Some part of this ignorance I hope to remove by my book which now draws towards its end, but which I cannot finish to my mind without visiting the libraries of Oxford which I therefore hope to see in about a fortnight. (*Letters*, vol. I, p. 81)

Johnson was evidently unable to "finish" the *Dictionary* "to [his] mind" for, in about a fortnight (the letter is not precisely dated), he wrote to his publisher William Strahan, "My journey will come to very little beyond the satisfaction of knowing that there is nothing to be done, and that I leave few advantages here to those that shall come after me" (vol. I, p. 82). This is patently untrue, and Johnson must have known it, unless he meant something very different from what he appears to mean in his remark to Strahan. There were, for example, manuscript resources in the Bodleian and in Oxford's college libraries, and Johnson knew it because he owned a copy of *Bernard's Catalogue*, which listed manuscript holdings all over Oxford.[3]

He also spent some time with Francis Wise, a Bodleian librarian, amidst his "nest of British and Saxon Antiquities" (*Letters*, vol. 1, p. 109). Johnson may have enjoyed the walk up to Wise's "nest" in Elsfield, but there is no evidence that he gathered any material on the trip. It appears that he also did not consult printed books; in Oxford he surely could have seen a copy of Edward Lye's edition of *Four Gospels, Evangelica Gothica* (1750), but the lacuna in his History shows that he did not know of it. (Johnson added the reference in his revised fourth edition of the *Dictionary*, which shows that he thought knowledge of Lye's edition belonged in his History, but he did not have that knowledge in 1755.) He also could certainly have seen a better edition than he used of *Tottel's Miscellany*. He complains about the many errors in the 1717 edition that "fell into his hands," and he makes many corrections. But he did not think far enough ahead to look at a better edition in Oxford. In fact, the only works that Johnson used in the History are ones he almost certainly owned already and were therefore ready to hand when he composed the work after returning to London in September 1754, about seven months before the publication of the *Dictionary* on 15 April.

The most influential work he encountered in Oxford, though not for the first time, was Warton's *Observations*.[4] Johnson selected six poets also selected by Warton in his thumbnail sketch of the history of English poetry (*Observations*, pp. 227–39). Both men called the poets "bards" and both treated, in the same order, Robert of Gloucester, John Gower, Chaucer, Lydgate, Thomas More, and Skelton. There are similarities between Johnson's remarks on these poets and Warton's; these similarities are not as striking as the choice and order of the examples, but they are enough to show the influence of Warton's written work on Johnson. The lexicographer may have had Warton's *Observations* near at hand when he composed his history, as he certainly did his copy of George Hickes's *Linguarum vetterum septentrionalium thesaurus* and James Greenwood's *Essay towards a Practical English Grammar*.[5] These latter works contain sections that provide the best generic antecedents for Johnson's History, and Hickes's *Thesaurus* provides actual texts. But whereas Johnson often copies Hickes verbatim, he seems merely to recall Warton: he indicates his knowledge of Warton's remarks not by paraphrasing them but by repeating a key word, such as "bard."

Warton was running through Johnson's mind as he wrote; but it was not necessarily the printed work any more than it was the conversations he must have had with Warton in Oxford. Warton says Chaucer "was the first who gave the English nation, in its own language, an idea of

HUMOUR" (*Observations*, p. 228). Johnson recalls the remark somewhat faintly or assimilates it to his own notion when he says, "the history of our poetry is generally supposed to commence" with Chaucer, and "he may perhaps, with great justice, be stiled the first of our versifyers who wrote poetically" (*1755*, sig. F1ᵛ). "First" is a key word in both judgments; the transformation of the creation of "humour" into writing "poetically" is a plausible activity of Johnson's generalizing mind. Although Warton's book might have been a regular and methodically assimilated source of Johnson's History, it seems more likely to me that both the book and Warton's conversation were extempore influences: they were running through his mind, as recent experience does, rather than laid out for analysis on his desk.

There is other evidence that Johnson composed his History in this unmethodical way. In one passage, for example, Johnson writes:

What was the form of the *Saxon* language, when, about the year 450, they first entered *Britain*, cannot now be known. They seem to have been a people without learning, and very probably without an alphabet; their speech therefore, having been always cursory and extemporaneous, must have been artless and unconnected, without any modes of transition or involution of clauses; which abruptness and inconnection may be observed even in their later writings. This barbarity may be supposed to have continued during their wars with the *Britains*, which for a time left them no leisure for softer studies; nor is there any reason for supposing it abated, till the year 570, when *Augustine* came from *Rome* to convert them to Christianity. (*1755*, sig. D1ʳ)

Johnson's 450 may be an approximation of the canonical date of 449, but 570 is clearly an indistinct memory of 597, the regularly given date easily derived from the standard work, Bede's *Historia eccelsiastica gentis Anglorum* (chapters 24–25). It is also odd that in this passage Johnson uses the word "inconnection," which is not in the *Dictionary*. The only other place it occurs in Johnson's works is in a footnote, probably but not assuredly by him, in the 1742 edition of *Monarchy Asserted* (Yale *Works*, vol. x, p. 77). I think it is a word he may have rejected had he been composing more methodically; its presence in the History marks that composition as somehow outside the regular realm of Johnsonian composition – it is a note rather than a composition.

In his Grammar, the last piece that Johnson composed before the publication of the *Dictionary*, there is even more evidence than in the History that he was noting rather than composing when he assembled the final parts of the *Dictionary*. At least nine words in the Grammar do not appear in the *Dictionary* proper. (Admittedly, most of these are words transcribed from the grammarian John Wallis, so one might conclude that Wallis is outside the world of Johnson's *Dictionary* without prejudice to the case of the Grammar; but then Wallis is such a large part of the Grammar that it is difficult to make this distinction.) Whereas the History cites passages from forty texts, twenty-seven of which are also used as sources of illustrative quotation in the *Dictionary*, the Grammar, in addition to other citations, uses forty-eight quotations illustrative of Johnson's remarks on orthography, grammar, and prosody. Twenty of these are also cited in the *Dictionary*, proportionally fewer than those cited in the History, and not all of these twenty are cited in precisely the same form in the Grammar. Twenty-eight of the quotations are new. Of the total of forty-eight citations, eight are from Milton and two from Shakespeare; these ten quotations are also cited in the *Dictionary*. The remaining quotations come from a total of twenty-six authors, several of whom are not cited at all in the *Dictionary*. As this summary suggests and a detailed examination of the body of illustrative quotation in the Grammar shows, a good deal of it is generated extempore rather than through Johnson's earlier, more methodical work on the *Dictionary*.

The largest number of quotations in the Grammar are in Johnson's Prosody. In adding a section on prosody at all, Johnson was departing from grammatical and lexicographical tradition, as he himself acknowledges: "It is common for those that deliver the grammar of modern languages, to omit their Prosody. So that of the Italians is neglected by *Buomattei*; that of the French by *Desmarais*; and that of the English by *Wallis, Cooper*, and even by [Ben] *Johnson* though a poet. But as the laws of metre are included in the idea of a grammar, I have thought it proper to insert them" (*1755*, sig. C2^r). Of the fifty-two English grammars published before 1754 in R. C. Alston's bibliography, only one – Alexander Gil's *Logonomia Anglica* (1619) – includes a list of metrical categories.[6] Several have sections on pronunciation, which is the first part of Johnson's Prosody but not the section with the illustrative quotations. Although Johnson cites Gil's work for the sake of illustrating the tradition of spelling reform in the seventeenth century, he does so derisively; it is unlikely, therefore, that he would have tried to follow Gil in adding his Prosody. It is more likely that he had a Latin work in mind, but it seems most likely of all that the Prosody, like much of its contents, is an extempore, last-minute addition to the *Dictionary*.

One sign that Johnson merely recalled his quotations illustrative of various prosodical forms is that he did not identify most of them in the first edition of the *Dictionary*, although he added references in the fourth edition. Even as vague a reference as "Old Ballad" is missing from the first edition; it was added to the fourth edition after three lines adduced to illustrate the five-syllable trochaic measure:

> In the days of old,
> Stories plainly told,
> Lovers felt annoy.
> (*1755*, sig. d1ʳ)

The lines come from a ballad by Thomas Deloney called "The King of France's Daughter." Thomas Percy printed it in *Reliques of Ancient English Poetry* (1765), but Johnson may have seen it in Percy's manuscript or in *A Collection of Old Ballads* (1723). In any case he omitted the line that follows the first line that he cites, presumably because it has six syllables rather than five. But would he have done so if he were looking at the book? Probably not. Probably he would have chosen another part of the ballad. This citation therefore looks very much as though it is remembered, and like most memories it is selective.

Also absent from the *Dictionary* and present in the Grammar is the author David Lewis. In his Prosody Johnson quotes a few lines of Lewis's poem "To Pope" as an example of a fourteen-syllable line typeset in a pattern of an eight-syllable line over a six:

> When all shall praise, and ev'ry lay
> Devote a wreath to thee,
> That day, for come it will, that day
> Shall I lament to see.
> (*1755*, sig. d1ʳ)

The poem originally appeared in print in a note to the second edition of Pope's *Dunciad* A (1729). In that publication, however, the clause "for come it will" is enclosed in parentheses. Johnson was unlikely, therefore, to have transcribed the lines. He probably recalled them, as he did on Sunday, 13 June 1784, along with the other three stanzas. On that occasion, Boswell records that Johnson incorrectly remembered the second half of the third stanza, saying, "When with thy Homer thou shalt shine / In one unclouded flame" instead of "In one establish'd fame" (*Life*, vol. IV, p. 307). Johnson "thought [that] was the reading in former editions," but Boswell believed it was "a flash of his own genius" and thought it "much more poetical than the other." "Unclouded flame" is visual in the broad, abstract sense that Johnson's poetry always is (consider "the clouded maze of fate" in *The Vanity of Human Wishes*), and it is surely better than "one established fame," which is thoroughly abstract. What does fame shining look like? A reader cannot make much of this phrase.

Directly below the lines from Lewis that flatter Pope for being above mere popularity, in the fourth edition Johnson placed Samuel Wesley's "Epitaph on an Infant." He also printed these lines, in just about exactly the same form (one capital letter is lower case), under *trump*. In both instances, however, Johnson gives a version of the first four lines that differs radically from the printed versions now available. Johnson has:

> Beneath this tomb an infant lies
> To earth whose body lent,
> Hereafter shall more glorious rise,
> But not more innocent.
>
> (*1773*, sig. d1^r)

In Wesley's *Poems on Several Occasions* (1743), the first four lines are:

> Beneath a sleeping Infant lies,
> To Earth whose Ashes lent,
> More glorious shall hereafter rise,
> Tho' not more innocent.

Perhaps the word "tomb," in substitution for "sleeping," added for Johnson a finality that he thought appropriate in any mention of death, and perhaps "body" is a doctrinal substitution for "ashes." Arguably, both changes put the poem more in Johnson's religious orbit than Wesley's, but not too much should be made of this.[7] It is obvious, however, that Johnson changed the lines, while keeping the meter intact, and it seems very probable that these changes were made extempore.

Next in his Prosody Johnson mentions "another measure very quick and lively, and therefore much used in songs, which may be called the *anapestick*, in which the accent rests upon every third syllable" (*1755*, sig. d1^r). As examples he adduces two lines from "Doctor Pope's Wish: A Ballad" (1685), sometimes entitled "The Old Man's Wish," a poem by Walter Pope, who is not cited anywhere in the first edition of the *Dictionary*. (He is cited once in *1773*, s.v. *pad-nag*.) The lines are the chorus of the poem:

> May I góvern my pássions with ábsolute swáy,
> And grow wíser and bétter as lífe wears awáy.
>
> (*1755*, sig. d1^r)

Bennet Langton reported to Boswell an undated incident in which Johnson, "rebuking" a "clergyman's" deliberate failure to quote Pope's "song" accurately, recited the lines correctly, laying special stress on "May I govern my passions with absolute sway" (*Life*, vol. IV, p. 19). The lines compose just the sort of moral injunction Johnson was often eager to print, and he indicated exactly how the lines should be stressed vocally as well as ethically in the *Dictionary*.

A line from another ballad follows, incorrectly attributed to Dr. Pope: "Diógenes súrly and proúd." The line comes from Edward Ward's poem "The Tipling Philosophers" (line 177). Johnson's memory must have furnished these lines, and I would like to believe that, as ballads do, they circulated both in his mind and in the society he kept. Morris Brownell has identified more than 150 songs mentioned in Boswell's *Life, Tour*, and *Journals* and fifty more of Boswell's own creation in manuscripts. As he points out, the presence of songs and ballads in the life of eighteenth-century intellectuals has been neglected, "perhaps because of traditional literary prejudice against the genre."[8] Although Johnson was demonstrably no music lover, he does seem to have had ballads running through his mind. His placement of them on the pages of his Prosody are not so much evidence of personality as they are indications of what he was hearing and remembering in conversation, in the theatre, and on the street.

Johnson could have read it as a broadside or seen it in the manuscript of Percy's *Reliques*, but it seems just as likely that Johnson heard and replayed occasionally in his mind the ballad "Admiral Hosier's Ghost" (1740) by Richard Glover. This political song contrasts the languishing death of the admiral and his men when, in 1726, they were forbidden to attack Porto Bello, a Spanish port in the West Indies, with the triumph of Admiral Edward Vernon's assault in 1739. Johnson recalls lines 49–52:

> For resistance I could fear none,
> But with twenty ships had done,
> What thou, brave and happy Vernon,
> Hast atchiev'd with six alone.

In 1739, when the ballad was first circulating, Johnson referred to Admiral Hosier in *Marmor Norfolciense* (Yale *Works*, vol. X, p. 41). He must have heard it or read it at that time (though it seems not to have been published until 1740). In the autumn of 1754 it returned to his mind, I conjecture, though his days as a "patriot" were over and Walpole long gone. Perhaps, however, the fact that the conflict between France and Britain in America was heating up in fall of 1754 brought patriotic songs to the streets. Though Johnson would then have heard them in a different key, since he opposed the war with France, he may well have heard them and recalled them when he needed them in another context.

Did Johnson go to the theatre and hear songs there? The evidence is scant. Certainly he went at times, but later in life, the period when his movements were much more carefully recorded, he did not hear well enough to enjoy the performances. Earlier in life he may have gone more often. The Prosody suggests that he knew songs recited in the theatre and had them in mind, whether he had read them only or heard them. He might have read in Dryden's play *Amphytrion* (4.1.490–91) or have heard in performance "Mercury's Song to Phaedra," a couplet of which he quotes in the fourth edition after "The Tipling Philosophers":

> When présent, we lóve, and when ábsent agrée,
> I thínk not of Iris, nor Iris of mé. (*1773*, sig. d1ʳ)

An auditory memory is also a plausible source for the lines from Addison's *Cato* (5.1.7–9) that Johnson also quotes; but it seems much more likely that Johnson heard in some kind of performance a tune in *The Beggar's Opera* adopted from a traditional song, the first four lines of which Johnson quotes:

> 'Twas when the seas were roaring,
> With hollow blasts of wind,
> A damsel lay deploring,
> All on a rock reclin'd.

More likely still to have been recalled from live performance is Johnson's excerpt from "The Sailor's Ballad" (stanza 2, lines 5–8):

> When terrible tempests assail us,
> And mountainous billows affright,
> Nor power nor wealth can avail us,
> But skilful industry steers right.

Even in the fourth edition of the *Dictionary* Johnson identified the work only as "Ballad." It may have been impossible to look up the source, especially if the lines had only been heard. They are in fact by Lewis Theobald, who is not quoted in the *Dictionary* (no surprise), and they are part of his dramatic entertainment *Perseus and Andromeda* (1730). There are slight differences between Johnson's and the printed version I have seen (5th ed., 1731); some printed versions of the play even omit the lines.[9] Theobald's little play was sometimes acted as an afterpiece to *King Lear*. It was performed, nearest Johnson's composition of the Grammar, on 16–17 October 1752 at Covent Garden.[10] Did Johnson attend? It was seven months after the death of his wife; he was finished with *The Rambler*; he may have been abroad, but there is no evidence one way or another. In any case, the song was part of the popular cultural life of London, and it must have been known to many of the people in Johnson's circle. Perhaps Garrick or Mr. Vincent, the manager of the Covent Garden Theatre, whom Johnson later consulted concerning his *Lives of the Poets*, sang it to Johnson. It must have been "in the air." The point I am trying to make is that Johnson breathed that popular air, and his composition of the History and Grammar seem to reflect that fact.

To argue that the Grammar and History are extempore compositions is not to deny that they also have places in time – specifically, in intellectual history. In fact, these places can be rather accurately described, although both works are somewhat unusual and quirky, especially in the context of a dictionary. Johnson's History is nearly unexampled in earlier English dictionaries. Of all the English dictionaries published before 1755, only Benjamin Martin's *Lingua Britannica Reformata* (1749) has anything resembling Johnson's History, but Martin's illustrative quotations are limited to ten versions of the Lord's Prayer written from *c.* 700 to 1610. Much more useful to Johnson than Martin's dictionary was George Hickes's collection of linguistic and bibliographical materials included in his *Linguarum vett[erum] septentrionalium thesaurus* (a repository of ancient northern languages) published in two volumes in Oxford (1703–05). From Hickes's sections on "Saxon" and "Semi-Saxon" Johnson borrowed several of his illustrative passages. The length of Johnson's illustrations also seems inspired by Hickes because his are much longer than those of any other book that Johnson might have used for compiling his History. He drew examples most importantly from Hickes, but Johnson seems to have modeled the number of his examples and the range of them on an augmented edition of James Greenwood's *Essay towards a Practical English Grammar.*[11]

Although many of Greenwood's examples are versions of the Lord's Prayer, and all of them are short, he has twenty-two different selections in his history (in the fourth and fifth editions), covering the period from the ninth century to the end of the sixteenth. Benjamin Martin may have taken his examples from Greenwood, but Johnson borrowed only Greenwood's concept of the required range and number of quotations needed to comprise a history of English. In sum, then, Johnson's History combines features of Hickes's *Thesaurus* and Greenwood's *Grammar* to comprise a history of the language, which is new because of its place in a dictionary and because of its presentation of so much early English in a book designed for non-experts. If the reliance of Johnson's History on extempore recollections of Warton's *Observations* (and other evidence of spur-of-the-moment composition) could be weighed in the balance against the reliance on Hickes and

Greenwood, perhaps a percentage could be assigned to the spontaneous part of Johnson's work, but the elements are not that easily separable.[12]

James Greenwood's *Grammar* has a position of double significance in Johnson's preliminaries to the *Dictionary*, because it provides a precedent not only for the examples in the History but also for Johnson's inclusion, in translation, of many parts of John Wallis's *Grammatica linguae anglicanae* (1653). Johnson was not, however, as passive in his use of Wallis as Greenwood. He made dozens of critical comments on Wallis, extempore notes such as that following his dutiful inclusion of Wallis's section on word formation: "Wallis's derivations are often so made, that by the same license any language may be deduced from any other" (*1755*, sig. c2^r). To his methodical reliance on Wallis, Johnson adds his extempore notes: this combination is representative of the way in which Johnson composed his Grammar.

In the history of English grammarians Wallis is usually credited with being the first to attempt a break with the tradition of reducing English to Latin grammatical categories. His progressiveness in this regard is evident when compared with the more traditional grammar by Ben Jonson. But Jonson too was progressive in his way: he tried to apply the principles of Petrus Ramus's Latin grammar to English and to base his work on actual linguistic experience. As Jonson says on the title page of his work, he drew his principles from "observation of the English Language as now spoken."[13] This is not so evident as he works his way through declensions and conjugations of English, but he does leave out the moods, presumably because they are not regularly marked by inflection as they are in Latin. Our Johnson restores the moods, and he follows Ben in writing up conjugations and declensions, although it means that he includes some forms that he never (or very rarely) used himself. Ben Jonson distinguishes "ye" as nominative singular and "you" as nominative plural. Samuel Johnson prints Ben's work and comments extemporaneously that "modern" writers use "you" for singular (*1755*, sig. b1^v), but he does not change the paradigm.

Ben Jonson and John Wallis help define Johnson's old-fashioned kind of progressivism in his Grammar of the English Tongue, while his extempore comments situate his thinking of the moment in relation to that stance. All in all, his Grammar is a step on the way to the more progressive Latin-based grammars that became dominant in the second half of the century. Robert Lowth's *Short Introduction to English Grammar* (1762) was the most influential of these. Johnson makes two respectful references to Lowth in his revised edition of the Grammar (*1773*, sig. b1^r), and he recommended

Lowth's grammar to the young Daniel Astle rather than his own (*Life*, vol. IV, p. 311).

The point of this essay is to throw light on the extempore elements in Johnson's composition of the Grammar and History. The other side of the coin, which I have discussed elsewhere, is the programmatic nature of the two works.[14] The two sides go together: the programmatic, mechanical copying of Wallis, for example, stimulates Johnson to make extempore comments. There is evidence of this same dynamic at work in the body of the *Dictionary*, and the likely method of composition makes the process easily imaginable: Johnson receives a page from the amanuenses with slips of quotations attached; he looks at the record and makes up his definitions, sometimes drawing on knowledge outside the results of methodical searches; finally, in some rare cases, he comments on what is in front of him. His notes are "inconnected"; they draw on his learning but also on what he has been thinking recently and what he has been hearing in journals, from friends, and on the street. The great work goes on in Johnson's *officina*, but it is interpenetrated with thoughts drawn from Johnson's daily stream of consciousness.[15] After his etymological entry on *cork* (Latin *cortex*), Johnson extemporaneously appends a few lines from Horace (*Odes* 3.8) that call for a drink to celebrate the kalends of March. Was it 1 March when Johnson made this entry? The end of a long day? Whatever the reason, it was not that his book needed an example of the use of the Latin word *cortex*. The reason could be called "personal," but the lines were very well known, part of a collective treasury of Latin verses not owned by Johnson in particular. The reason for inclusion is also not Johnson's wish to make his *Dictionary* a guide to classical learning or even a humanist project: the lines are slight, though memorable, convivial more than pedagogical. Horace's ode ends with the exhortation "cape laetus . . . ac linque severa" (take pleasure and leave off hard work). It is not especially personal (as *carpe diem* also is not), but in the context of Johnson's *Dictionary* it is certainly spontaneous and perhaps stimulated by the present circumstances of hard work.

Carelessness and haste are possible causes for the state in which Johnson published his History and Grammar. Moreover, all the errors in the History as well as all the faults Johnson finds in Wallis, even as he includes him, make the imputation hard to deny. On the other hand, these pieces can teach us a good deal about Johnson's method of composition in the *Dictionary* and perhaps in some of his other works. They also, I think, alert us to the importance of the casual, the accidental, the circumstantial, and the spontaneous in literature. Awareness of these features in writing humanizes authors as well as texts because human life is full of the accidental. Everyone who writes or reads closely knows that sometimes a word choice is based on a reaction (often imitative) to a word used or heard earlier (sometimes just minutes earlier); we echo our linguistic experience. The point is that writers are often reacting rather than planning when they write, and Johnson provides a good example. For all his traditional humanistic aspirations and for all his mastery of humanistic commonplaces, he is a spontaneous writer capable of imitating many voices and interjecting asides of many tones. A study of Johnson's Grammar and History demonstrates that he reveals these qualities in two of his least-read compositions.

NOTES

1. In "Johnson's *Dictionary* and Dictionary Johnson," *Yearbook of English Studies* 28 (1998), 19–43, Gwin Kolb and I apply some of the evidence used in this present paper to acknowledge counter-indications to our proposition that Johnson's work in the *Dictionary* is largely corporate and collaborative, rather than individual. We had not at that time differentiated the extempore from the larger concept of individual expression.

2. For further discussion of the composition of all of the preliminaries, see Gwin J. Kolb and Robert DeMaria, Jr., eds., *Johnson on the English Language*, vol. xviii of the Yale *Works*. Everything I have to say about the *Dictionary* is pervasively influenced by my long collaboration with Gwin Kolb on this volume.

3. *Catalogi librorum manuscriptorum Angliae et Hiberniae in unum collecti indice alphabetico*, 2 vols. (Oxford, 1697). Johnson used the book to request copies of manuscripts by Sir Thomas More in August 1755 (see *Letters*, vol. i, pp. 112–13).

4. Thomas Warton, *Observations on the Faerie Queene of Spenser* (London and Oxford, 1754). For a detailed discussion of the influence of Warton on Johnson and vice versa, see Gwin J. Kolb and Robert DeMaria, Jr., "Thomas Warton's *Observations on the 'Faerie Queene' of Spenser*, Samuel Johnson's 'History of the English Language,' and Warton's *History of English Poetry*: Reciprocal Indebtedness?," *Philological Quarterly* 74 (1995), 327–35.

5. George Hickes, *Linguarum vett[erum] septentrionalium thesaurus* (2 vols., 1703–5); James Greenwood, *An Essay towards a Practical English Grammar, Describing the Genius and Nature of the English Tongue* (1711; 5th ed., 1753).

6. Robin C. Alston, *A Bibliography of the English Language from the Invention of Printing to the Year 1800*, vol. i, *English Grammars Written in English* (Leeds: privately printed, 1965).

7. The doctrinal change could have been introduced by an amanuensis, perhaps the same person who bowdlerized Sir Thomas More's "Merry Iest," which is quoted at length in the History. See Kolb and DeMaria, "Johnson's *Dictionary* and Dictionary Johnson," pp. 31–32, and Yale *Works*, vol. xviii.

8. Brownell has a note on his work in the *Johnsonian News Letter* 54, no. 1 (September 2003), 50–51, but for a fuller explanation of his work, see "Boswell's

Ballads, A Life in Song," in *Boswell in Scotland and Beyond*, ed. Thomas Crawford (Glasgow: Association for Scottish Literary Studies, 1999), pp. 119–45.

9. *Literature on Line* (Chadwyck-Healey) has a different version of the poem.

10. Linda Troost helped me identify the source of Johnson's lines and directed me to the information about the performance of Theobald's entertainment.

11. Greenwood, *Essay towards a Practical English Grammar*.

12. For information on the paucity of Latin and Continental precursors to Johnson's History, see Kolb and DeMaria, Yale *Works*, vol. xviii.

13. *The English Grammar*, in *Ben Jonson*, ed. C. H. Herford and Percy and Evelyn Simpson, 11 vols. (Oxford: Clarendon Press, 1947), vol. viii, pp. 453–553, on p. 453.

14. Kolb and DeMaria, "Johnson's *Dictionary* and Dictionary Johnson."

15. I take the word "interpenetrated" from a talk by Pat Rogers about the contemporary references and influences in Pope's *Windsor-Forest*.

CHAPTER 6

Johnson the prescriptivist? The case for the prosecution

Geoff Barnbrook

Johnson's *Dictionary of the English Language* has, according to its author's own arguments in both the *Plan* and the Preface to the work itself, an overtly prescriptive purpose, a characterization which was largely accepted well into the twentieth century. In recent years this simple view of the *Dictionary* has been undermined to some extent by changes in attitude to Johnson, which seem to reflect a desire to rehabilitate him and to relocate the *Dictionary* within the history of descriptive linguistics. This essay explores the evidence of contemporary texts and uses it to reassess the case for seeing Johnson's project as prescriptive both in declared intention and in effect. This evidence is taken both from texts chosen by Johnson as part of the highly selective and personal corpus from which he drew his illustrative quotations – "the wells of English undefiled," as he calls them in the Preface (1825 *Works*, vol. v, p. 39) – and the many areas of contemporary writing largely ignored by him.

INTRODUCTION

In some ways no case needs to be made for this particular prosecution: Johnson is a self-confessed prescriptivist, glorying in both the *Plan* and the Preface in his intention to arrest or at least to slow the process of decay in English through the example of his commentary. People have been known, however, to confess to crimes that they have not committed and to fail in their intentions; and in the ranks of those who fail in their intentions lexicographers have a strong claim for inclusion, if not for prominence. Because of this, if for no other reason, Johnson's claims need to be investigated so that an objective assessment can be made of his role in relation both to his own *Dictionary* and the subsequent development of English-language lexicography.

The present attempt to carry out this investigation has resulted in what I have called "the case for the prosecution." There is an inescapable element of moral judgment in this description, and I hope to show not only that Johnson's aims and practice were significantly prescriptive, but also that such an approach is culpable in the context of lexicography.

THE BACKGROUND: ATTITUDES TO JOHNSON

That the *Dictionary* was seen by its contemporary audience as prescriptive can hardly be in doubt. The famous statement by Chesterfield in *The World* in 1754, even more famously reacted to by Johnson, uses the metaphors of political order and disorder:

> The time for discrimination seems to be now come. Toleration, adoption and naturalization have run their lengths. Good order and authority are now necessary. But where shall we find them, and at the same time, the obedience due to them? We must have recourse to the old Roman expedient in times of confusion, and chuse a dictator. Upon this principle I give my vote for Mr. Johnson to fill that great and arduous post. And I hereby declare that I make a total surrender of all my rights and privileges in the English language, as a free-born British subject, to the said Mr. Johnson, during the term of his dictatorship.[1]

While this statement of the concept of the dictionary anticipated publication, those subsequent to it confirmed Chesterfield's prediction. As an example, *The London Chronicle* in 1757 spoke of

> his Dictionary, in which he hath supplied the Want of an Academy of Belles Lettres, and performed Wonders towards fixing our Grammar, and ascertaining the determinate Meaning of Words, which are known to be in their own Nature of a very unstable and fluctuating Quality. To his Labours it may hereafter be owing that our Drydens, our Addisons, and our Popes shall not become as obsolete and unintelligible as Chaucer.[2]

Wells also quotes Robert Nares's comment in his *Elements of Orthoepy* in 1784: "The English Dictionary appeared; and, as the weight of truth and reason is irresistible, its authority has nearly fixed the external form of our language; and from its decisions few appeals have yet been made."[3] In all of these contemporary comments we have a wholly positive view of prescriptivism, with Johnson seen as the champion of stability and the preserver of a vulnerable language in a threatening environment. By the mid nineteenth century, though, attitudes were changing, and Trench's comments on Johnson are less favorable, while maintaining the view that his was a prescriptivist approach. In his discussion of the first identified deficiency of existing English dictionaries, that of the inconsistent treatment of obsolete words, Trench condemns both Johnson's criteria for inclusion or exclusion, and his application of them:

"Obsolete words," says Johnson, "are admitted when they are found in authors not obsolete, or when they have any force or beauty that may deserve revival." I will not pause here to inquire what a lexicographer has to do with the question whether a word deserves revival or not; but rather call your attention to the fact that Johnson does not even observe his own rule of comprehension, imperfect and inadequate as that is.[4]

Whether viewed favorably or otherwise, Johnson's identification with a prescriptive approach to lexicography seems more or less complete up to this point. Trench's criticisms, of course, arise from an approach to linguistics which is rather more specialized than that favored by the majority of interested parties of the nineteenth or twentieth centuries. The continued popularity of editions of Johnson's *Dictionary* and of its more recent successors in the prescriptive tradition shows this very clearly. The *Oxford English Dictionary*, the great offspring of Trench's discussion of deficiencies, was at the time of its production, and remains to the present day, unique in its attempt to describe the English language with a minimum of prescription. In the context of traditional dictionary development it represents a magnificent and monumental cul-de-sac.

A change in attitude to Johnson seems to arise in the mid twentieth century as the concept of prescriptivism becomes more unfashionable in mainstream linguistics. An explicit attempt at Johnson's rehabilitation can be seen in Brian O'Kill: "Although his defining technique is rather inconsistent by modern standards, Johnson's definitions often attain that quality of unobtrusive inevitability which makes them almost impossible to improve on."[5] Less explicitly, Robert DeMaria, Jr. compares Johnson's notion of diction to that of the great descriptive lexicographer James A. H. Murray. After presenting Murray's well-known diagram representing the range and subsets of English vocabulary, he comments:

In terms of this diagram, Johnson locates the center of English to the west and north of Murray: both in the direction of the "Scientific" and "Technical" as opposed to the "Foreign" and "Dialectal," and in the direction of the "Literary" as opposed to the "Colloquial." Moreover, Johnson sees the central area of "Common Words" as more tightly focused, and he finds more ways than does Murray for a word to diverge from the center of pure "Anglicity."[6]

This comparison implies a difference of emphasis or of orientation between the two lexicographers, rather than the fundamentally different projects in which they seem to have been engaged. DeMaria similarly sees Johnson's editorial remarks, the explicit comments on the usage and value of words which are examined in more detail below, as displaying "the great variety of special languages he perceived within the general body of English" (DeMaria, *Johnson's "Dictionary,"* p. 176). Among his examples of editorial remarks that show Johnson's perception of these "special languages" are "a cant word not used in pure or grave writings" (*bamboozle*), "a woman's word" (*frightfully* 2), and "a barbarous term of heraldry" (*gules*). It might seem to the unbiased observer that these all seem to represent an approach both prescriptive and subjective, fully appropriate to Chesterfield's desired dictator of the language.

These assessments are all, of course, based on the reaction of others to the *Dictionary*. As evidence they are almost entirely inadmissible: perhaps they only show that the work is so well regarded that it is generally seen to reflect whatever is held to be the best linguistic attitude at the time. In order to proceed with the case we need to examine the nature of the charge and the evidence provided by the *Dictionary* itself, rather than by popular opinion.

THE NATURE OF THE OFFENSE: THE CONCEPT OF PRESCRIPTIVISM

In order to assess the validity of the charge against Johnson we need a definition of the crime. David Crystal, a linguist of impeccable credentials in the modern descriptive tradition, offers the following definition for *prescriptive*: "A term used by linguists to characterize any approach which attempts to lay down rules of correctness as to how language should be used. Using such criteria as purity, logic, history or literary excellence, prescriptivism aims to preserve imagined standards by insisting on norms of usage and criticizing departures from these norms."[7] Crystal's definition seems almost to be specially bespoke for Johnson's approach. R. L. Trask's longer article on the subject of prescriptivism begins with a shorter but similar definition: "The imposition of arbitrary norms upon a language, often in defiance of normal usage."[8] Both definitions agree on the imposition of norms: Trask emphasizes their arbitrariness (and frequent variation from normal usage) while Crystal sets them in a context of the preservation of imagined standards. There seem to be two possible types of behavior here: any attempt to lay down rules of correctness constitutes basic prescriptivism, while the attempt to impose norms in defiance of normal usage can be seen as an aggravated form of the offense.

In order to prove Johnson guilty of basic prescriptivism it would be enough to show that he attempts to lay down rules of correctness. Even a very superficial survey of the *Dictionary* shows that there are places where he does this, and examples have already been shown in the comments on his approach in the previous section. In order to assess his approach objectively, however, the extent and significance of his prescriptive commentary needs to be assessed. The basic approach for this aspect of the investigation, through an exploration of the explicit comments on word usage contained in the *Dictionary*, is described below.

To assess any defiance of normal usage involved in the imposition of norms requires a further element of evidence: we must establish the nature of normal usage. Johnson describes his own sources for linguistic authority in both the *Plan* and the Preface to the *Dictionary*. The very act of selecting a corpus such as Johnson's "wells of English undefiled" is potentially prescriptive. The modern corpus is normally designed primarily to achieve representativeness of the variety of language being explored.[9] Once the corpus is assembled its use is also subject to variation, and Tognini-Bonelli identifies two main approaches: corpus-based and corpus-driven (chapters 4 and 5). The major difference she identifies between them is the use made of the corpus data: in the corpus-driven approach it is of primary importance and "the commitment of the linguist is to the integrity of the data as a whole" (E. Tognini-Bonelli, *Corpus Linguistics at Work*, p. 84), while in the corpus-based approach the corpus is used "mainly to expound, test or exemplify theories and descriptions that were formulated before large corpora became available to inform language study" (p. 65). Johnson's approach is, at best, corpus-based, and the investigation of this aspect of his suspected prescriptivism, performed through an exploration of texts both from his own selection and from other contemporary sources, is described below.

THE INVESTIGATION

Assessing the prescriptiveness of usage notes

Johnson's explicit comments on word usage are generally contained in notes placed toward the end of the entry for a particular sense of the word. During the process of digitizing the text of the first and fourth editions of the *Dictionary* for Anne McDermott's electronic edition,[10] these usage notes, along with the other elements of the dictionary entries, were assigned distinctive tags. The original text produced in this process has been made available for this research and, with the aid of simple text processing programs, it has been possible to extract all the usage notes together with the headwords to which they relate. This has provided a basis for assessing these notes for the types of comments in them, and allocating them to prescriptive and descriptive categories.

Selecting words from the Dictionary

Words have been selected for comparison with the test corpora from the headwords associated with the usage notes, extracted as described above. The selection was based on the type of comment made in the note. As explained in detail below, the notes have been categorized according to the presence of particular keywords in their text. The vocabulary Johnson uses to condemn delinquent vocabulary, for example – "low," "cant," "barbarous," etc. – has been used to identify the specifically evaluative comments. A selection was made from the notes which were seen as prescriptive, and the results are discussed below.

The corpus for comparison

There are as yet no general reference corpora adequate to the needs of the linguist investigating the eighteenth century: there is nothing approaching the scale of the British National Corpus at 100 million words or the Bank of English with its more than 450 million words, nor their comprehensive coverage of language from a wide range of genres.[11] There are archives containing significant quantities of texts appropriate to the period, but they are generally skewed to the literary side of language in much the same way as Johnson's "wells." The Diachronic part of the Helsinki Corpus of English Texts has the advantage that it contains a wide range of text genres and, although it is small by modern standards (containing only 551,000 words of Early Modern English and fewer than 200,000 words within the period corresponding to Johnson's date boundaries), it is still the most useful general basis for a comparison of this sort.[12]

The Helsinki Corpus provides a set of texts which fall largely outside the criteria set by Johnson: many are non-literary and lack the authority that Johnson allocates to his "writers of the first reputation" (1825 *Works*, vol. v, p. 21). It thus provides an opportunity to assess Johnson's norms against language use beyond his narrowly defined area. To test his comments against his own authorities, texts by Alexander Pope, a writer extensively quoted in the *Dictionary*, were used as a representative sample.

Details of the methodology

Simple text processing programs in the awk language[13] were run against the annotated dictionary text files described above to extract the elements of the dictionary entries explicitly tagged as usage notes, together with the headword with which the usage note was associated.[14] During the processing the total number of headwords contained in each letter was counted, together with the number of headwords for which usage notes existed. Both totals were output to a separate file to allow statistical comparison.

It is difficult to distinguish between prescriptive and descriptive usage notes automatically using the computer, and far too unwieldy a process to do so manually. As a compromise, therefore, words which seemed likely from an initial survey of the usage notes to be indicative of the underlying nature of the comments were searched for within the files produced for the two editions of the *Dictionary*, and lines containing them were extracted into separate files.

A manual examination of the *Dictionary* text made it evident that certain words were closely associated with highly evaluative comments on usage, which could therefore be evidence of prescription. These were "low," "barbarous," and "cant" as descriptions of words or senses, and "properly" and "improperly" as comments on usage. Lines from the files of notes which contained these words were extracted to separate files for further examination. Here, for example, is part of the file of notes containing the word "low" extracted from *1755*:[15]

ABOMINABLE. In low and ludicrous language, it is a word of loose and indeterminate censure.
ABOMINABLY. A word of low or familiar language, in the ill sense.
ADORER. A term generally used in a low sense; as, by lovers, or admirers. In a serious sense.
ADVENTURESOME. A low word, scarcely used in writing.
ALAMODE. A low word. It is used likewise by shopkeepers for a kind of thin silken manufacture.
AS. In a consequential sense. answering to like or same. In a reciprocal sense, answering to as. Going before as, in a comparative sense; the first as being sometimes understood. Answering to such. Having so to answer it; in a conditional sense. So is sometimes understood. Answering to so conditionally. Before how it is sometimes redundant; but this is in low language. It seems to be redundant before yet; In a sense of comparison, followed by so.
To BANG. A low and familiar word.

These files formed the initial basis for categorizing the usage notes. This procedure was repeated in a guided process of trial and error until the majority of the notes had been categorized successfully into various types of prescriptive and descriptive comment.[16] The files produced from this exercise were then examined to assess the evidence for prescription in the *Dictionary* and to provide a basis for sampling word senses to be compared to usages exhibited in contemporary texts. The exploration of the texts was carried out using standard concordancing software. The results of these operations are described in detail in the next section.

RESULTS

Usage note statistics

The table below shows the total number of headwords and the number of those headwords with associated usage notes for each of the letter sections of the first and fourth editions of the *Dictionary*.

	1755		1773	
	Headwords	Notes	Headwords	Notes
A	2965	570	2968	570
B	2360	302	2307	335
C	4493	521	4529	576
D	2706	252	2728	389
E	1768	156	1803	260
F	2006	235	2028	308
G	1303	176	1310	227
H	1527	164	1537	233
IJ	2299	246	2307	360
K	220	34	224	42
L	1314	134	1321	185
M	2128	209	778	80
N	645	82	648	98
O	1480	136	1049	106
P	3228	389	3435	406
Q	254	32	259	42
R	1961	189	2000	252
S	4669	497	4780	665
T	1936	214	1963	259
UV	2616	153	2645	197
WXYZ	1187	184	1216	236
Totals	43065	4875	41835	5826

These figures show that overall more than 10 percent of the headwords in both editions (11.3 percent in the first, 13.9 percent in the fourth) contain usage notes of one sort or another. Since all notes associated with the senses of one headword are grouped together in this count the actual density of notes is, if anything, understated.

Not all of the usage notes, of course, are necessarily prescriptive within our previously stated definition. Of the first ten notes extracted from the first edition, only one would come strictly within our previously established definition of prescription, using the phrase "a barbarous corruption" to condemn a usage seen as incorrect. Of the other nine within this sample, four of them give guidance on pronunciation, while the other five seem to describe current usage rather than making any distinction between correctness and incorrectness. This may seem to make the original accusation somewhat less convincing, except that the claim is not that Johnson is prescriptive in every possible case, but that the overall program of the *Dictionary* is prescriptive. For this to be shown to be true, a significant amount of prescription needs to be found within the text.

The process by which significant words within the notes were used to identify the nature of their commentary has been described above. Notes containing these diagnostic words and their frequencies in the two editions are given in the table below, in order of their frequency of appearance in the first edition. The notes identified by these significant words amount to 82.2 percent of the complete set from the first edition and 85.5 percent from the fourth. (The notes left unidentified by these routines are labeled "*remainder*" in the table.) Where appropriate, the computer program that extracts the words from the complete sets of notes has been constructed so that it also extracts other inflected forms of the words. For example, the frequency given for *signification* includes the forms *signify, signifies, signification,* and *significations.*

Word	1755	1773
used	1470	2080
as	446	451
obsolete	266	367
low	223	238
sense	192	209
proper	187	259
applied	116	90
signification	107	76
cant	92	98
improper	90	94
common	66	89

(*cont.*)

Word	1755	1773
particle	66	78
sometimes	65	83
ludicrous	61	94
general	44	34
corruption	42	48
only	40	37
accent	39	43
plural	38	45
old	37	38
perhaps	35	42
familiar	29	24
bad	27	21
barbarous	26	26
often	26	38
pronounce	22	23
usual	20	20
whence	20	18
disused	17	19
singular	14	19
figurative	13	16
contraction	12	7
rather	12	15
mere	11	7
vicious	10	11
poetic	8	7
frequent	7	11
false	4	3
redundant	3	1
abbreviation	2	0
vile	2	3
remainder	868	944
Totals	4875	5826

The words shown in the table may not seem very informative in themselves, but they were selected because they are associated with patterns of comment that can be assigned to prescriptive and descriptive categories. The words most obviously associated with fully prescriptive patterns are given in the table below. The notes containing these words, all of which have strongly evaluative and mostly negative implications, represent 15.9 percent of all the notes extracted from the first edition and 15.5 percent of those from the fourth.

Word	1755	1773
low	223	238
proper	187	259
cant	92	98
improper	90	94
ludicrous	61	94
corruption	42	48
bad	27	21
barbarous	26	26
mere	11	7
vicious	10	11
false	4	3
vile	2	3
Totals	775	902

The following words also tend to be used judgmentally, though less strongly so, usually allocating their headwords to different levels of the language. These represent a further 1.9 percent of both the first and fourth edition notes.

Word	1755	1773
common	66	89
familiar	29	24
Totals	95	113

Finally for the prescriptive markers, the following words all represent ways of expressing the lack of currency of particular headwords or their senses. These can probably only be seen as marginally prescriptive, if at all. Together they represent a further 6.7 percent of first edition notes and 7.3 percent of those from the fourth edition. It is certainly arguable that these comments are not genuinely prescriptive, since they could be used to reflect the current lexis of the language rather than imposing arbitrary norms on it. However, given the restricted chronological extent of the corpus of texts that Johnson claims for his authorities, comments on currency savor more of personal decision than of genuine observation over a sufficiently long term. They have therefore been included in the prescriptive notes to allow full comparison with the test corpora.

Word	1755	1773
obsolete	266	367
old	37	38
disused	17	19
redundant	3	1
Totals	323	425

The remaining words identify notes which are either specifically aimed at areas of normal descriptive comment (such as accompaniment by a "particle") or else are made sufficiently tentative by their introductions (such as "sometimes," "perhaps," and "usual") to defuse their overtones of correctness or the imposition of arbitrary standards. Taken together these represent 57.7 percent of the first edition notes and 59.1 percent of the fourth edition set.

Word	1755	1773
used	1470	2080
as	446	451
sense	192	209
applied	116	90
signification	107	76
particle	66	78
sometimes	65	83
general	44	34
only	40	37
accent	39	43
plural	38	45
perhaps	35	42
often	26	38
pronounce	22	23
usual	20	20
whence	20	18
singular	14	19
figurative	13	16
contraction	12	7
rather	12	15
poetic	8	7
frequent	7	11
abbreviation	2	0
Totals	2814	3442

In the table below, under each edition the prescriptive notes are divided into their three main categories (total prescriptive, descriptive, and unidentified) in the left-hand column, and the totals for prescriptive, descriptive, and unidentified notes are given:

	1755	%	1773	%
Prescriptive				
Evaluative	775		902	
Language level	95		113	
Currency	323		425	
Total prescriptive	1193	24.5	1440	24.7
Descriptive	2814	57.7	3442	59.1
Unidentified	868	17.8	944	16.2
Totals	4875	100	5826	100

It cannot be denied, therefore, that the usage notes to both editions of the *Dictionary* contain a strong element of purely descriptive comment. Nor, on the other hand, can it be denied that there is also a significant prescriptive element: this amounts to about 24 percent in each edition (or 17 percent if the comments on currency are ignored). The first part of the charge can be fairly laid at Johnson's door, though not without qualification (and, no doubt, mitigation), which will be discussed in more detail in the conclusions.

COMPARISON WITH THE CORPUS

To explore the second part of the charge, that Johnson's comments are not merely prescriptive but are made in defiance of normal usage, it is necessary to establish the nature of that usage. As already explained above, this was achieved using a corpus for comparison with selected usage notes. The notes extracted into their individual files by the process described in the previous section provided the basis for selection, which was made using a standard random-number generation process within a simple extraction program. Thirty of the prescriptive usage notes from each edition were selected by this process and Johnson's comments on the headwords involved were assessed against their observed usage in the corpora. The list of headwords extracted from the first edition, together with the results of the comparison with the appropriate part of the Helsinki Corpus, is given below. For each of these headwords a concordance was generated using standard software (Microconcord, developed by Mike Scott and Tim Johns in 1993), and the behavior of the headword as evidenced by the concordance lines was compared to the comments made in the usage notes.

For each headword, a decision is shown in the table below: "A" where the usage note seems to agree with the corpus evidence, "D" where it seems to disagree with it, and "U" (for "unproven") where it was impossible to decide either way because of a lack of appropriate data in the corpus. Where no occurrences of a headword were found the word is prefixed in the table by an asterisk.

Headword	A	D	U	Note[17]
*adorer			✓	A term generally used in a low sense; as, by lovers, or admirers. In a serious sense.
grievous	✓			Sometimes used adverbially in low language.
grum			✓	A low word.
*to shail			✓	A low word.
*to sling			✓	Not very proper.
*unition	✓			A word proper, but little used.
*ruff	✓			Obsolete. This seems to be the meaning of this cant word.
*whynot			✓	A cant word for violent or peremptory procedure.
*privacy			✓	Privacy in this sense is improper.
*casted	✓			But improperly, and found perhaps only in the following passage.
*me		✓		Me is sometimes a kind of ludicrous expletive. It is sometimes used ungrammatically for I; as, methinks.
*to moble			✓	Sometimes written mable, perhaps by a ludicrous allusion to the French je m' habille.
extreme			✓	This word is sometimes corrupted by the superlative termination, of which it is by no means capable, as it has in itself the superlative signification.
*to proselyte			✓	A bad word.
way		✓		A familiar phrase. Way and ways, are now often used corruptly for wise.
wondrous	✓			Wondrous is barbarously used for an adverb.
confoundedly			✓	A low or ludicrous word.
faxed	✓			Now obsolete.
*crud			✓	Commonly written curd.
*benempt	✓			An obsolete word.
to defect	✓			Obsolete.
*guidon	✓			Obsolete.

(cont.)

Headword	A	D	U	Note[17]
lack		✓		Lack, whether noun or verb, is now almost obsolete.
to malice		✓		Obsolete.
pendant	✓			Obsolete.
riched	✓			Obsolete.
sprong		✓		Obsolete.
suit	✓			Obsolete. In Spenser it seems to signify pursuit; prosecution.
wheras	✓			Obsolete. Always referred to something different.
to obey	✓			It had formerly sometimes to before the person obeyed, which Addison has mentioned as one of Milton's latinisms; but it is frequent in old writers; when we borrowed the French word we borrowed the syntax, obeir au roi.
Totals	14	5	11	

The corresponding table for the fourth edition is given below:

Headword	A	D	U	Note
adventuresome	✓			A low word, scarcely used in writing.
to guttle	✓			A low word.
agreeable			✓	It has the particle to, or with. In the following passage the adjective is used by a familiar corruption for the adverb agreeably. It is used in this sense both of persons and things.
barleybroth			✓	A low word, sometimes used for strong beer.
scrape			✓	This is a low word.
to bait			✓	Perhaps this word is more properly bate.
ought		✓		This word is therefore more properly written aught.
to sympathize			✓	Not proper.
Bilingsgate			✓	A cant word.
poachy			✓	A cant word.
to squiny			✓	A cant word.
to gargle			✓	An improper use
ginnet			✓	Hence, according to some, but, I believe, erroneously, a Spanish gennet, improperly written for ginnet.
to skim			✓	Improper. Perhaps originally skin.
trendle			✓	Now improperly written trundle.
dan			✓	The old term of honour for men; as we now say Master. I know not that it was ever used in prose, and imagine it to have been rather of ludicrous import.

(cont.)

Headword	A	D	U	Note
ambassadour			✓	Ambassadour is, in popular language, the general name of a messenger from a sovereign power, and sometimes, ludicrously, from common persons. In the juridical and formal language, it signifies particularly a minister of the highest rank residing in another country, and is distinguished from an envoy, who is of less dignity.
to line		✓		A sense rather ludicrous.
*unnervate			✓	A bad word.
to deal			✓	This seems a vitious use.
*coexistence			✓	With to. Locke, who in the preceding lines has coexisted with, has here coexistence to. More commonly followed by with.
to spear			✓	This is commonly written spire.
to admire		✓		Generally in a good sense. It is sometimes used, in more familiar speech, for to regard with love. It is used, but rarely, in an ill sense.
lief			✓	Now used only in familiar speech.
*goel	✓			An old word.
*to accourage	✓			Obsolete.
*belamour	✓			Obsolete.
*cark	✓			This word is now obsolete.
*to dirke	✓			Obsolete.
to forbid	✓			Now obsolete. To bid is in old language to pray; to forbid therefore is to curse.
Totals	8	3	19	

A summary of the results of this analysis for each of the two editions is given in the table below:

	1755	1773	Total
Agreed	14	8	22
Disagreed	5	3	8
Unproven	11	19	30
Total	30	30	60

As can be seen, for half of the notes overall there was insufficient evidence to decide on the validity of the comment contained in them, usually quite simply because the headword itself did not occur in the corpus. This is the case, for example, with the headword *adorer* in the first edition. Johnson's note claims that this is "a term generally used in a low sense; as, by lovers, or admirers." Since the word was not found at all in the Helsinki Corpus it is impossible to assess whether this represents a true description of its usage at the time. In other cases where the headword is not found, its very absence from the corpus suggests that Johnson's comment may have been valid. As an example, take the headword *adventuresome* in the fourth edition, which Johnson calls "a low word, scarcely used in writing." In this case its absence from the Helsinki Corpus, though not providing conclusive confirmation, is at least consistent with the comment and does nothing to invalidate it. A similar attitude has been adopted in assessing the validity of Johnson's descriptions of words as "obsolete," such as *guidon* in *1755* or *to accourage* in *1773*: their absence from the corpus has been interpreted in Johnson's favor, and these items have been included in the "agreed" totals rather than the "not proven."

An overall assessment of the results from the Helsinki Corpus, then, suggests that there is insufficient evidence for the more serious charge that Johnson's prescriptions are in defiance of normal usage. It also suggests, perhaps more strongly, that the corpus may be inadequate for the demands of the investigation and that this work should be repeated on a corpus of larger scale, more broadly based on the writings of the period, when such a resource becomes available.

COMPARISON WITH JOHNSON'S AUTHORITIES

The full list of Johnson's sources for the illustrative quotations is both extensive and indeterminate, and the set of authorities which he used as the basis for his decisions in the *Dictionary* is, if anything, even less accessible. When corpus resources for eighteenth-century English are more systematically available it will be possible to carry out proper investigations into the behavior of the language that underlies the *Dictionary*, but in the meantime it is possible to use the immense literary resources available through the Web as a representative sample. The works of Alexander Pope were selected as a means of comparison with the Helsinki Corpus since they are easily available,[18] they are extensively used by Johnson for illustrative quotations, and they do not overlap with the texts included in the Helsinki materials.

Each of the words selected for examination in the Helsinki Corpus was also searched for within the Literature Online database, restricting the author to Alexander Pope. In almost all cases no occurrence of the word was found in the Pope texts. This is in itself fairly unsurprising: the basis for most of the usage notes associated with these words is either that they are considered unworthy in some way of use by educated people, or that they are obsolete. In this sense the non-occurrence of these words supports Johnson's selection of them for comment of this sort. The following words in the selection were found in Pope (the frequency of occurrence is given in parentheses after each word). From *1755*: *adorer* (1), *ruff* (2), *me* (30), and *lack* (1); from *1773*: *ought* (8), *Bilingsgate* (1), *dan* (3), and *unnervate* (1). These results need some commentary. The sense of *adorer* castigated by Johnson as "low" is that related to "lovers, or admirers," exactly the sense in which Pope uses it. The two occurrences of *ruff*, a word not found in the Helsinki Corpus, cast doubt on the obsolete status accorded it by Johnson's comment. The word *me* is condemned in its usage note when it is used as "a kind of ludicrous expletive," a usage not found in Pope, and also when "used ungrammatically for I; as, methinks."[19] The thirty occurrences in Pope are all examples of this usage. The word *lack*, categorized by Johnson as almost obsolete both as a noun and a verb, seems to be hanging on in Pope as in the Helsinki Corpus. The spelling *ought*, said by Johnson to be "more properly written aught," turns up eight times in Pope against four occurrences of *aught*, bearing out the disagreement noted from Helsinki. The word *Bilingsgate* does occur in Pope, though in a context that suggests that Johnson's categorization of it as "a cant word" is not unreasonable. *Dan* is used by Pope exactly as a "term of honour for men," though there is no reason to suppose that his use of it is "rather of ludicrous import." Finally, *unnervate*, condemned by Johnson as "a bad word," is used once by Pope, though it is in a reference to a quotation from Scaliger in a footnote, rather than his own words.

This is again a rather inconclusive set of results. The few items highlighted above where Pope and Johnson disagree spectacularly are outweighed by the majority of words which, condemned by Johnson to linguistic limbo of one sort or another, do not occur at all in Pope's texts.

CONCLUSIONS

There seems to be clear and incontrovertible evidence in the sheer volume and nature of Johnson's usage notes that the prescriptive approach promised in the *Plan* and detailed, though with reservations, in the Preface, informed the construction of the *Dictionary* to a significant extent. Thus far the first part of the charge made at the beginning of this essay seems to be fully supported: Johnson has used an "approach which attempts to lay down rules of correctness as to how language should be used" (Crystal, *Dictionary*

of Linguistics, p. 369). The second part of the charge, the suggestion that
the norms imposed might be "in defiance of normal usage" (Trask, *Key
Concepts*, p. 246), seems much less clear. There is little evidence to support
this as a general criticism, and the few cases where Johnson appears to have
gone against normal usage can be seen as the inevitable slips associated with
such a complex and onerous task.

Having accepted this, the reader may be forgiven for wondering what all
the fuss is about. Johnson's audience, as evidenced by the earlier quotations,
sought prescription explicitly and eagerly. The agitation for an English body
corresponding to the Accademia della Crusca or the Académie Française
shows a general desire to have the English language firmly policed, a desire
which the *Dictionary* seems to have gone some of the way to satisfying.
If Johnson's approach is prescriptive, then it was surely the only approach
available to him, given the social and linguistic background of the period.

This justification is, of course, true up to a point, and it provides some of
the mitigation mentioned earlier. Earlier dictionaries, however, had managed largely to avoid the prescriptive approach, while dictionaries after
Johnson, with one or two notable exceptions, seem to take prescription as
a natural and thoroughly positive aspect of lexicography, growing effort-
lessly into their new powers as linguistic guardians. Johnson did not create
the environment that transferred power in this way, but he colluded with
it and, in so doing, helped to change the attitudes of lexicographers and
dictionary users, as well as the nature of lexicography, in ways which can
only be seen as negative.

The new wave of learners' dictionaries of English, based on usage data
taken from major reference corpora, began only in 1987 with the publication of the *Collins Cobuild English Language Dictionary*,[20] and that
fully descriptive approach is only now beginning to influence the ways in
which native-speaker dictionaries are constructed. Johnson's prescriptivism,
though understandable in the context of his time and audience, has had
far-reaching negative effects which we forget at our peril.

NOTES

1. *The World* 100 (28 November 1754), 601–02. This passage is also discussed in
   R. A. Wells, *Dictionaries and the Authoritarian Tradition: A Study in English
   Usage and Lexicography* (The Hague: Mouton, 1973), pp. 39–40.
2. *The London Chronicle*, 12–14 April 1757, p. 358.
3. Robert Nares, *Elements of Orthoepy: Containing a Distinct View of the Whole
   Analogy of the English Language* (London, 1784), pp. 269–70.

4. Richard Chevenix Trench, *On Some Deficiencies in Our English Dictionaries*, 2nd ed. (London, 1860), p. 10. A facsimile is available at http://athens.oed.com/archive/paper-deficiencies/.
5. Brian O'Kill, *The Lexicographic Achievement of Johnson*, in the facsimile edition of *1755* (Harlow: Longman, 1990), p. 11.
6. Robert DeMaria, Jr., *Johnson's "Dictionary" and the Language of Learning* (Oxford: Oxford University Press, 1986), p. 177.
7. David Crystal, *A Dictionary of Linguistics and Phonetics*, 5th ed. (Oxford: Blackwell, 2003), p. 369, all cross-references removed.
8. R. L. Trask, *Key Concepts in Language and Linguistics* (London: Routledge, 1999), p. 246.
9. See E. Tognini-Bonelli, *Corpus Linguistics at Work* (Amsterdam: John Benjamins, 2001), pp. 52–55, for a discussion of these issues.
10. *A Dictionary of the English Language on CD-ROM*, ed. Anne McDermott (Cambridge: Cambridge University Press, 1996).
11. For details of the BNC see http://www.natcorp.ox.ac.uk/; for the Bank of English see http://www.cobuild.collins.co.uk/boe_info.html.
12. It is fully documented in Merja Kytö, *Manual to the Diachronic Part of the Helsinki Corpus of English*, 3rd ed. (1996), at http://khnt.hit.uib.no/icame/manuals/HC/INDEX.HTM.
13. For details of the awk language see A. V. Aho, B. W. Kernighan, and P. J. Weinberger, *The AWK Programming Language* (Reading: Addison Wesley, 1988). For a very brief introduction to the use of awk in language analysis see Geoffrey Barnbroook, *Language and Computers* (Edinburgh: Edinburgh University Press, 1996), pp. 177–85.
14. The first part of the annotated text file for the letter A in *1755*, for example, reads:

@1 A,
@4 The first letter of the European alphabets,
@9 has, in the English language, three different sounds, which may be termed the broad, open, and slender.
The broad sound resembling that of the German <cf2>a<cf1> is found, in many of our monosyllables, as <cf2>all, wall, malt, salt;<cf1> in which <cf2>a<cf1> is pronounced as <cf2>au<cf1> in <cf2>cause,<cf1> or <cf2>aw<cf1> in <cf2>law.<cf1> Many of these words were anciently written with <cf2>au,<cf1> as <cf2>fault, waulk;<cf1> which happens to be still retained in <cf2>fault.<cf1> This was probably the ancient sound of the Saxons, since it is almost uniformly preserved in the rustic pronunciation, and the Northern dialects, as <cf2>maun<cf1> for <cf2>man, haund<cf1> for <cf2>hand.<cf1>
@1 <<a>>A
@9 open, not unlike the <cf2>a<cf1> of the Italians, is found in <cf2>father, rather,<cf1> and more obscurely in <cf2>fancy, fast,<cf1> &c.

The corresponding section of the file of usage notes extracted from this file reads:

A, 1 has, in the English language, three different sounds, which may be termed the broad, open, and slender.

<<a>>A 5 open, not unlike the <cf2>a<cf1> of the Italians, is found in <cf2>father, rather,<cf1> and more obscurely in <cf2>fancy, fast,<cf1> &c.

The numbers preceded by the "@" symbol are the tags assigned to the different elements of the dictionary entry (@1 for headword, @9 for usage notes), while the tags in angle brackets, such as <cf1> and <cf2>, represent changes in font or other aspects of the appearance of the text. In the file of usage notes output from the *Dictionary* text the note is separated from the headword by a tab character, making further processing easier. The number immediately following the headword is internally generated and used to control the accuracy of processing.

15. Capitalization has been regularized and angle bracket tags have been removed for clarity.

16. The method was similar to that described for the analysis of definition sentence types in Barnbrook, *Defining Language: A Local Grammar of Definition Sentences* (Amsterdam: John Benjamins, 2002), pp. 118–21.

17. The capitalization and terminal punctuation of the usage notes have been regularized here and in the next table for clarity.

18. See the *Literature Online* resources at http://lion.chadwyck.co.uk.

19. Those with a little more historical perspective than Johnson will recognize that he has misunderstood both the syntax and the meaning here: it is an example of the older sense of the word expressed in the *OED*, s.v. *think v*[1] – "to seem, to appear." In this sense it can be used with no expressed subject and takes the dative, so that *methinks* is equivalent to "it seems to me." While this usage is marked as obsolete in the *OED*, there is a citation from the seventeenth century.

20. J. M. Sinclair, ed., *Collins Cobuild English Language Dictionary* (London and Glasgow: Collins, 1987).

CHAPTER 7

Johnson the prescriptivist? The case for the defense

Anne McDermott

It is commonly acknowledged among historians of language that the eighteenth century was a period of authoritarianism, prescription, and standardization in language, and Johnson is often pointed to as the arch-exponent and ideologue of those views. In volume IV of the *Cambridge History of the English Language*, covering the period 1776–1997, for instance, Suzanne Romaine presents the common view of Johnson's *Dictionary* as a heavily prescriptive text, based on a narrow (and narrowing) view of the English language which favored the usage of the written over the oral, the high-born over the vulgar, and the conservative over the radical.[1] These views of the language attributed to Johnson are implicitly connected with his political views by several commentators. Gwyn Williams's history of the French Revolution, for example, harnesses Johnson with Robert Lowth and John Harris and claims that

They made the "national language" into a class language. Grounded in a theory of universal grammar which reflected qualities of the mind and in a veneration of Latin and Greek, they rigorously defined a "refined language," strong in abstraction; it alone could be the vehicle of intellectual endeavor, including the political. Spoken English and the "vulgar" in general was dismissed as the reflection of inferior minds, incapable of expressing anything of consequence, certainly of nothing political – "cant" as Johnson called it.[2]

The hitching of Johnson with Lowth and Harris (the latter an especially odd bedfellow) makes Johnson appear as the representative of a linguistic *ancien régime* that needed to be toppled by a popular revolution in language. It is undoubtedly true that these views were held by some writers and commentators on the language in the eighteenth century, and were perhaps widely held. I would like, however, to challenge the view that many of them were held by Johnson.

The mood of the times certainly favored a prescriptive attitude to the language: Johnson was employed to produce a dictionary with the aim of

fixing the language, of prescribing certain usages and spellings and of proscribing others.[3] This expectation had grown more strident since Swift had
published his *Proposal for Correcting, Improving and Ascertaining the English
Tongue*, arguing that "some Method should be thought on for *ascertaining*
and *fixing* our Language for ever, after such Alterations are made in it as
shall be thought requisite."[4] Johnson was certainly aware of this expectation when he began the *Dictionary*, and he acknowledges and appears
to comply with his contracted task in the *Plan*: "The chief intent of [this
dictionary] is to preserve the purity and ascertain the meaning of our English
idiom" (1825 *Works*, vol. v, p. 3). His declaration in the Preface to the
Dictionary, however, written nine years later, that he "do[es] not form,
but register the language" (1825 *Works*, vol. v, p. 44) ought at least to
make us enquire whether the prescriptive expectation was carried out in
practice.

The many possible models and determinants of correctness in language
may be listed as follows:

etymology (e.g., the claim that *dilapidated* can only be used of things
made of stone because of the derivation of the word from Latin *lapis*,
stone);

application of the rules of Latin (e.g., the supposition that the same
moods and cases exist in English as in Latin);

logic (e.g., the double-negative rule);

analogy (i.e., the parallel between an expression and some established
pattern of usage, e.g., the supposition that *earlily* is the correct form
of the adverb by analogy with other adverbs adding the suffix *-ly*);

the "expert opinion" (i.e., the preferred usage of grammarians, lexicographers, or a language academy).

Clearly the preference in the early eighteenth century was for the "expert
opinion" brand of prescriptivism, whether in the form of a language
academy or the edicts of a lexicographer, and slowly the preference for
the latter prevailed in Britain. So Johnson knew when he accepted the
commission for the *Dictionary* that a cloud of prescriptive expectation was
hovering over him.

He seemed only too willing to comply with this expectation when he
wrote the section on etymology in his *Plan*:

By tracing in this manner every word to its original, and not admitting, but with
great caution, any of which no original can be found, we shall secure our language
from being over-run with *cant*, from being crouded with low terms, the spawn of
folly and affectation, which arise from no just principles of speech, and of which
therefore no legitimate derivation can be shewn. (1825 *Works*, vol. v, p. 11)

Not only does this passage express the view that there is such a concept as "legitimate derivation," but there is a corresponding illegitimacy attributed to "cant" words, which are branded with infamy as the "spawn of folly and affectation" and are said to "arise from no just principles of speech." This comment suggests that etymology and analogy (the rules of speech and paradigms underlying a language) are the true parents of English and that to neglect one or the other will lead to bastard words crawling all over the language.

However, even at this early stage, Johnson seems unwilling to exercise the kind of prescriptive jurisdiction that was expected of him, and uncomfortable with the expectation that he will exercise authority in his judgments on the language. He deflects authority onto others, notably Lord Chesterfield, his supposed patron; the writers whose works he will quote from; and Pope, who has chosen those writers:

> With regard to questions of purity, or propriety, I was once in doubt whether I should not attribute too much to myself in attempting to decide them . . . I may hope, my Lord, that since you, whose authority in our language is so generally acknowledged, have commissioned me to declare my own opinion, I shall be considered as exercising a kind of vicarious jurisdiction . . . as the delegate of your Lordship. (1825 *Works*, vol. v, p. 19)

Johnson significantly calls the writers whose works he will quote from his "authorities," but is still anxious to defer authority by one further stage onto Pope: "It has been asked, on some occasions, who shall judge the judges? And since with regard to this design, a question may arise by what authority the authorities are selected, it is necessary to obviate it, by declaring that many of the writers whose testimonies will be alleged, were selected by Mr. Pope" (1825 *Works*, vol. v, p. 20).

Johnson, however, seems to have been fully aware before embarking on his sea of words that they will not conform neatly to "just principles of speech" and that the aspiration to make the language accord with principles of analogy will ultimately fail:

> To our language may be with great justness applied the observation of *Quintilian*, that speech was not formed by an analogy sent from heaven. It did not descend to us in a state of uniformity and perfection, but was produced by necessity and enlarged by accident, and is therefore composed of dissimilar parts, thrown together by negligence, by affectation, by learning, or by ignorance. (1825 *Works*, vol. v, p. 11)

The reference to Quintilian makes the meaning here clear. In the *Institutio oratoria* Quintilian rejects reason, which underlies appeals to etymology and analogy, as a reliable guide to the language and argues that all judgments must ultimately be based on usage:

Non enim, cum primum fingerentur homines, Analogia demissa caelo formam loquendi dedit, sed inventa est postquam loquebantur, et notatum in sermone quo quidque modo caderet. Itaque non ratione nititur sed exemplo, nec lex est loquendi sed observatio, ut ipsam analogian nulla res alia fecerit quam consuetudo.

Analogy was not sent down from heaven to frame the rules of language when men were first created, but was discovered only when they were already using language and note was taken of the way in which particular words ended in speech. It rests therefore not upon Reason but upon Precedent; it is not a law of speech, but an observed practice, Analogy itself being merely the product of Usage.[5]

An emphasis on etymology as the primary linguistic principle in a dictionary will tend to lead to decreased marking of polysemy and differentiation of senses, whereas a focus on usage as the primary linguistic principle will tend to lead in the opposite direction to increased polysemy and differentiation of senses. The very fact that Johnson focuses increasingly on polysemy and differentiation of senses at the expense of etymology is itself a strong indication that his primary focus was on usage.

That Johnson based so much of his *Dictionary* on the illustrative quotations is another indication of his commitment to the centrality of usage in ascertaining and codifying the language. He refers to the citations as "authorities" but treats them as though they are evidences of particular usages. The difference between Johnson and Noah Webster in this regard is very noticeable. Webster saw no need for the inclusion of quotations:

One of the most objectionable parts of Johnson's Dictionary . . . is the great number of passages cited from authors, to exemplify his definitions. Most English words are so familiarly and perfectly understood, and the sense of them so little liable to be called in question, that they may be safely left to rest on the authority of the lexicographer without examples . . . Numerous citations serve to swell the size of a Dictionary without any adequate advantage.[6]

Webster was clearly influenced by the "expert opinion" brand of prescriptivism and thought the authority of the lexicographer ranked higher than any other lexicographic principle. Even Joseph Priestley regards analogy as the higher lexicographic principle when "good authors" disagree in their usage: "since good authors have adopted different forms of speech, and in a case that admits of no standard but that of *custom*, one authority may be of as much weight as another; *the analogy of language* is the only thing to which we can have recourse, to adjust these differences."[7] Only Johnson places reliance on the reader to judge the meanings of words from the context of the cited passages and to decide between competing usages.

There is a widespread recognition that Johnson's view of the language was altered by the experience of attempting to codify it in writing his *Dictionary*. This is undoubtedly true, but it seems clear that he was already aware, even before he started his lexicographic work, that ultimately any judgments about the language must be founded on usage. His comments in the *Plan* use a metaphor taken from the law and suggest that he was using concepts from the law, specifically the division between common law (generally accepted law based on custom and practice) and statute law (laws enacted by governments and legislatures), to express his recognition that language does not conform to any written rules, but must depend on and be measured by usage. William Blackstone writes of the common law that it is "doctrines that are not set down in any written statute or ordinance, but depend merely upon immemorial usage, that is, upon common law, for their support." He makes it clear that courts will allow reliance on custom only when the custom meets the criteria of antiquity (no man can remember the beginning of it) and continuity (the rights claimed under it have never been abandoned or interrupted).[8] Lord Campbell's assessment of the state of the common law in England in the years before publication of the *Dictionary* (and before the influential decisions of Lord Mansfield) is: "If an action turning upon a mercantile question was brought in a court of law, the judge submitted it to the jury, who determined it according to their own notions of what was fair, and no general rule was laid down which could afterwards be referred to for the purpose of settling similar disputes."[9] Johnson's practice in relation to the *Dictionary* could perhaps be described as the laying down of general rules (based on custom) which could afterwards be referred to for the purpose of settling disputes.

In speaking of syntax Johnson makes the point that it is "not to be taught by general rules, but by special precedents," and adds: "it is not in our power to have recourse to any established laws of speech, but we must remark how the writers of former ages have used the same word" (1825 *Works*, vol. v, p. 13). Johnson evidently considered the quotations drawn from these writers to be acting not merely as "authorities," in and of themselves *authorizing* certain usages, but also as testimonies, attesting to and *exemplifying* usage.

The concept of "special precedents" refers to the reported decisions of courts and judges which make new interpretations of the law and therefore can be cited as precedents and, in this context, seems to refer to the kind of judicial decision that Lord Mansfield, Chief Justice of the King's Bench from 1756 to 1788, was later famous for making which returned to the roots of custom in established social practice: "as the usages of society alter, the law must adapt itself."[10] Johnson is using the phrase to apply to the usage of the writers he quotes as if they were the testimonies of witnesses in a court of law and that their primary function is evidentiary. His use of the metaphor is therefore closer to the functioning of common law.[11] The emphasis of common law is less on finding an applicable rule to fit new facts than on treating case precedents as *evidences* about unwritten law.[12] Opposing legal briefs are treated as adversarial hypotheses about the application of the law underlying custom and practice to a new set of facts. The underlying principle of the application of common law is the same blend of empiricism and inductivism as underlies the development of modern scientific thought. This should give us some insight into the way in which Johnson thought of his illustrative quotations as functioning as testamentary witnesses providing evidence of previous writers' usage. When these disagree, as he anticipated they would, he envisages that we will act as linguistic judges, weighing up the evidence and coming to our own judgment:

> we usually *ascribe* good, but *impute* evil; yet neither the use of these words, nor perhaps of any other in our licentious language, is so established as not to be often reversed by the correctest writers. I shall therefore, since the rules of stile, like those of law, arise from precedents often repeated, collect the testimonies on both sides, and endeavour to discover and promulgate the decrees of custom, who has so long possessed, whether by right or by usurpation, the sovereignty of words. (1825 *Works*, vol. v, p. 16)

The implication is that, regardless of any prior notions of correctness we may have, if the testimonies on one side outnumber the testimonies on the other, we should follow the predominant usage.

Johnson's presentation of usage in the *Plan* covers three separate but overlapping concepts: usage of the best writers, who are regarded as models of style and "authorities"; usage from the period "since the accession of Elizabeth," which Johnson calls "the golden age of our language" (1825 *Works*, vol. v, p. 18); and common usage or custom. I have indicated that even the presentation of the usage of the best writers, the "authorities," is, in practice, not so much prescriptive as evidential, but it is also true that the presentation of the usage of Johnson's "golden age," from the accession of Elizabeth to the Restoration, is not so much a draught of pure water drawn from "the wells of English undefiled" (1825 *Works*, vol. v, p. 39) as an extended glossary on the texts Johnson is quoting from. His intent as well as his actual practice is best described in the *Plan*, where he explains that "many [antiquated or obsolete words] might be omitted, but that the reader may require . . . that no difficulty should be left unresolved in books which he finds himself invited to read, as confessed and established models of stile" (1825 *Works*, vol. v, p. 18). The notion of these books as "models of stile" may be prescriptive, though they were selected not on Johnson's authority but because they are "confessed and established"; in other words, it is generally agreed that these texts are models of style. Johnson is very careful here not to present these works as *his* choice: he had earlier deflected authority for the choice of sources onto Pope and now he uses a passive construction to suggest that a reader "finds himself invited to read" certain works, but does not say by whom. This seems to me to be a conscious and very careful avoidance of prescriptive authority, even in an area where readers of the *Dictionary* would have expected that Johnson *should* exert such authority.

Johnson retains the notion of a "golden age" of language when he comes to write the Preface, but his reasons for choosing usages from this period have a more nationalistic emphasis than in the *Plan*. He opposes calques (literal translations of foreign expressions) in the *Plan*,[13] but develops in the Preface a notion of England as a proud and independent nation, reflected in its language:

Our language, for almost a century, has . . . been gradually departing from its original *Teutonick* character, and deviating towards a *Gallick* structure and phraseology, from which it ought to be our endeavour to recal it, by making our ancient volumes the groundwork of stile, admitting among the additions of later times, only such as may supply real deficiencies, such as are readily adopted by the genius of our tongue, and incorporate easily with our native idioms. (1825 *Works*, vol. v, pp. 39–40)

There is an undeniable prescriptive flavor to all this, which would seem to favor English usage over French usage, Elizabethan usage over contemporary usage, and polite usage (the "groundwork of stile") over common usage, but it is not carried through into practice in the ways one might expect from this comment. The remark seems aimed at meeting the expectations of Johnson's contemporary readers, rather than an accurate and fair reflection of the contents of the *Dictionary*. If such notions of nationalistic purity were Johnson's primary intention, why would he include words or phrases, admittedly in italic, which he regarded as not yet assimilated into English? It seems a fairer reflection of his intentions as carried into practice when he comments in the Preface, "Some of the examples have been taken from writers who were never mentioned as masters of elegance or models of stile; but words must be sought where they are used" (1825 *Works*, vol. v, p. 40). Here, as elsewhere, his primary concern is with usage.

Finally, there is the area of common usage or custom. It is common usage that modern lexicographers believe should be reflected in dictionaries, rather than the preferences of the lexicographer or the social class he represents, and it has usually been assumed that Johnson's *Dictionary* deliberately excludes common usage in favor of that of the polite classes. His allusion to Quintilian in the *Plan*, however, ought to alert us to the fact that Johnson did not disregard common usage even at the outset of his lexicographic labors, and we ought also to pay some attention to his claim: "I shall . . . endeavour to discover and promulgate the decrees of custom, who has so long possessed, whether by right or by usurpation, the sovereignty of words" (1825 *Works*, vol. v, p. 16). The contention that it was only *after* he had grappled over nine long years with the language that Johnson reluctantly accepted the primacy of common usage has been overdetermined by his own confessions in the Preface of failure to regulate the language. Johnson was clearly alert to the primary demands of custom even in 1747. The remarks in the Preface register not so much a radical change of program as a confession that the constantly fluctuating nature of usage makes it almost impossible to record schematically in a dictionary: "it must be remembered, that while our language is yet living, and variable by the caprice of every one that speaks it, these words are hourly shifting their relations, and can no more be ascertained in a dictionary, than a grove, in the agitation of a storm, can be accurately delineated from its picture in the water" (1825 *Works*, vol. v, p. 35).

Johnson found himself more and more driven to record the language wherever he found it, without regard to notions of style or correctness, and to read the *Dictionary* is to encounter an enormously wide variety of texts, by no means predominantly "high" literature, written by several hundred writers, both famous and obscure, forming collectively a corpus of seventeenth- and eighteenth-century usage: "Many quotations serve no other purpose, than that of proving the bare existence of words" (1825 *Works*, vol. v, p. 39).

In the Preface Johnson discusses the problem of polysemy, a perennial lexicographer's anxiety, and, in particular, the problem of where to set the boundaries in discriminating the various sub-senses of a word. In some cases the illustrative quotations do not help because some writers' usage is itself confused, with the result that "some examples might be indifferently put to either signification," but Johnson asserts that "this uncertainty is not to be imputed to me, who do not form, but register the language; who do not teach men how they should think, but relate how they have hitherto expressed their thoughts" (1825 *Works*, vol. v, p. 44). A lexicographer who "do[es] not form, but register the language" is hardly one driven by a prescriptive program.

Given Johnson's apparent acceptance of the task of distilling a purer language from the briny sea of words, one might expect that he would proscribe certain usages much more frequently than he does. He states quite openly in the *Plan* that "Barbarous or impure words and expressions, may be branded with some note of infamy, as they are carefully to be eradicated wherever they are found; and they occur too frequently even in the best writers" (1825 *Works*, vol. v, p. 19). This is overt prescriptive intention and one might expect it to be carried through into the *Dictionary* by means of usage labels, or perhaps even typographical marks, such as daggers or asterisks, by which "beauties" or barbarisms were sometimes marked in eighteenth-century texts. No such marks appear in the text, however, and the labels are sparingly used.[14]

Latin grammarians had divided grammatical errors (*vitiae orationis*) into two main categories: barbarisms and solecisms.[15] Barbarisms were errors in single words (usually of orthography or phonology), whereas solecisms were errors in syntax or morphology, where words were put together contrary to the norms of grammar. Johnson draws attention to this distinction in the entry for *solecism*: "Unfitness of one word to another; impropriety in language. A barbarism may be in one word, a solecism must be of more." One would expect, then, that if Johnson were to proscribe usages he would do so using these familiar terms. However, what one finds in the *Dictionary* is that he rarely uses either term. There is a mere handful of entries out of a total exceeding 40,000 which contain such proscriptions. A single example exists of Johnson proscribing a usage on the grounds of solecism, and that is the entry for *never* 2:

It is used in a form of speech handed down by the best writers, but lately accused, I think, with justice, of solecism; as, *he is mistaken though never so wise*. It is now maintained, that propriety requires it to be expressed thus, *he is mistaken though ever so wise*; that is, *he is mistaken* how *wise* soever *he be*. The common mode can only be defended by supplying a very harsh and unprecedented ellipsis; *he is mistaken though so wise*, as *never was* any: such however is the common use of the word among the best authors.

This comment is followed by eight illustrative quotations from writers committing this supposed solecism.

The terms "barbarism" and "barbarous" are used slightly more frequently, but even then only twenty-one usages are so labeled in *1755*. Among them is the entry for *disannul*: "This word is formed contrary to analogy by those who not knowing the meaning of the word *annul*, intended to form a negative sense by the needless use of the negative particle. It ought therefore to be rejected as ungrammatical and barbarous." Yet such judgments are rare in the *Dictionary*; much more common is the kind of comment Johnson makes in the entry for *nought*: "as therefore we write *aught* not *ought* for any thing, we should, according to analogy, write *naught* not *nought* for *nothing*; but a custom has irreversibly prevailed of using *naught* for bad, and *nought* for *nothing*." This custom is then exemplified by the addition of five quotations. Johnson's most significant comment occurs in the entry for *latter*:

This is the comparative of *late*, though universally written with *tt*, contrary to analogy, and to our own practice in the superlative *latest*. When the thing of which the comparison is made is mentioned, we use *later*; as, *this fruit is* later *than the rest*; but *latter* when no comparison is expressed, but the reference is merely to time;
— — *Volet usus*
Quem penes arbitrium est, & vis, & norma loquendi.

The quotation is from Horace's *Ars poetica*, lines 71–72, and may be translated as: "[if] that is what use should dictate, in whose power is the judgment and the law and the rule of speech." The passage from Horace reflects a linguistic controversy of antiquity, as to whether words were formed by "analogy" or by "anomaly," by nature or custom, and Horace comes down clearly on the side of custom.[16]

What is noteworthy about this passage, and is rarely rendered in translations of it, is the parallel that Horace makes between the operations of language and the operations of the law.[17] The maxim underpinning the concept of common law is *communis error facit jus*: what was at first illegal, if it is repeated many times, is presumed to have acquired the force of custom and practice, and then it would be wrong to depart from it.[18] Similarly barbarisms and solecisms in language, if they are repeated many times, are presumed to have acquired the force of custom and usage, and then it would be wrong to depart from them. The lines Johnson quotes are immediately preceded in Horace by:

Multa renascentur quae iam cecidere, cadentque
Quae nunc sunt in honore vocabula, si volet usus . . .

This whole passage was translated by Ben Jonson:

> Much phrase that now is dead, shall be reviv'd;
> And much shall dye, that now is nobly liv'd,
> If Custome please; at whose disposing will
> The power, and rule of speaking resteth still.[19]

It is evidently this line of thought that Johnson has in mind when he writes in the Preface to the *Dictionary*: "As any custom is disused, the words that expressed it must perish with it; as any opinion grows popular, it will innovate speech in the same proportion as it alters practice" (1825 *Works*, vol. v, p. 47).

Johnson makes the Horatian distinction between nature and custom in a *Rambler* essay, written in 1751 as he was compiling the entries for the *Dictionary*: "It ought to be the first endeavour of a writer to distinguish nature from custom, or that which is established because it is right, from that which is right only because it is established" (Yale *Works*, vol. v, p. 70). That which is right only because it is established is the common law, and in language it is custom and usage. It seems likely also that when Johnson states in the Preface, "It has been asserted, that for the law to be *known* is of more importance than to be *right*" (1825 *Works*, vol. v, p. 27), he is making another claim for the importance of common law and another implicit parallel with custom and usage. His assertion of the primacy of anomaly over analogy, or custom and usage over any supposed rules of the language, occurs in the Preface, when he concedes that "Every language has its anomalies, which, though inconvenient, and in themselves once unnecessary, must be tolerated among the imperfections of human things" (1825 *Works*, vol. v, p. 24).

Johnson found the language recalcitrant, unruly, and impossible to squeeze into the neat exigencies of analogy or etymology. By the time he came to write his Preface to the *Dictionary*, after he had had the experience of attempting to trace every word back to its derivation and trying to establish the "just principles of speech," he acknowledged the force of custom and usage: "Even in words of which the derivation is apparent, I have been often obliged to sacrifice uniformity to custom; thus I write in compliance with a numberless majority, *convey* and *inveigh, deceit* and *receipt, fancy* and *phantom*" (1825 *Works*, vol. v, p. 26).

Several comments in the Preface betray a lexicographic concern to reflect and record usage, wherever and however found, rather than a prescriptivist's concern to select only certain approved usages or to mark usages approvingly or disapprovingly. It is this lexicographic concern which leads Johnson to remark, "I . . . have often inserted . . . words which are supported perhaps only by a single authority, and which, being not admitted into general use, stand yet as candidates or probationers, and must depend for their adoption on the suffrage of futurity" (1825 *Works*, vol. v, p. 31). Comments such as this indicate an uncertainty about whether or not such words could be regarded as belonging to the core of the language, and such doubts afflict modern lexicographers when they are making selections of headwords.

It is also common for modern lexicographers to have uncertainties about lemmatization. Lemmatization is a process in which all the inflectional and variant forms of a word are reduced to and grouped under a single lemma, their base form. So, for example, *am, are*, and *is* would be recorded in a modern dictionary under the single lemma *be*.[20] Since the overall number of words in a dictionary is thereby reduced this is a very useful technique, but it can also lead to uncertainty: it requires a certain level of linguistic competence on the part of the user. The syntactic counterpart of lemmatization is parsing, whereby part of speech and syntactical function are labeled. Johnson's exclusions often tell us more about his intentions and purpose than his inclusions, and so it is significant that among the classes of words which he excludes are compounded forms (such as *thieflike* or *coachdriver*), words formed by addition of a suffix (adjectives such as *greenish*, adverbs such as *dully*, adjectival nouns such as *vileness*, verbal nouns such as *keeping*), and participles, past or present (such as *bringing* or *stayed*). The reason he gives for omitting these word classes is that "their signification cannot be mistaken" (1825 *Works*, vol. v, p. 32). The fact that Johnson's *Dictionary* is relatively unlemmatized and often includes parts of speech of single words as separate entries suggests to me that Johnson has an "ordinary" user very much in mind, the linguistic counterpart of the "common reader."

Johnson's concern in the *Dictionary* was to reflect what he regarded as the core of the language. It is for this reason that he includes common words rather than concentrating on hard words, and he excludes a great many "terms of art" not for reasons of snobbery because they were associated with trade or with the working classes, but because they were specialized and technical words and so belong in a technical dictionary.[21] He includes words that are attested in written texts not through a prejudice in favor of the written over the oral, but because speech is notoriously difficult to record. Johnson recognizes, in fact, that it is speech that tends to innovate usage: "Copiousness of speech will give opportunities to capricious choice, by which some words will be preferred, and others degraded; vicissitudes of fashion will enforce the use of new, or extend the signification of known terms . . . pronunciation will be varied by levity or ignorance, and the pen must at length comply with the tongue" (1825 *Works*, vol. v, pp. 47–48). If anything, this comment appears to give primacy to the oral over the written. In Johnson's Preface to Giuseppe Baretti's *Easy Phraseology . . . of the Italian Language* (1775), however, the oral and the written are presented as two equally important aspects of the language:

> Of every learned and elegant people the language is divided into two parts: the one lax and cursory, used on slight occasions with extemporary negligence; the other rigorous and solemn, the effect of deliberate choice and grammatical accuracy. When books are multiplied and style is cultivated, the colloquial and written diction separate by degrees, till there is one language of the tongue, and another of the pen.
> No language can be said to have been learned till both these parts are understood: but to reach the colloquial without the opportunities of familiar conversation, is very difficult. By reading great Authors it cannot be obtained, as books speak but the language of books. (*Prefaces and Dedications*, p. 10)

In *Rambler* 177, written at the same time as the first edition of the *Dictionary*, Johnson presents Vivaculus, who retires to study in solitude, and gives a very unflattering portrait of a man who knows only the language of books and loses touch with the oral language: "My ease and elegance were sensibly impaired; I was no longer able to accommodate myself with readiness to the accidental current of conversation, my notions grew particular and paradoxical, and my phraseology formal and unfashionable; I spoke, on common occasions, the language of books" (Yale *Works*, vol. v, p. 169).

The words Johnson selects for inclusion in the *Dictionary* are rarely marked by expressions of approval or disapproval and the reason for inclusion seems to have been predominantly usage. Johnson seems to have been applying a test to the words of the language which is not one of supposed "purity," but a linguistic parallel to his literary test of time. Words which have endured for the 100–150 years since the age of Elizabeth are the most likely to form the core of the language, rather than the fleeting and fluctuating forms of usage of the polite *beau monde*. The expression of this view is clearest in Johnson's Preface to Shakespeare:

> If there be, what I believe there is, in every nation, a stile which never becomes obsolete, a certain mode of phraseology so consonant and congenial to the analogy and principles of its respective language as to remain settled and unaltered; this stile is probably to be sought in the common intercourse of life, among those who

speak only to be understood, without ambition of elegance. The polite are always catching modish innovations, and the learned depart from established forms of speech, in hope of finding or making better; those who wish for distinction forsake the vulgar, when the vulgar is right; but there is a conversation above grossness and below refinement, where propriety resides. (Yale *Works*, vol. VII, p. 70)

This is the language selected for inclusion in Johnson's *Dictionary*.

NOTES

1. Suzanne Romaine, ed., *The Cambridge History of the English Language*, *vol. IV: 1776–1997* (Cambridge: Cambridge University Press, 1998), Introduction, especially p. 7.
2. Gwyn Williams, *Artisans and Sans-Culottes: Popular Movements in France and Britain during the French Revolution* (London: Routledge, 1989), cited by Romaine, *Cambridge History of the English Language*, p. 8. A similar view is expressed by John Barrell, *English Literature in History, 1730–80: An Equal, Wide Survey* (London: Hutchinson, 1983), p. 148.
3. This example from Warburton, published in the same year as Johnson's *Plan*, expresses a common view of the language:

   And its being yet destitute of a Test or Standard to apply to, in cases of doubt or difficulty, shews how much it wants that attention. For we have neither GRAMMAR nor DICTIONARY, neither Chart nor Compass, to guide us through this wide sea of Words. And indeed how should we? since both are to be composed and finished on the Authority of our best established Writers. But their Authority can be of little use till the Text hath been correctly settled, and the Phraseology critically examined. As, then, by these aids, a *Grammar* and *Dictionary*, planned upon the best rules of Logic and Philosophy, (and none but such will deserve the name) are to be procured. (William Warburton, ed., *The Works of Shakespear*, 8 vols. [London, 1747], vol. I, pp. xxv–xxvi)

4. Jonathan Swift, *A Proposal for Correcting, Improving and Ascertaining the English Tongue* (London, 1712), p. 31.
5. *Institutio oratoria*, 1.6.16, in *Quintilian: The Orator's Education*, ed. Donald A. Russell, 2 vols. (Cambridge, Mass., and London: Harvard University Press, 2001), vol. I, pp. 168–69.
6. Noah Webster, *An American Dictionary of the English Language* (New York, 1828), p. 7. Richard J. Moss describes Webster's attitude to his own authority as a lexicographer:

   In most of these cases, Webster maintained that the public generally used the term incorrectly; he, however, had traced back the word to its true meaning. This desire to set himself up as the authority on the use of language and thus give himself a position of power in all areas of human action was a central reason for his devotion to the study of language. (*Noah Webster* [Boston: Twayne, 1984], p. 97)

7. Joseph Priestley, *The Rudiments of English Grammar* (London, 1761), p. vi.
8. William Blackstone, *Commentaries on the Laws of England*, 9th ed., 4 vols. (London, 1783), vol. I, pp. 48, 76. I am indebted to John Stone, who first

suggested to me the connection between Johnson's lexicographic work and areas of the law, specifically law dictionaries.

9. Lord John Campbell, *The Lives of the Chief Justices of England, from the Norman Conquest till the Death of Lord Tenterden* (London, 1849–57), p. 299.

10. William Murray, Lord Mansfield, quoted in John Stone, "Law and the Politics of Johnson's *Dictionary*," *The European English Messenger* 12 (2003), 54–58, on p. 56.

11. John Stone comments: "'Collecting testimonies' points to something like Mansfield empanelling special juries of merchants to get their opinion on questions of accepted usage in commercial dealings. In both cases, Mansfield's and Johnson's, testimony in itself is not authoritative, but helps in the study of custom, which is" (personal communication).

12. On this issue see J. C. Hogan and M. D. Schwartz, "On Bacon's 'Rules and Maximes' of the Common Law," *Law Library Journal* 76 (1984), 48–77.

13. Expressions are often taken from other languages, some apparently, as to *run a risque, courir un risque*; and some even when we do not seem to borrow their words; thus, to *bring about* or accomplish, appears an English phrase, but in reality our native word *about* has no such import, and it is only a French expression, of which we have an example in the common phrase, *venir à bout d'une affaire*. (1825 *Works*, vol. v, p. 11)

14. Pope uses such typographical features, for example, in his edition of Shakespeare to mark "beauties" or usages that he particularly approves of: "Some of the most shining passages are distinguish'd by comma's in the margin, and where the beauty lay not in particulars but in the whole a star is prefix'd to the scene" (*The Works of Shakespear*, ed. Alexander Pope, 6 vols. [London, 1723–25], vol. i, p. xxiii).

15. Works which deal with this issue include Stanley F. Bonner, *Education in Ancient Rome: From the Elder Cato to the Younger Pliny* (Berkeley: University of California Press, 1977), pp. 198–211, and Raija Vainio, *Latinitas and Barbarisms according to the Roman Grammarians: Attitudes towards Language in the Light of Grammatical Examples* (Turku: Painosalama Oy, 1999).

16. For this ancient linguistic controversy see E. Rawson, *Intellectual Life in the Roman Republic* (London: Duckworth, 1988), pp. 117–31, especially pp. 120–23; D. L. Blank, "Analogy, Anomaly and Apollonius Dyscolus," in *Language*, ed. Stephen Everson (Cambridge: Cambridge University Press, 1994), pp. 149–69; and Michael Frede, "Principles of Stoic Grammar," in *The Stoics*, ed. John M. Rist (Berkeley: University of California Press, 1978), pp. 27–75.

17. The phrase quoted by Johnson is translated by C. H. Sisson as "For nothing but use determines the fate of words" (*The Poetic Arts: A Translation of Horace's Ars Poetica* [Cheadle: Carcanet, 1978], p. 95), but this misses the parallel with the law that Horace has in his text. An exception among translators might be Byron, who renders the passage, "Though those shall sink, which now appear to thrive, / As Custom arbitrates, whose shifting sway / Our life and language must alike obey" ("Hints from Horace," in *The Works of Lord Byron, with his Letters and Journals*, 14 vols. [London: John Murray, 1832–33], vol. ix, p. 113).

"Life" goes some way to translate the ideas of custom and practice, though not
explicitly in relation to the law.

18. See Arthur R. Hogue, *Origins of the Common Law* (Bloomington: Indiana
    University Press, 1966), p. 176.
19. "Horace, of the Art of Poetry," in *Ben Jonson*, ed. C. H. Herford and Percy and
    Evelyn Simpson, 11 vols. (Oxford: Clarendon Press, 1947), vol. VIII, p. 309.
20. Johnson includes these as individual entries in the first, the fourth, and the
    abridged editions.
21. His lack of prejudice towards such words may be demonstrated by the fact that
    Johnson wrote the Preface to Richard Rolt's *Dictionary of Trade and Commerce*
    (London, 1756). See Allen T. Hazen, *Samuel Johnson's Prefaces and Dedications*
    (New Haven: Yale University Press, 1937), pp. 198–99.

CHAPTER 8

Johnson's encyclopedia

Jack Lynch

Johnson's professed goal was "a dictionary, common or appellative," but it may be worthwhile to ask what exactly he meant by *dictionary*. In his Preface, he expressed his desire "to pierce deep into every science, to enquire the nature of every substance . . . and exhibit every production of art or nature in an accurate description" – in short, to compose a book that "might be in place of all other dictionaries." He hoped "that every quotation should be useful to some other end than the illustration of a word," and therefore "extracted from philosophers principles of science; from historians remarkable facts; from chymists complete processes." These grand plans he finally dismissed as "the dreams of a poet doomed at last to wake a lexicographer" (1825 *Works*, vol. v, pp. 31, 42–43, 38). And yet, despite the "hasty detruncation" of quotations he regretted as necessary, hundreds of entries are longer than simple definition demands – they are, in other words, more in keeping with our notion of an encyclopedia than a dictionary. This essay examines some of the ways in which Johnson moved between the two forms.

Other critics have considered the *Dictionary*'s encyclopedism, most notably Robert DeMaria, Jr., who points out that "Johnson makes few attempts to disguise the encyclopedic qualities of his book."[1] He argues convincingly that the large body of quotations turns the *Dictionary* into an encyclopedic survey of knowledge, and places Johnson's work in an important tradition of European learning. My focus, though, is both more narrow and more literal: the points of contact between Johnson's *Dictionary of the English Language* and actual encyclopedias. The distinction so often taken for granted is not so clear as many readers assume.

The traditional distinction maintains that an encyclopedia is concerned with things, a dictionary with words; an encyclopedia describes the world, and a dictionary describes the words we use to discuss the world. In his handbook on lexicography Ladislav Zgusta insists on the need to "differentiate *encyclopedic dictionaries* from linguistic ones. The latter are primarily concerned with language . . . [Encyclopedias] are primarily concerned with the denotata of the lexical units (words): They give information about the extralinguistic world."[2] This distinction is, however, notoriously difficult to maintain, since the relationship between word and world is rarely straightforward. Although it is often a simple matter in practice to distinguish encyclopedic from linguistic information, the borderline is difficult to draw with precision, and it may be no simple matter to tell whether a definition describes a word or the thing to which the word refers.

Before getting bogged down in theoretical problems, it may help to begin with the clear practical differences between the two forms, at least as they have developed in the tradition of which Johnson is a part. Encyclopedias, for instance, are usually concerned especially with noun phrases, whereas general dictionaries include all parts of speech. Modern encyclopedias as a rule give more attention to proper names than dictionaries.[3] Encyclopedias also tend to have longer entries than dictionaries. These generalizations about actual works, however, serve only to stave off the theoretical problems of the word–thing dichotomy: in excluding verbs and proper names we are still left with the question of how to define common noun phrases.

The problem is that there is no end to the kinds of information a reference work might provide, and it is easy for a dictionary definition to swell until it is indistinguishable from an encyclopedia entry. Most lexicographers have tried to provide just enough information to allow readers to associate a word with a thing already in their experience. A definition, in this scheme, allows readers to recognize the thing being defined – the *definiendum* – but offers no information beyond what is necessary for the reader to associate the word with the thing. The lexicographer's task is therefore to describe a minimal set of attributes both necessary and sufficient to identify the *definiendum*. As Zgusta notes, "A good part of the lexicographer's research is concerned with establishing *criteriality*, with the task to find what is criterial and what is not" (*Manual of Lexicography*, p. 29). If it is not criterial, it is the business of an encyclopedia, not a dictionary.

The first problem with identifying a finite set of criteria is that it depends on the lexicographer's ability to separate the criterial qualities, those that determine the *definiendum*'s identity, from the non-criterial ones – a distinction that maps neatly onto the Scholastic distinction of essence and accident.[4] Although modern philosophers and linguists are justly wary of such categories, these conceptions were dominant when the modern reference work began to take shape in the Middle Ages. For Scholastic philosophers, definition should be a straightforward matter: a definition identifies the essence of a thing, leaving the accidents for more extended discussions.

Aristotle's discussion of logical definition in the *Posterior Analytics* B13 (96a20–97b37) was influential, especially as interpreted by Porphyry in his *Isagoge* and Boethius in his commentary. From this Scholastic tradition emerged the "genus–differentiae" mode of definition, summarized as "Definitio fit per genus proximum et differentiam specificam": a definition identifies the kind and offers a means of distinguishing it from other examples of that kind. The genus and a minimally adequate number of differentiae provide a definition; the accidents can be left for other kinds of description. Much lexicographical practice even today employs some version of this genus–differentiae definition. A modern dictionary defines *drake* as "a male duck": the genus is "duck," and the drake is distinguished from other ducks by being male.[5] But in order for this mode of definition to work for all *definienda*, one needs a strictly hierarchical conception of reality. Each thing must be an example of a single kind, each kind in turn being an example of a single higher kind.

This conception was widespread among medieval scholars, and it is no coincidence that many works of the time were organized on hierarchical Porphyrian principles. But problems with the Scholastic scheme soon became apparent. Hierarchies depend on each species belonging to one, and only one, genus, but as writers began classifying knowledge, they discovered that many species seemed to belong to multiple genera. An axe is a kind of weapon and a kind of tool; a whale is a mammal and a sea creature. Umberto Eco describes the logical consequence: "if the tree is not hierarchically organized, one has no guarantee of dealing with a finite number of markers." The result is that "The tree of genera and species, the tree of substances, blows up into a dust of differentiae, in a turmoil of infinite accidents, in a nonhierarchical network of *qualia*. The dictionary is dissolved into a potentially unordered and unrestricted galaxy of pieces of world knowledge. The dictionary becomes an encyclopedia, because it was in fact *a disguised encyclopedia*."[6]

This may have contributed to the decline of thematically organized reference works popular in the Middle Ages and the corresponding rise of alphabetically – which is to say, arbitrarily – organized works, and by the eighteenth century the hierarchy of knowledge had had its day as a practical macrostructure. Many hierarchical schemes of knowledge were proposed in the seventeenth century, but all the large-scale general dictionaries relied on the alphabet.[7] A century after Johnson, in 1852, Peter Mark Roget would attempt a new kind of work on hierarchical principles; by 1879, however, his son was forced to add an alphabetical index to make it usable. Without a firm belief in the Porphyrian tree, it was no longer clear which facts were criterial and which accidental, and definitions could no longer depend on simple notions of genera and differentiae. Although genus–differentiae definition often remained possible in practice, the theoretical problems had become increasingly worrisome.

In recent decades, another problem has proved even more worrisome. Structuralist linguistics, the movement that dominated much of the twentieth century, tended to treat language as a comparatively self-contained domain, separable from other modes of cognition. As long as knowledge of words could be separated from knowledge of things, the distinction between dictionaries and encyclopedias persisted more or less unchallenged. Beginning, however, in the 1960s – spurred by research into natural-language processing by computers, and aided by conceptions of language developed by analytical philosophers – a new movement, cognitive linguistics, conceived of language not as a self-contained domain but as a faculty inseparable from the rest of cognition. If our understanding of words and our understanding of things cannot be sharply distinguished, the boundary between the two forms that take their origin from that division begins to look nebulous.[8] As Geeraerts has argued, "The distinction between semantic and encyclopedic knowledge . . . is based on the distinction between an autonomous linguistic conceptual structure . . . and conceptual memory in the broadest sense. If the latter distinction is discarded, the former also falls" ("Cognitive Grammar," p. 656).

After some stirrings in the 1960s and 1970s, therefore, there arose among some linguists a critical attack on any principled distinction between the two forms. John Haiman's essay of 1980, while not the first to insist the demarcation of the genres was illusory, was still the most forceful and influential early attack on the traditional conception of the two genres.[9] His argument that all dictionaries are really encyclopedias prompted many responses pro and con, and the two camps have ever since engaged in often fervent arguments over the "lexicon–encyclopedia interface."

Johnson falls between the Scholastics and the cognitive linguists, both chronologically and temperamentally. Though he was not yet plagued by modern linguistic hand-wringing, the older onomasiological tradition was moribund, and Johnson had little patience with those whose notions of reality were strictly hierarchical. He expressed in his Preface a desire "to limit every idea by a definition strictly logical" (1825 *Works*, vol. v, p. 42), but unlike the over-confident Wilkins he recognized that hierarchies would be difficult to respect in practice. As he explained to Boswell:

"Sometimes things may be made darker by definition. I see a *cow*. I define her, *Animal quadrupes ruminans cornutum*. But a goat ruminates, and a cow may have no horns. *Cow* is plainer." BOSWELL. "I think Dr. Franklin's definition of *Man* a good one – 'A tool-making animal.'" JOHNSON. "But many a man never made a tool." (*Life*, vol. iii, p. 245)

Eighteenth-century readers and writers recognized a difference between dictionaries and encyclopedias, even though the terms were not always respected in book titles. Many works we would call encyclopedias were published as dictionaries or lexicons (such as John Harris's *Lexicon Technicum* of 1704, the *New Royal and Universal Dictionary of Arts and Sciences* of 1769–71, and, across the Channel, Bayle's *Dictionnaire historique et critique* of 1697), and many works called themselves by both names apparently indiscriminately (such as Ephraim Chambers's *Cyclopædia; or, An Universal Dictionary of Arts and Sciences* and the *Encyclopædia Britannica; or, A Dictionary of Arts and Sciences* of 1771).[10] Still, the distinction was generally recognized, and when Johnson included encyclopedic information he knew he was crossing a generic boundary. In the Preface he expresses a familiar eighteenth-century conception of the relationship between words and things, insisting he was "not yet so lost in lexicography, as to forget that *words are the daughters of earth, and that things are the sons of heaven*" (1825 *Works*, vol. v, p. 27). More to the point, his definition of *dictionary* suggests it is concerned only with linguistic information: "A book containing the words of any language in alphabetical order, with explanations of their meaning; a lexicon; a vocabulary; a word-book."[11] But even as he insisted that dictionaries are concerned with words, he confessed to a strong desire to talk about things. "When first I engaged in this work," he notes in his Preface, "I resolved to leave neither words nor things unexamined, and pleased myself with a prospect of the hours which I should revel away in feasts of literature" (1825 *Works*, vol. v, p. 42). Likewise, "When I had thus enquired into the original of words, I resolved to show likewise my attention to things; to pierce deep into every science, to enquire the nature of every substance of which I inserted the name" (1825 *Works*, vol. v, p. 42).

Such information, he later realized, would have to be omitted. But the omission was not complete, and from the beginning he recognized that some encyclopedic information would be unavoidable:

It was some time doubted whether it be necessary to explain the things implied by particular words. As under the term *baronet*, whether instead of this explanation, *a title of honour next in degree to that of baron*, it would be better to mention more particularly the creation, privileges and rank of baronets; and whether under the word *barometer*, instead of being satisfied with observing that it is *an instrument to discover the weight of the air*, it would be fit to spend a few lines upon its invention, construction and principles. (1825 *Works*, vol. v, p. 14)

Such entries, he admits, will strike experts as superficial – "It is not to be expected that with the explanation of the one the herald should be satisfied, or the philosopher with that of the other" – but "common readers" will need this sort of information, since "without some attention to such demands the dictionary cannot become generally valuable." His treatment of the lexicon–encyclopedia interface is fundamentally pragmatic.

Whatever his theory, in practice his work was more encyclopedic than any earlier general dictionary. English dictionaries conventionally emphasized their encyclopedic contents. Dictionary title pages were notoriously wordy, even in an age famous for wordy title pages, and it was *de rigueur* to catalogue there the various fields of knowledge covered in the volume. Thomas Blount's *Glossographia* promises that "the Terms of Divinity, Law, Physick, Mathematicks, and other Arts and Sciences [will be] explicated." John Kersey's *Dictionarium Anglo-Britannicum* is bolder, offering an "Explication . . . of all Terms relating to Arts and Sciences, both Liberal and Mechanical, *viz. Divinity, Law, Philosophy, Physick, Surgery, Anatomy, Chymistry, Pharmacy, Botanicks, Mathematicks, Grammar, Rhetorick, Logick, Musick, Heraldry, Maritime Affairs, Military Discipline, Traffick, Husbandry, Gardening, Handicrafts, Confectionery, Cookery, Horsemanship, Hunting, Hawking, Fowling, Fishing*, &c." Thomas Dyche goes further, promising to explicate the words from "ANATOMY, ARCHITECTURE, ARITHMETICK, ALGEBRA, ASTRONOMY, BOTANY, CHYMISTRY . . ." with a total of twenty-eight fields of inquiry; Edward Phillips promises to cover "*Theology, Philosophy, Logick, Rhetorick, Grammer, Ethicks, Law, Natural History, Magick, Physick, Chirurgery, Anatomy* . . ." and so on through forty-one. Nathan Bailey is the winner in this competition, promising to "Explai[n] hard and technical Words, or Terms of Art, in all the *ARTS, SCIENCES*, and *MYSTERIES* following . . . *VIZ.* IN AGRICULTURE, ALGEBRA, ANATOMY, ARCHITECTURE, ARITHMETICK, ASTROLOGY, ASTRONOMY, BOTANICKS, CATOPTRICKS, CHYMISTRY, CHIROMANCY, CHIRURGERY, CONFECTIONARY, COOKERY . . ." through fully sixty-two fields of inquiry.[12]

Now compare Johnson's title page: "A Dictionary of the English Language: In Which the Words Are Deduced from Their Originals, and Illustrated in Their Different Significations by Examples from the Best Writers. To Which Are Prefixed, a History of the Language, and an English Grammar." Next to his predecessors, Johnson's title page is positively spare, and all the information he describes is strictly linguistic. Despite these more modest claims, though, his *Dictionary* is in fact more extensive than any earlier English dictionary. Much of this bulk comes from his careful discrimination of senses for each word, which is especially evident in his treatment of the polysemous words and the phrasal verbs. It also comes through in his illustrative quotations, which, as DeMaria argues, serve to make the *Dictionary* a more encyclopedic work. But even without the multiple quotations, Johnson's *Dictionary* was among the most encyclopedic of English dictionaries because many of his definitions are themselves encyclopedic. A few samples of earlier definitions will show the extent of Johnson's encyclopedism. Consider *algebra*. Phillips's *New World of Words* dispenses with etymology and definition in eleven words: "a Syriac word, signifying the art of figurative numbers, of equation." Kersey's *New English Dictionary* is even more terse: "*Algebra*, or the Art of figurative numbers." Nathan Bailey, the only contemporary to rival Johnson's encyclopedism,[13] is more comprehensive, with a definition of seventy-five words, followed by a number of hyponyms: "*Numeral* ALGEBRA," "*Vulgar* ALGEBRA," "*Literal* ALGEBRA," "*Specious* ALGEBRA," and so on.

Johnson, by contrast, provides a definition of fully 242 words.[14] He begins by characterizing the "peculiar kind of arithmetick" in language similar to Bailey's (both definitions are adapted from Chambers, although Bailey does not acknowledge the fact). He also draws on both Chambers and the Trevoux dictionary to provide a brief history of algebra as it developed in India and moved from Persia to Arabia to Greece; he discusses its arrival in fifteenth-century Europe and concludes by noting that "After several improvements by Vieta, Oughtred, Harriot, Descartes, Sir Isaac Newton brought this art to the height at which it still continues."

Another word, *daffodil*, makes the case even more clearly. For Phillips it is "a kinde of flowr, otherwise called *Narcissus*" (s.v. *daffadill*). For Kersey, it is merely "a flower" (s.v. *daffodell*), which provides the genus without a single differentia. Even the normally expansive Bailey defines it as "a Flower, commonly called a Daffy-down-dilly" (s.v. *daffodil*). Johnson, however, provides a comprehensive discussion of the plant's physiology in an entry adapted from Philip Miller:

This plant hath a lily-flower, consisting of one leaf, which is bell-shaped, and cut into six segments, which incircle its middle like a crown; but the empalement, which commonly rises out of a membranous vagina, turns to an oblong or roundish fruit, which is triangular, and gapes in three parts; is divided into three cells, and full of roundish seeds.

Clearly this sort of information goes far beyond the genus–differentiae model; "oblong or roundish fruit" cannot be considered a criterial quality. In entries like this, Johnson has left lexicography behind in favor of an encyclopedia.

Of course not all nouns require encyclopedic treatment. Some are easily defined with synonyms or paraphrases, long the favored mode of early English monolingual dictionaries. Cawdrey, for instance, generally resorted to one- or two-word synonyms – "medicine, remedie, or cure"; "longitude, length" – and Johnson continued the tradition with definitions like *aria*, "An air, song, or tune," and *gleek*, "Musick; or musician." Other modes of definition are available when synonymy is not. Johnson tends to define simple artifacts with reference to a few categories: the purpose for which they have been devised (*book*, "A volume in which we read or write"), the materials from which they are made (*salad*, "Food of raw herbs"), the means by which they are put together (*cheese*, "A kind of food made by pressing the curd of coagulated milk, and suffering the mass to dry"), or their structure or organization (*chain*, "A series of links fastened one within another").[15] Some artifacts, though, are more complicated than books, salads, cheese, or chains; their materials, construction, and organization may be too complex to describe in a short compass, and a reference to their purpose threatens to swell into a long discussion of history, philosophy, or natural science. The structure of an *airpump* or *barometer*, for example, is difficult to describe in a few words, and to describe their function requires considerable background in chemistry. In the Preface Johnson disavows any intention of covering all the terms of art from commerce, navigation, law, and so on, but in fact he includes many hundreds.

More difficult even than complex artifacts are natural objects, for which no obvious purpose is evident, the materials and means of construction are inscrutable, and the structure or organization is often too complicated to describe. In such cases Johnson sometimes resorts to the Scholastic mode of definition, offering a genus and a minimal number of differentiae: a *moose*, for instance, is "The large American deer; the biggest of the species of deer," which identifies the genus ("deer") and provides two differentiae ("American," "biggest") to situate the moose among other examples of the genus. But there is not always an obvious set of criterial differentiae, and often Johnson judges that non-criterial information will prove useful to his audience. A *cat*, for instance, is "A domestick animal that catches mice, commonly reckoned by naturalists the lowest order of the leonine species," which identifies the genus ("leonine") and offers two criterial differentiae ("domestic" and "lowest order" in the species), but also provides the non-criterial information that such animals catch mice. A few entries seem to offer nothing but encyclopedic differentiae: *dog* n.s. 1 is "A domestick animal remarkably various in his species; comprising the mastiff, the spaniel, the buldog, the greyhound, the hound, the terrier, the cur, with many others. The larger sort are used as a guard; the less for sports." He offers the hyperonym "animal" and the hyponyms of the various kinds, but never specifies the criterial qualities that serve to distinguish dogs from other animals.

Perhaps the most challenging entries, though, are neither artifacts nor natural objects but complex human activities and fields of inquiry. Terms like *algebra, chemistry*, and *jury* require definitions even in a general dictionary, as do related terms like *logarithm, quicksilver*, and *demurrer*. Such do not lend themselves at all well to the Scholastic mode of providing a genus and differentiae; since human institutions are always bound up with their history and the ends to which they are put, it is notoriously difficult to find a minimally adequate set of criterial differentiae.

The *Dictionary* entries that strike us as "encyclopedic" therefore tend to fall into three groups: those dealing with complicated artifacts (*airpump, geneva, grenade, orrery*), those dealing with natural objects and phenomena (*crocodile, diamond, epilepsy, gravity*), and those dealing with human institutions and fields of learning (*architecture, arithmetick, astronomy, baron*).

There are many dozens of these encyclopedic entries in the *Dictionary*, but most were taken from other reference works.[16] Ephraim Chambers's *Cyclopædia*, for instance, provides a 250-word essay on architecture, and John Cowell explains jury systems in nearly 600 words. From John Ray comes a long table of animal taxonomy; John Arbuthnot is quoted at length on the causes of gout and John Quincy on the symptoms of lumbago; John Harris not only explains logarithms but offers a table of base-2 logs for numbers from 1 to 512.

And yet these encyclopedic entries have been met by silence from most Johnsonians. Commentators on the *Dictionary* have tended to agree with Boswell's assessment of Johnson's original definitions: "The definitions have always appeared to me such astonishing proofs of acuteness of intellect and precision of language, as indicate a genius of the highest rank" (*Life*, vol. 1, p. 293). But even those who praise his original definitions extravagantly shuffle uncomfortably when confronted with these borrowed definitions. The assumption seems to be that Johnson simply lifted them uncritically, with none of his characteristic "acuteness of intellect." A comparison of the source material and the published *Dictionary* entries, though, shows that his borrowings were rarely mechanical, and that he selected and reworked his material meticulously and with the needs of the common reader in mind.

Johnson selected his sources with care. There were many works from which he could have lifted simple definitions but, as a rule, he tried to use the source with the most complete, accurate, and current information. Chambers's *Cyclopædia* is among his most important sources, at least in the early part of the alphabet.[17] Johnson admired Chambers's work; he told Boswell that Chambers was one of the models for his own style, and he regretted that he was unable to work on the revision of the *Cyclopædia* in the 1770s.[18] And he drew much of his specialized knowledge from other influential reference books. Terms of art he found especially in John Harris's *Lexicon Technicum*; for botany, he turned to Philip Miller's *Gardeners Dictionary*; he found much of his medical information in John Quincy's *Lexicon Physico-Medicum*. Some antiquarian and zoological information came from the English translation of Augustin Calmet's Bible dictionary.[19] Not every encyclopedic work he used was properly an encyclopedia. John Hill's *General Natural History* and *Materia Medica* provided many of his entries on animals, plants, and minerals ("fossils"); their organization, though, was topical rather than alphabetical, and they are synoptic treatises rather than reference books. Likewise John Woodward's *Naturalis historia telluris*, which in its English translation provided much of Johnson's information on natural phenomena, ranging from geology (*earthquake, fossil*) and chemistry (*petrol, salt* n.s. 1) through medicine (*eructation, heart-burning* 1) and botany (*bohea, tobacco*). John Arbuthnot's *Essay concerning the Nature of Aliments* was a source of medical information not in Quincy. For astronomy and chronology he often used William Holder's *Discourse concerning Time* and John Harris's *Descriptions*.[20] Sometimes he would range even further afield, looking not in comprehensive "secondary" treatises but in original "primary" contributions to a science. His definition of *chymistry*, for instance, comes not from another reference book but from Herman Boerhaave's *New Method of Chemistry*, and the first illustrative quotation under *rainbow*, which supplements his brief definition, comes directly from Newton's *Opticks*.[21]

Even when he drew on what scientists would today call secondary sources, his handling of them was not strictly mechanical. It would have been easy to lift definitions of botanical terms directly from earlier general dictionaries, but he turned instead to Miller's *Gardeners Dictionary*, which required extensive cross-referencing. His definition of *daffodil* comes from Miller's entry from *narcissus*, and a reader who turns to Miller for *daffodil* will find only a cross-reference to *narcissus*. Likewise *daisy*, which Miller defines under *bellis* (with a cross-reference from *daisy*), and *elm*, which refers to *ulmus*. Miller does not always offer references from familiar to scientific names: although Johnson quotes Miller under *licorice*, the reader who looks under *L* in Miller will find nothing. The quoted entry appears instead under *glycyrrhiza*. Johnson has worked to make a specialist's book accessible to a general audience.

His adapted entries are almost always abridged. He defines *daffodil* with sixty-two words and acknowledges Miller as his source, but these sixty-two words are drawn from Miller's entry of nearly four thousand, which is typical of his practice. In such cases much information must be lost, for even the most skilled abridger cannot condense the sense of thousands of words into dozens. Where Miller's discussion of the narcissus lists thirty-six varieties and describes several methods for raising them, Johnson has room only for a description of the plant's physiology. When he adapts Hill's entry for *diamond*, he retains the discussion of the largest diamond ever discovered but omits the notes on their shapes, structure, and place in classical literature and mythology.[22] These abridgments deserve to be studied closely because they reveal the kind of information Johnson thought most important for a general audience. The entry on *arithmetick*, for instance, comes from Chambers; Johnson's definition of 91 words is selected from roughly 2,000 in Chambers. Most of this compression comes from omitting all the hyponyms (which had been so important to Bailey), the information on the various kinds of arithmetic – practical arithmetic, instrumental arithmetic, logarithmical arithmetic, and so on – which together account for about 1,500 words in Chambers. But Johnson still carries off a considerable feat of compression, turning the remaining 500 or so words into fewer than a hundred, which he manages partly through writing more tightly, and partly by eliminating the many qualifications and attributions of various opinions.

The entry for *kidney*, taken from Quincy's *Lexicon Physico-Medicum*, provides a good example of Johnson's method of abridgment. Quincy begins with the shape, size, and placement of the kidneys. Then comes a comment on their ontogeny – "In a *Fœtus* their external Substance is divided into several Lobes" – and a long section, roughly 200 words, on their structure ("There are in the Kidneys Lymphatick Vessels . . . Veins and Arteries . . . are divided into several Branches"). Then comes a discussion of their function: "The use of the Kidneys is to separate the Urine from the Blood" (Quincy, *Lexicon Physico-Medicum*, s.v. *kidneys*). Johnson reduces this long entry to just over 100 words: he preserves the information on their shape, size, placement, and function, but omits the discussion of their ontogeny and structure.

In abridging long encyclopedia entries Johnson follows no hard-and-fast rules, but it is possible to identify some general habits. He almost always omits citations of authorities and cross-references to hyperonyms and hyponyms. When encyclopedias provide long lists of names who have supported a position Johnson removes them, sometimes altogether, sometimes replacing them with a formula like "Some believe." Many technical terms are removed: when he copies Miller's entry for *bellis* in his own entry for *daisy*, "the Calyx (or Cup) of the Flower" becomes simply "the cup of the flower." As a rule, though, he preserves information about the physiology of plants and animals, the purposes of complicated artifacts, and the history of each field of inquiry, which seem to constitute for him the most important facts for a general audience.

Sometimes abridgment comes at the expense of precision. Qualifications are often lost: Miller's "Seed, for the most part of the same Shape" (s.v. *ulmus*) becomes in Johnson a "seed of the same shape" (s.v. *elm*). Miller chose his words with care; the seed is not always or exactly of the same shape, but only "for the most part." Johnson cannot afford such niceties. Miller's scientific nomenclature is also left by the wayside, as are some of his editorial comments on less adept botanists: "ULMUS; *folio latissimo scabro*. Ger. Emac. The Witch-Hazel *or* broad-leav'd Elm, by some unskilful Persons called the British elm" becomes "the witch hazel, or broad-leaved elm, by some called the British elm." And some revisions are harder to explain. Miller identifies eleven species of oak (s.v. *quercus*); Johnson copies the entry s.v. *oak*, but writes, "The species are five."[23]

Not all the adaptations of the earlier works, though, represent losses in precision or accuracy; sometimes Johnson actually improves his sources. He regularly improves their style. He does not, as a rule, preserve the punctuation and capitalization of any of his quotations; but these adapted entries are repunctuated extensively, often resulting in considerable improvements in clarity. He also often combines information from several reference works to provide a more comprehensive definition than can be found in any one of them. Under *chocolate*, for instance, he quotes 77 words from Miller's botanical description of the plant, and another 35 words from Chambers's *Cyclopædia* on the drink derived from it. *Coffee* gets the same treatment: 71 words from Miller on the plant followed by 142 from Chambers on the beverage.

On a few occasions, Johnson even makes small additions to his sources, suggesting a more thorough knowledge of his subject than his habit of borrowing would suggest. It shows he approached his sources critically, and was not content merely with transcribing and abridging. Chambers, for instance, calls *astronomy* "properly a mixed mathematical science, whereby we become acquainted with the celestial bodies, their magnitudes, motions, distances, periods, eclipses, *&c.*" Johnson trims some of Chambers's wordiness, but he also is unsatisfied with his "*&c.*" and therefore replaces it with a more specific term: "A mixed mathematical science teaching the knowledge of the celestial bodies, their magnitudes, motions, distances, periods, eclipses, and order." And he famously updates Quincy's information on electricity with an up-to-the-moment reference to the "philosophers . . . now endeavouring to intercept the strokes of lightning."

Although the *Plan* reveals that Johnson had encyclopedic information in mind from the beginning of his labors, the fourth edition of the *Dictionary* (1773) shows a rather different attitude toward these long encyclopedic entries: many are trimmed substantially. The complete entry for *ahouai* in the first edition, taken from Miller, runs to 169 words, describing the physiology, the various species and their ranges, and the properties of the fruit, including the nut containing "a most deadly poison; to expel which, the Indians know no antidote, nor will they use the wood for fuel." Compare the same entry in the fourth edition: "The name of a poisonous plant." The 169 words of *1755* are reduced to 6 in *1773*, and Johnson rejects all of Miller's information except that the plant is poisonous. Similar abridgments can be seen in many of the revised botanical entries: the 113-word definition of *alexanders* is reduced to "The name of a plant"; *archangel* is reduced from 114 words to 9; *arse-smart* from 57 to 2; *basil* from 157 to 5; *bear's-ear* from 142 to 2; *carrot* from 185 to 3; and so on. Not every encyclopedic entry is abridged, and the botanical entries seem to have been shortened more drastically than most of the others. The condensations, moreover, tend to be more extreme in the early letters of the alphabet. But it is difficult to find any encyclopedic definitions that grew between the first and fourth editions, and many dozens are reduced, often by as much as 60 percent.[24] The reasons for this abridgment is unclear. Perhaps it was merely a practical decision, enforced by the need to make room for the new and enlarged entries. Perhaps, on the other hand, it represents Johnson's reconsideration of the value of these entries, as he realized they were the dreams of an encyclopedist doomed at last to wake a dictionary-maker.

Even in the fourth edition, though, there is far more information than strict criterial definitions would require; the *Dictionary* of 1773 is largely still an encyclopedia, as it was from the initial conception in the *Plan*. The lessons of this examination of the encyclopedic entries are several. First, Johnson's conscious use of elements from both forms of reference book shows that, for all his awareness of generic conventions, he did not allow any a priori conception of what a dictionary should be to interfere with his mission of serving his readers. As he insisted in his *Life of Pope*, "To a thousand cavils one answer is sufficient; the purpose of a writer is to be read."[25] He noted in his *Plan* that "without some attention to such demands the dictionary cannot become generally valuable" (1825 *Works*, vol. v, p. 14), and would not therefore be read.

These entries also show his talent as an editor and abridger. The Johnson of myth is famous for never blotting a line, but the Johnson of fact held revision in high esteem. He insisted that he might improve any *Rambler* essay; Boswell, dubious, assumed they could be improved only through additions. "Nay, Sir," said Johnson; "there are three ways of making them better; – putting out, – adding, – or correcting" (*Life*, vol. iv, p. 309). "Putting out" was particularly valuable. He remembered Waller's remark that "poets lose half their praise, because the reader knows not what they have blotted" (*Lives*, vol. iii, p. 136). The encyclopedic entries in the *Dictionary* let us see exactly what Johnson has blotted.

Perhaps most important, these encyclopedic entries reveal the encyclopedic scope of Johnson's mind – the extent of his learning, curiosity, and industry. It is true that few of the encyclopedic entries are original with Johnson. He did, however, consistently strive to work with the best sources, and he synthesized, juxtaposed, and reworked material from multiple works to provide information that could not be found in any one of them. The very range of sources he adapted demonstrates his familiarity with works in medicine, gardening, botany, zoology, chemistry, electricity, mathematics, heraldry, law, divinity, commerce, cookery – a catalogue of fields of knowledge that never appeared on his title page, but which is evident on every succeeding page of the *Dictionary*. He speculated in the *Plan* that "I may at last have reason to say, after one of the augmenters of Furetier, that my book is more learned than its author" (1825 *Works*, vol. v, p. 14). In producing a book more learned than himself, he paradoxically demonstrated just how learned he was.

NOTES

1. Robert DeMaria, Jr., *Johnson's "Dictionary" and the Language of Learning* (Chapel Hill: University of North Carolina Press, 1986), p. x.
2. Ladislav Zgusta, *Manual of Lexicography* (Prague: Academia; The Hague: Mouton, 1971), p. 198.
3. Eighteenth-century practice in this respect was variable: Bayle includes both personal and place names, whereas the first edition of the *Encyclopædia Britannica* (Edinburgh, 1771) has only place names. Edward Phillips includes both personal and place names in what is ostensibly a dictionary, *The New World of English Words; or, A General Dictionary* (London, 1658).
4. On the mapping of the lexical–encyclopedic distinction onto the essence–accident distinction, see Dick Geeraerts, "Cognitive Grammar and the History of Lexical Semantics," in *Topics in Cognitive Linguistics*, ed. Brygida Rudzka-Ostyn (Amsterdam: John Benjamins, 1988), pp. 647–77. Geeraerts's insights into the matter are especially valuable, as he is both a theoretical linguist and a working lexicographer, an editor of both the *Woordenboek der Nederlandsche taal* and the *Van Dale groot woordenboek der Nederlandse taal*.
5. *The American Heritage Dictionary of the English Language*, 4th ed. (Boston: Houghton Mifflin, 2000), s.v. *drake* 1.
6. Umberto Eco, *Semantics and the Philosophy of Language* (Bloomington: Indiana University Press), pp. 57, 68.
7. Werner Hüllen discusses the older topical works in "A Great Chain of Words: The Onomasiological Tradition in English Lexicography," in *Anglistentag 1993 Eichstätt*, ed. Günther Blaicher and Brigitte Glaser (Tübingen: Niemeyer 1994), pp. 32–46, and *English Dictionaries, 800–1700: The Topical Tradition* (Oxford: Oxford University Press, 1999). He notes their disappearance in favor of the more familiar semasiological works. Some dictionaries and encyclopedias still attempted to map the fields of knowledge hierarchically; John Wilkins employs such a scheme in his *Alphabetical Dictionary, Wherein All English Words according to Their Various Significations Are Either Referred to Their Places in the Philosophical Tables, or Explained by Such Words as Are in Those Tables* (London, 1668), and Robert Darnton discusses the "mappemonde" of Diderot and d'Alembert in "Philosophers Trim the Tree of Knowledge: The Epistemological Strategy of the *Encyclopédie*," in *The Great Cat Massacre and Other Episodes in French Cultural History* (New York: Basic Books, 1984), pp. 191–213. These schemes, however, were not functional parts of the macrostructure, which remained firmly alphabetical. And even Wilkins recognized that "The chief Difficulty and Labour will be to contrive the Enumeration of things and notions, as that they may be full and *adequate*, without any *Redundancy* or *Deficiency* as to the Number of them, and *regular* as to their Place and Order" (*An Essay towards a Real Character, and a Philosophical Language* [London, 1668], p. 20).

8. For an overview of quarrels over the boundary between dictionaries and ency-clopedias see Bert Peeters, "Setting the Scene: Some Recent Milestones in the Lexicon–Encyclopedia Debate," in *The Lexicon–Encyclopedia Interface*, ed. Peeters (Amsterdam: Elsevier, 2000), pp. 1–52.

9. John Haiman, "Dictionaries and Encyclopedias," *Lingua* 50 (1980), 329–57.

10. See *The Oxford Companion to the English Language*, ed. Tom McArthur (Oxford: Oxford University Press, 1992), s.v. *encyclopaedia*.

11. A *lexicon* is likewise "A dictionary; a book teaching the signification of words," and a *lexicographer* not only the famous "harmless drudge," but also one "that busies himself in tracing the original, and detailing the signification of words." His definitions of *cyclopædia* and *encyclopedia* are less useful because they give no hint the words refer to books: the former is "A circle of knowledge; a course of the sciences," and the latter "The circle of sciences; the round of learning."

12. Thomas Blount, *Glossographia; or, A Dictionary Interpreting All Such Hard Words of Whatsoever Language, Now Used in Our Refined English Tongue*, 2nd ed. (London, 1661); John Kersey, *Dictionarium Anglo-Britannicum; or, A General English Dictionary* (London, 1708); Thomas Dyche, *A New General English Dictionary; Peculiarly Calculated for the Use and Improvement of Such as Are Unacquainted with the Learned Languages* (London, 1740); Edward Phillips, *New World of English Words* (London, 1658); Nathan Bailey, *Dictionarium Britannicum*, 2nd ed. (London, 1736). In preparing his *Dictionary* Johnson used the second edition of Bailey's *Dictionarium Britannicum*: see W. K. Wimsatt, *Philosophic Words: A Study of Style and Meaning in the "Rambler" and "Dictionary" of Samuel Johnson* (New Haven: Yale University Press, 1948), p. 21 and n. 4.

13. Bailey clearly exceeds Johnson's encyclopedism in one respect: he includes a number of graphic elements, including unusual typography (s.v. *alembick*), illustrations (s.v. *crown, diapre*, etc.), and line graphs (s.v. *logarithmetick curve*). Johnson rarely includes such graphical or typographical elements, though there are at least two exceptions: under *brevier* and *pica* he relates the size of the type to that used in his *Dictionary* itself, in the first case providing a sample of brevier type and in the second indicating that "This dictionary is in small pica."

14. All quotations from Johnson's *Dictionary* come from *1755*, except where noted below.

15. Johnson's inclination is to define artifacts according to their purpose; their organization or structure is the category on which he relies least often. Even when an object seems to have an obvious structural definition, he prefers to explain the reason for that structure, defining *shelf*, for instance, as "A board fixed against a supporter, so that any thing may be placed upon it," and *table* as "A horizontal surface raised above the ground, used for meals and other pur-poses." Many terms which describe a structure itself – *quincunx*, for example – are defined in the quotations from other writers, suggesting Johnson found such definitions the most difficult to compose.

16. In such entries it can be difficult to draw the line between definitions and quotations. Sometimes Johnson provides a very short definition – "A flower,"

for instance – and allows a long quotation to provide further details. In other cases he provides no original definition at all, just an attributed quotation that does the work of a definition.

17. Ephraim Chambers, *Cyclopædia; or, An Universal Dictionary of Arts and Sciences*, 4th ed. (London, 1741), p. ix. This seems to be the edition Johnson used: the sale catalogue of his library dates his copy to 1741, though it could be the fifth edition, which appeared from 1741 to 1743. Chambers is cited by name 171 times in the first edition, but the distribution is far from even. He appears 70 times under *A*, 18 times under *B*, and 76 times under *C*, but just 4 times under *D* (*damaskening, declinatory, deferents,* and *deficient numbers*), once under *M* (*mummy*), once under *Q* (*quicksilver*), and once under *S* (*steel* n.s.). Not every borrowing from Chambers, however, acknowledges him by name; *abacus* n.s. 2, for instance, is taken from the *Cyclopædia* (perhaps at second hand) but attributed only to "Dict."

18. For Johnson modeling his style on Chambers, see Boswell, *Life*, vol. i, pp. 218–19, and *Johnsonian Miscellanies*, ed. G. B. Hill, 2 vols. (Oxford: Clarendon Press, 1897), vol. ii, pp. 347–48. For his desire to revise the *Cyclopædia*, see *The Memoirs of the Life, and Writings of Percival Stockdale*, 2 vols. (London, 1809), vol. ii, p. 179, and *Letters*, vol. ii, p. 4. Johnson revised the first sheet printed: see John Nichols, *Illustrations of the Literary History of the Eighteenth Century*, 8 vols. (London, 1817–58), vol. iv, pp. 800–19. Paul Tankard summarizes the evidence in "'That Great Literary Projector': Samuel Johnson's *Designs*, or Projected Works," *The Age of Johnson: A Scholarly Annual* 12 (2001), 103–80, on pp. 154–55.

19. Wimsatt discusses some of Johnson's sources; see *Philosophic Words*, esp. pp. 28–31 and Appendix B. It is difficult, perhaps impossible, to determine which editions of these works Johnson used. The editions listed here are the ones I consulted, and may not have been those he worked with: John Harris, *Lexicon Technicum: or, An Universal English Dictionary of Arts and Sciences* (London, 1704); Philip Miller, *The Gardeners Dictionary: Containing the Methods of Cultivating and Improving the Kitchen, Fruit and Flower Garden*, 2nd ed. (London, 1733); John Quincy, *Lexicon Physico-Medicum; or, A New Physical Dictionary, Explaining the Difficult Terms Used in the Several Branches of the Profession*, 3rd ed. (London, 1726); Augustin Calmet, *An Historical, Critical, Geographical, Chronological, and Etymological Dictionary of the Holy Bible*, trans. Samuel D'Oyly and John Colson, 3 vols. (London, 1732).

20. John Hill, *A General Natural History*, 3 vols. (London, 1748); *A History of the Materia Medica, Containing Descriptions of All the Substances Used in Medicine* (London, 1751); John Woodward, *The Natural History of the Earth, Illustrated, and Inlarged*, trans. Benjamin Holloway (London, 1726); John Arbuthnot, *An Essay concerning the Nature of Aliments, and the Choice of Them, according to the Different Constitutions of Human Bodies*, 3rd ed. (London, 1735); William Holder, *A Discourse Concerning Time, with Application of the Natural Day, and Lunar Month, and Solar Year, as Natural; and of Such as Are Derived from Them* (London, 1694); John Harris, *The Description and Use of the Globes and the*

Orrery, 5th ed. (London, 1740); John Harris, *The Description and Uses of the Celestial and Terrestrial Globes*, 5th ed. (London, 1720).

21. Herman Boerhaave, *A New Method of Chemistry; Including the Theory and Practice of That Art* (London, 1727); Sir Isaac Newton, *Opticks; or, A Treatise of the Reflexions, Refractions, Inflexions and Colours of Light* (London, 1704).

22. See Hill, *General Natural History*, vol. I, pp. 585–86.

23. Perhaps Johnson was concerned strictly with domestic oaks, since Miller notes that species six through eleven "have been brought from *Amazon*."

24. A sample of encyclopedic entries abridged between the first edition and the fourth includes *aqua fortis*, which is shortened from 172 words to 79; *airpump*, from 227 to 194; *algebra*, from 242 to 179; *architecture* 1, from 268 to 33; *arithmetick*, from 91 to 8; *astronomy*, from 121 to 71; *differential method*, from 73 to 57; *elk*, from 153 to 71; *evolution* 4, from 58 to 30; *fibre* 2, from 186 to 120; *geneva*, from 103 to 56; *geometry*, from 186 to 72; *ginseng*, from 150 to 72; *grenade*, from 100 to 62; *milky-way*, from 185 to 100; *mummy* 1, from 391 to 249; *plaid*, from 53 to 26; and *seacow*, from 192 to 106.

25. *Lives of the English Poets*, ed. G. B. Hill, 3 vols. (Oxford: Clarendon Press, 1905), vol. III, p. 240.

CHAPTER 9

The law, the alphabet, and Samuel Johnson

John Stone

The law is its language; the language itself carries the law . . . The
language of law is of itself the memory and the movement of the law.
— Peter Goodrich, *Languages of Law*

. . . for such a body of law, the alphabet is the only workable expedient.
— W. S. Holdsworth, *A History of English Law*

Dictionary entries come in two basic shapes. Most common are jagged
series of short blocks of text formed by headword and etymology, explanations of senses, and illustrative quotations; far rarer are justified paragraphs
of encyclopedic information, quoted (often in lieu of a definition) from
reference works on such subjects as pharmacology, botany, animal husbandry, and construction. The longest such extracts, running to over eight
hundred words, are often entries-within-entries, listing various sub-senses
(twenty-two in the case of *cabbage* n.s.) or glossing scientific controversies
(e.g. *mildew* n.s.).[1] They effectively remove Johnson from disputes as to
word meaning in specific domains, leaving the explanation of scientific
rather than popular senses to specialists. Others are clearly meant to teach
science: *animal* n.s. 1, *flower* n.s. 1, and *plant* n.s. 1 feature detailed taxonomy lessons (*animal* reproduces complex hierarchies in two tables), while
retrograde 3 advises readers that retrograde orbits are "only apparent and
occasioned by the observer's eye being placed on the earth." Johnson's desire
to impart accurate knowledge is such that he juxtaposes complementary
extracts from two works (see, for example, *stockgilly flower*), quotes warnings
against shoddy workmanship (e.g. *mortar* n.s. 2), and relays tips on how
to amputate a limb (*amputation*), as well as appending his own updating
commentary to a dated source (*electricity*).

Yet this concern manifests itself spottily, shaped by happenstance rather
than systematic design, guided by Johnson's interests (music is underrep-
resented and musical terms sometimes poorly defined) and resources (far
more plants than animals are accorded detailed treatment). Johnson's choice

147

of sources, and their coverage, were decisive in this respect. A handful of authorities – John Mortimer, Philip Miller, John Quincy, John Cowell, John Harris, and Ephraim Chambers – furnished most of the encyclopedic content, and their fortes are accordingly Johnson's. Lesser sources may make a strong showing in a short alphabetical range: the *Builder's Dictionary*, to give one example, is cited on twelve occasions, of which nine are between *as-* and *br-*. Slips may have been lost, the work itself laid aside or simply mislaid. Whatever the reason for such patterns, they lead to surprising anomalies: the 130-word entry for *beam* n.s. includes exact building-code specifications, while a column is merely "a round pillar" (s.v. *column* 1), and a pillar, "a column" (s.v. *pillar* 1). A further anomaly, given Johnson's concern with the advancement of knowledge, is the decision to leave the *Dictionary's* encyclopedic content largely undisturbed in later editions. John Ray and Miller, and not Linnæus, speak for botanists in the fourth edition, though their works were over half a century old.

The use of authorities that are themselves word-books, or well-indexed subject guides, saved Johnson from excessive "fortuitous and unguided excursions into books" (1825 *Works*, vol. v, p. 31). Even when field-specific texts by authors Johnson admired were available, he relied on sources facilitating quick word searches. The *Dictionary's* legal sources are a case in point. Johnson read and marked up the third volume of a four-volume edition of Francis Bacon's collected works in preparing the *Dictionary*,[2] later citing him well over two thousand times. As the quotations are not consistently attributed to particular titles, it is difficult to estimate the weight of legal passages, of which I have counted over fifty. A further thirty-three quotations in the first edition are labeled as having been drawn from Matthew Hale's *History and Analysis of the Common Law of England*;[3] seventy-three others, though unlabeled, are taken from the same source. Bacon and Hale are thus the fourth and third most frequently cited legal authors in the *Dictionary*, yet their contributions are dwarfed by John Cowell's early law dictionary, *The Interpreter*, and John Ayliffe's indexed guide to English canon law, the *Parergon Juris Canonici Anglicani*,[4] cited 284 and 474 times respectively.

By setting aside the term "dictionary," we may get a more accurate picture of Johnson's use of alphabetically arranged works. Seventeenth- and eighteenth-century law dictionaries, for instance, glossed procedure and substantive points while explaining terms, in interaction with the broader category of legal reference works. They drew references from abridgments of statutes and case law, for which in turn they furnished both definitions and illustrations, making the border between genres unclear.

Johnson's work on the *Harleian Catalogue* (which lists over one thousand English law books) illustrates this: he and his fellow bibliographer William Oldys were reluctant to classify Cowell's *Interpreter* as a dictionary, including "interpreter" as a genre in a broader heading.[5] Works catalogued as abridgments might nonetheless feature (and advertise, in their titles) thousands of definitions, as is the case of William Sheppard's *Epitome of All the Common & Statute Laws of this Nation . . . Wherein More than Fifteen Hundred of the Hardest Words or Terms of the Law are Explained.*[6]

Johnson's familiarity with the English legal literature and extensive use of *The Interpreter* in compiling the *Dictionary* suggest a wider context and more tangled genealogy than have hitherto featured in accounts of the *Dictionary*. Since the publication of Starnes and Noyes's landmark study in 1946, comprehensive monolingual English dictionaries have generally been portrayed as having grown out of the hard-word tradition. Technical dictionaries and glossaries, including those of the law, were ancillary, mentioned in passing as sources of material for more central works. Though John Considine and Jürgen Schäfer have done much to end this needless segregation,[7] the extent of the general monolingual dictionary's debt to its more specialized counterparts has yet to be gauged. Consider one instance of Starnes and Noyes's praise for Nathaniel Bailey's *Dictionarium Britannicum* (1730): "Here also for the first time a painstaking attempt is made to build up complete families of words arranged in an orderly fashion with all derived and related expressions. Thus, the explanation of the various forms and uses of the word *Action* extend to almost a page."[8] Fourteen of Bailey's thirty-two entries for *action* describe legal usages;[9] of these, eleven are defined in *The Interpreter* (indeed, four of Bailey's entries quote *The Interpreter*), and thirteen in Thomas Blount's law dictionary, the *Nomo-Lexicon* of 1670.[10] (The missing sense is present, and indexed, in Sheppard's *Epitome*.) Lexical sets of law terms, then, could be found in works compiled for a professional readership long before the *Dictionarium Britannicum*; an innovation which Starnes and Noyes attribute to Bailey is legal (though perhaps not exclusively legal) in origin.

Behind much work on the history of lexicography lies a checklist of features and procedures destined to become either prevalent (such as numbered senses) or highly prestigious (such as the *OED*'s historical method). As the most striking feature of a dictionary – its coverage, and exponential growth in the selection of headwords – may be charted from Cawdrey's *Table Alphabeticall* to, say, *Webster's Third*, scant attention has been paid to the features of works representing only a determined portion of the lexis.

Yet in assembling encyclopedic content, eighteenth-century lexicographers acquainted themselves with and may have learned from the example of technical dictionaries. For the originality of each compiler to be seen in its proper light, inventories of shared features – that is, studies of the *linguistics* of technical dictionaries – will be needed. Much of what has hitherto been considered sophisticated about Johnson's *Dictionary* will prove, I believe, to have analogues in earlier law dictionaries; and if legal lexicography, historically the preserve of legal historians and bibliographers, may be studied from a linguistic perspective, Johnson's own choice of legal sources for the *Dictionary* will be thrown into relief. In what follows I apply a Johnsonian checklist to a group of law dictionaries and related works from the seventeenth and eighteenth centuries. This discussion will in turn provide the context for closer scrutiny of the two legal reference works Johnson quotes most often, *The Interpreter* and John Ayliffe's *Parergon*.

Though the tradition of English legal glossaries stretches back to the twelfth century, the first English law dictionary (indeed, the first dictionary printed in England) did not appear until 1523. The *Expositiones terminorum legum Anglorum*, also known by the later title *Termes de la ley*, compiled by John Rastell in law French (to which a parallel English translation was soon added), at first comprised one hundred and sixty-nine entries, couched in what one scholar has called "plain terms."[11] Practical in design and dogmatic in tone, Rastell seldom refers to his sources, though later editors would alter the *Termes* in both respects as it swelled, by its twenty-sixth edition (1742), to over one thousand entries.

Rastell was without competition until the appearance, in 1607, of Cowell's *Interpreter*. More ambitious in scope and scholarly in method, Cowell cites abridgments, law reports, statutes, and treatises, as well as extra-legal sources, and had clearly amassed his materials before composing his entries. With *The Interpreter* citation becomes central to the development of the law dictionary. The citation-free common-law primers of the fifteenth and sixteenth centuries date, in this sense, from before the flood. Printing had made specific references possible and so helped foster "the addiction to citations which has beset the English lawyer ever since."[12] In this respect *The Interpreter* and its successors are methodologically related to the abridgments of law reports to which pleaders turned as case-law burgeoned: both seem to have been modeled on law students' commonplace books.[13] The student's method was described in the mid seventeenth century by Matthew Hale:

After two or three years so spent [reading introductory texts], let him get a large Common-place Book, divide it into Alphabetical-Titles, which he may easily gather up, by observing the Titles of Brook's Abridgment, and some Tables of Law-Books . . . Afterwards it might be fit to read the Yearbooks . . . and to come down in order and succession of time to the latter law . . . What he reads in the course of his Reading, let him enter the abstract or substance thereof, especially of Cases or Points resolved into his Common-place Book under severall titles, and it can be conveniently Broken, let him enter each part under its proper Title.[14]

Three aspects of Johnson's original procedure are present here: a pre-existing word list; a reading program, chronologically bracketed; and the atomizing "breaking up" of digested text into discrete points. If Hale's more general "Alphabetical-Titles" are respected, the result will combine alphabetical with thematic arrangement, definitions of lesser terms being nested in overarching entries (e.g., Sheppard's four-page chapter "Of an Advowson," *Epitome*, pp. 84–87, which nests thirty-nine definitions). Alternatively, if entries for the index terms are arranged alphabetically and commentary on substantive points limited, the result is a law dictionary. The former scheme is superficially clumsy for a word-book. Yet by providing an index with page number references, and marking each term with the catch-word "what," Sheppard guides readers to the definitions they need. Many subsequent abridgments were likewise indexed, in what the legal historian W. S. Holdsworth dubbed "the double application of the alphabetical principle."[15]

Lexicographers and abridgment writers alike refer to process and product in analogous terms: Sheppard, for example, speaks of his "industrious search of thirty six years" (*Epitome*, sig. a1ʳ); Cowell, employing a medieval image, likens the legal lexicographer to "a laborious Bee" which "hath gathered from all the former, the best iuyce of their flowers, and made up a hive of delectable honey" (*The Interpreter*, sig. *3ʳ); and Blount, whose law dictionary was the fruit of thirty years' work, imagined "the student would make a further use of it, as a *Repertory* or *Common-Place*" (*Nomo-Lexicon*, sig. a2ᵛ). Hybrid works combining the features of both dictionaries and abridgments, such as Giles Jacob's *New Law-Dictionary* (1729), portrayed both kinds of collection – philological and jurisprudential – as a single process: "This large Work now publish'd, contains the *Derivations* and *Definitions* of *Words* and *Terms* used in the LAW, and likewise the *whole Law*, with the *Practice* thereof, abstracted from all other Books in an easy concise Method."[16] It might be objected that these works explain things rather than words; they construe referents, rather than defining semantic concepts. While this may hold for less inherently hermeneutical fields, the very notion of legal usage – which the law lexicographers consistently contrast with "our Language generally" (*The Interpreter*, sig. 3Q4ᵛ) – precludes it. Put bluntly, jurists refined their concepts before putting "things" to the test. The distinction between, say, principal and accessory might be germane to a ruling; the definition of such legal categories and their application to the social world were intertwined. Thus Edward Leigh, in his *Philologicall Commentary*, supplements his definitions of *accessory* with a series of illustrative examples culled from case law.[17] In the last of these, a maid had planned, with a man, to rob her mistress; she opened the door to her mistress's bedroom and held a candle, while the man murdered the woman. Was she an accessory to the crime, or a principal?[18] The question is both semantic and juridical, for the law as it stood was partly a question of usage.

A further distinction from works more properly encyclopedic lies in the amount of "low linguistics" contained in the law dictionaries. By the 1670s, their features could be remarkably similar to Johnson's, as this entry from Blount illustrates:

𝕮𝖔𝖛𝖊𝖓𝖆𝖇𝖑𝖊 (Fr. *Convenable*) Fit, convenient, or suitable. – 𝕿𝖍𝖆𝖙 𝖊𝖛𝖊𝖗𝖞 𝖔𝖋 𝖙𝖍𝖊 𝖘𝖆𝖒𝖊 𝖙𝖍𝖗𝖊𝖊 𝖘𝖔𝖗𝖙𝖘 𝖔𝖋 𝖋𝖎𝖘𝖍, 𝖇𝖊 𝖌𝖔𝖔𝖉 𝖆𝖓𝖉 𝖈𝖔𝖓𝖛𝖊𝖓𝖆𝖇𝖑𝖊, 𝖆𝖘 𝖎𝖓 𝖔𝖑𝖉 𝖙𝖎𝖒𝖊 𝖍𝖆𝖙𝖍 𝖇𝖊𝖊𝖓 𝖚𝖘𝖊𝖉. 31 Edw. 3. Stat. 3 cap. 2. Plowden, fol. 472.a. (*Nomo-Lexicon*, sig. Vɪʳ)

Here are etymology, gloss, and a quotation which could not be construed as encyclopedic content. Missing is reference to the part of speech. Though such references are rare, law dictionaries abound in entries for verbs, along with many adjectives and the occasional adverbial. Usage notes are provided to help the reader discriminate synonyms and analogous words: Cowell, Blount, and Manley contrast *convicted* and *attainted*,[19] quoting statute to prove that a distinction exists, just as Johnson would work out careful distinctions in such entries as *ancient* adj. 1, where the headword and *old* are discussed. Compounds receive more extensive treatment than they do in the *Dictionary*: Cowell glosses *woolwinders* as "such as winde vp euery fleece of wooll" (*The Interpreter*, sig. 4C2ʳ) because he has found the term in three statutes; Johnson excludes it, no doubt on the grounds that "the primitives contain the meaning" (1825 *Works*, vol. v, p. 32). Phrases and idioms are typically subordinated to the weightiest word they contain, rather than being listed under their first word; and, as in Johnson (see, for example, the idiom *upon that matter*, s.v. *matter* n.s. 14), they typically round off entries. Cowell accordingly reserves *by the verge* for the conclusion of his entry for *verge*, which Johnson reproduces (s.v. *verge* 3). The arrangement of senses shows a consistent pattern, albeit a less systematic one than Johnson's.

Whenever possible, a central or prototypical sense is glossed first, as when Cowell writes, "stuard, alias steward . . . is a word of many applications: yet alway signifieth an officer of cheife accoumpte within the place of his sway" (*The Interpreter*, sig. 3Q3ᵛ). This central sense need not be peculiar to the law: Cowell's entry for *stranger* moves on from "it signifieth in our language Generally" to "in the law, it hath an especiall signification" (sig. 3Q4ᵛ). In the absence of a single central sense, Cowell constructs a branching hierarchy: *assise*, for example, features four ordinally numbered general senses (over 140 years before Benjamin Martin made separate, numbered definitions a standard feature in the *Lingua Britannica Reformata*), the first of which is "a writ directed to the Shyreeue . . . of foure sorts" (sig. E3ᵛ–E4ʳ). Wedged in between the first and second senses and clearly appendant on the former are paragraphs on the four writs. Cowell nonetheless proceeds directly to peculiarly legal usage in entries that are "falsely" headed by a headword that is never explained in isolation. Thus:

Goe, is vsed sometime in a speciall signification in our common lawe: as to go to God, is to be dismissed the court . . . Goe forward, seemeth also to be a signe giuen by a Iudge to the Sergeant or Counceler, pleading the cause of his client, that his cause is not good. For when he standeth vpon a point of lawe, and heareth those words of the Iudges mouth, he taketh vnderstanding, that he looseth the action. (sig. 2K3ᵛ)

Cowell's interest lies with the meanings of the idiom *go to God* and the phrasal verb *go forward* that arise from the contextual and interpersonal situation of speaker and listener. Though it is doubtful whether Cowell could have articulated his insight theoretically, he had clearly arrived at an understanding of *to go forward* that foreshadows pragmatics. Johnson, in the *Dictionary* Preface, reflects on similar phenomena: expletives, he writes, "are easily perceived in living tongues to have power and emphasis, though it be sometimes such as no other form of expression can convey" (1825 *Works*, vol. v, p. 35).

The use of authorities affords a further parallel with Johnson's practice. It is for his choice and use of quotations, along with his definitions, that Johnson has most often been lauded: for collected examples allowed him to study what Allen Reddick has termed the "contextual life of words."[20] In law dictionaries and some abridgments, authorities already served many of the functions ascribed to *Dictionary* quotations – justifying the inclusion of a word, supporting a definition or illustrating word meaning, tracing semantic change, and conveying knowledge. They precede and inform definitions, as when Cowell, in introducing a generic definition of *assise*, states that "my collections have served me thus" (*The Interpreter*, sig. E3ᵛ). They often justify the inclusion of a headword, as in Cowell's entries for *salarie* (sig. 3N1ᵛ), *roode of land* (sig. 3M3ʳ), and *stalkers* ("a kind of net," sig. 3Q1ʳ), which do not feature any commentary on points of law. Where a single authority is proffered, Cowell's explanation glosses the passage in question, making such entries akin to Johnson's treatment of words peculiar to one author (e.g., *conspicuity, enwheel, exsuffolate, fedary*, all from Shakespeare). Quotations from authorities are also offered as evidence of the accuracy of definitions, as when Cowell writes, "And so is this word Triall understood in the statute, *anno* 33 *H*. 8, *cap*. 23, where it saith thus" (*The Interpreter*, sig. 3V4ᵛ); as supplements to a definition, as in Cowell's entry for *woodward* (sig. 4C1ᵛ), later reproduced by Blount (*Nomo-Lexicon*, sig. 3Z1ʳ), and Manley (*Nomothetes*, sig. 4A2ʳ), where the woodman's oath makes clear the function of this "officer of the forest"; or, in a fashion reminiscent of Johnson's use of technical dictionaries, because they are themselves definitions (see the sub-entry *statute merchant*, under *statute*, in *The Interpreter*, sig. 3Q2ʳ; and *conspirators* in the *Nomo-Lexicon*, sig. S2ᵛ). Cowell's entry for *murder* mentions a condition without which, according to customary law, a killing would not be murder, but adds "this point is altered by the statute, *anno* 14 *Ed*. 3 *cap*. 4 and murder is now otherwise defined" (*The Interpreter*, sig. 2Y1ᵛ). In such cases, statutory definitions supplant customary usage as an authority, obviating the need to collect examples and proceed inductively.

Of course, in abstracting from collected data there is necessarily an element of interpretation. Having reviewed some of the thornier problems of distinguishing senses, Johnson concludes that "The solution of all difficulties, and the supply of all defects, must be sought in the examples, subjoined to the various senses of each word, and ranged according to the time of their authours" (1825 *Works*, vol. v, p. 38). The onus is implicitly on the reader to do the seeking, to solve the difficulties and supply the defects, to compare, interpret, and continue the very task the lexicographer has simultaneously undertaken and facilitated. According to Nancy Wright, *The Interpreter* features a strikingly similar deferral to readers, for whom the lexicographer has "provided the basis . . . to make interpretative acts."[21] Wright might be discussing Johnson rather than Cowell when she portrays him as the compiler of "a diachronic catalogue of past and co-existing usages" ("John Cowell and *The Interpreter*," p. 15); and Blount's observation that Cowell is sometimes "too prolix . . . setting down several Authors Opinions, without categorically determining which is the true" (*Nomo-Lexicon*, sig. aʳ) seems to be echoed by the lexicographer Charles Richardson, for whom Johnson's *Dictionary* was not much more than "a collection . . . of usages" (quoted in Reddick, *The Making of Johnson's Dictionary*, p. 48).

Paradoxically, Johnson's awareness of jurists' interest in precision is itself written into the *Dictionary*: Francis Bacon reminds the reader repeatedly that "the unjust judge is the capital remover of landmarks, when he defineth amiss" (s.v. *define* v.n., *mere* n.s. 2, *mislayer, remover*). The basic shapes of the definition in monolingual English dictionaries until Johnson had been a list of synonyms, and bare reference to a genus or superordinate (e.g. "a kind of tree").[22] Cowell, Blount, and Manley sometimes define verbs by reference to equivalent verbs in non-specialist registers: for example, *abet* is defined in Cowell (*The Interpreter*, sig. A2^r) and Manley (*Nomothetes*, sig. B1^v) as "to encourage or set on," which Blount expands to "encourage, incite or set on" (*Nomo-Lexicon*, sig. B2^r). The dominant pattern, though, is that of definition by genus and both descriptive and functional differentiae, Johnson's model for such words as *desk* ("an inclining table for the use of writers or readers, made commonly with a box or repository under it"). To cite but a few: *addition*, in Cowell, is "a title given to a man ouer and aboue his Christian and surname, shewing his estate, degree, occupation, trade, age, place of dwelling, &c" (*The Interpreter*, sig. B2^v); *moot*, in Blount, is "that exercise, or arguing of Cases, which young *Barrasters* and Students perform, at certain times, for the better enabling them for practice, and defence of Clients Causes" (*Nomo-Lexicon*, sig. 2Y1^r); while Sheppard defines *common* (in the first of two senses) as "that Soil, Water, or other thing, the use whereof is common to this or that Town, Lordship, or Person" (*Epitome*, p. 263). In a passage Johnson in all likelihood read (he used the following sentence as an illustrative quotation, s.v. *provocation*), John Ayliffe remarked on one of his own definitions in terms suggesting the care taken in formulating them: "In this Definition the Term *Provocation* is made use of as a Genus, because the Word *Provocation* is a more comprehensive Term than the word *Appeal*" (*Parergon*, p. 72). It is worth noting that while such logical definitions were not unique to the law, they grew common in the hard-word dictionary tradition in the work of a barrister and law-lexicographer-to-be, Thomas Blount, who regularly plagiarizes Cowell in the *Glossographia* (see *deforsour, denizen, parliament, pickage, subsidy, wage*).

There is something of a paradox in Johnson's use of Cowell. Both as a law-book and a word-book, *The Interpreter* was dated. Semantic evolution had made some of Cowell's entries antiquated; and where Johnson knowingly reproduces such material, he is obliged to supplement it with a contemporary source (e.g., *attorney*, which pairs Cowell with Chambers). Yet among writers of reference books, Cowell's contribution to the *Dictionary* is quantitatively perhaps second only to the botanist Phillip Miller's: in the letter A alone, *The Interpreter* furnishes some 3,500 words of text, listed almost exclusively as definitions. If Johnson was taking his botany from the 1720s, his medicine from the 1710s, and his pharmacology from the 1750s, what drove him to rely on a legal source first published in 1607?

Three explanations suggest themselves. Johnson may have been satisfied with a source that had come into his hands early, whether from his father's stock or during his work writing parliamentary debates. Michael Johnson is known to have sold his son's foremost source for canon-law terms, Ayliffe's *Parergon*, to Johnson's friend Gilbert Walmesley soon after its appearance.[23] As the *Parergon* is also listed in the sale catalogue of Johnson's library, he may have remained familiar with it for nearly sixty years. Considered inferior to both the earlier *Repertorium Canonicum* by John Godolphin and the nearly contemporary *Ordo Judiciorum* by Thomas Oughton, the *Parergon* has been criticized for both its "rather ornate style of English" and "failure to analyze or draw conclusions from the heaps of materials which are piled into each heading."[24] Johnson seems not to have detected the deficiencies of the work: knowing it to be well indexed, and knowing himself to be reasonably familiar with its structure, he used Ayliffe as best he could. Of course much of this is speculative, as is the assumption that Johnson was familiar with *The Interpreter* before setting about compiling his *Dictionary* authorities.

On the other hand, Johnson's preference for *The Interpreter* may have been more political than philological. Some of Cowell's definitions and commentary had proved polemical. In 1610, the dictionary itself was suppressed (how many copies were burned is unclear) and Cowell resigned his regius professorship of civil law at Cambridge. Among Cowell's prominent critics was Sir Edward Coke, a key figure in English constitutional history whom Johnson considered "a mere lawyer" (*Life*, vol. II, p. 158). Coke is conspicuous by his near-absence as an authority in the *Dictionary*, despite the centrality of his *Institutes* and *Reports* to common-law education and the authority accorded them by eighteenth-century courts. Reliance on one of Coke's rivals may be a veiled snub. Most convincing, perhaps, is a properly philological explanation: of the lexicographers of the law, it is Cowell who is most keenly interested in the law as language. Rastell and his editors were sometimes content to begin an entry with a statement of the "Assets be of two sorts" type, subordinating consideration of terms to the explanation of the law, while Blount, in plagiarizing Cowell (and Blount is largely derivative of Cowell), more often than not omits his predecessor's purely linguistic

commentary (cf. *Nomo-Lexicon*, s.v. *assets, faint pleader, withernam*), providing parenthetical etymologies after the headword in contrast to Cowell's
scholia.[25] Moreover, Cowell's lack of a common-law training obliged him
to study his examples *as examples.* As a professor of civil law, he was a
visitor from an allied field, broadly familiar with the conceptual apparatus
of the common lawyers but without the practitioners' ready grasp of their
terms. Thus his attempts to ascertain the root meaning of words of ramified
signification by reference to a historical record of usage (albeit a selective
one): Cowell, like Johnson, was a student of word meaning in context who
presented words as the end-products of linguistic and intellectual evolution.

   This is not to say that Cowell was a legal Johnson *avant la lettre.* The
features I have portrayed as innovative in the law dictionaries are met with
frequently, though not systematically; more often than not, they are motivated by a desire to systematize legal knowledge and to help practitioners
determine where the law stood on a particular point – and legal knowledge
could not be separated from legal history, and with it the history of the law's
words. Coupled with the dual character of the language of the law – both
hermeneutical and performative – this produced a special sensitivity to a
range of linguistic phenomena noted by the lexicographer in his study of
his collections. As a lexicographical technique, the inductive study of words
was an occasional by-product of the inductive study of the law: collections
of legal commonplaces were effectively (though haphazardly) approached
as corpora. Cowell's example, then, may have been instrumental in leading Johnson to proceed in a similarly inductive manner, for "the rules of
stile, like those of law, arise from precedents often repeated" (1825 *Works*,
vol. v, p. 16).

NOTES

I would like to thank Professor Sir J. H. Baker of St. Catharine's College,
Cambridge, for his assistance in this essay.
1. Except where noted, all *Dictionary* entries come from *1755*.
2. Francis Bacon, *Works*, 4 vols. (London, 1740). The third volume of the copy
   Johnson used to prepare the *Dictionary* survives at Yale, shelfmark Yale–Im.
   J637.+755a.
3. Referred to in the *Dictionary* as "Hale's *Common Law of England*," "Hale's
   Common Law," "Hale's *Laws of England*," and "Hale's *Hist. of the Common Law
   of England*."
4. John Cowell, *The Interpreter; or, Booke Containing the Signification of Words*
   (Cambridge, 1607); John Ayliffe, *Parergon Juris Canonici Anglicani; or, A Com-
   mentary, by Way of Supplement to the Canons and Constitutions of the Church of
   England* (London, 1726).

5. Samuel Johnson and William Oldys, *Catalogus bibliothecæ Harleianæ, in locos distributus cum indice auctorum*, 5 vols. (London, 1743–45), vol. II, p. 673.

6. William Sheppard, *An Epitome of All the Common & Statute Laws of This Nation, Now in Force, Wherein More than Fifteen Hundred of the Hardest Words or Terms of the Law are Explained; and All the Most Useful and Profitable Heads or Titles of the Law by Way of Common Place, Largely, Plainly, and Methodically Handled* (London, 1656). See *Harleian Catalogue*, vol. II, p. 657.

7. John Considine, "Narrative and Persuasion in Early Modern English Dictionaries and Phrasebooks," *The Review of English Studies* n.s. 52, no. 206 (May 2001), 195–206; Jürgen Schäfer, *Early Modern English Lexicography* (Oxford: Clarendon Press, 1989). See, for example, Considine's description of *The Interpreter* as "the most substantial monoglot English dictionary of its day" ("Narrative and Persuasion," p. 204).

8. Dewitt Starnes and Gertrude Noyes, *The English Dictionary from Cawdrey to Johnson, 1604–1755*, new ed. (Amsterdam: John Benjamins, 1991), pp. 119–20.

9. Nathaniel Bailey, *Dictionarium Britannicum; or, A More Compleat Universal Etymological English Dictionary than Any Extant*, 2nd ed. (London, 1736).

10. Thomas Blount, Νομο-Λεξικον [*Nomo-Lexicon*]: *A Law Dictionary, Interpreting Such Difficult and Obscure Words and Terms as Are Found either in Our Common or Statute, Ancient or Modern Lawes: With References to the Several Statutes, Records, Registers, Law-Books, Charters, Ancient Deeds, and Manuscripts, Wherein the Words are Used: And Etymologies, Where They Properly Occur* (London, 1670).

11. John D. Cowley, *A Bibliography of Abridgments, Digests, Dictionaries and Indexes of English Law to the Year 1800* (London: Selden Society, 1932), p. lxxxi.

12. J. H. Baker, "The Books of the Common Law," in *The Cambridge History of the Book in Britain*, vol. III, ed. Lotte Hellinga and J. B. Trapp (Cambridge: Cambridge University Press, 1999), pp. 411–32, on p. 431.

13. See *ibid.*, p. 417; and Cowley, *A Bibliography of Abridgments*, p. lxxvi.

14. Matthew Hale, "The Publisher's Preface Directed to the Young Students of the Common-Law," in Henry Rolle, *Un Abridgment de Plusieurs Cases et Resolutions del Common Ley: Alphabeticalment Digest Desouth Severall Titles*, 2 vols. (London, 1668), vol. I, sig. a1ʳ–c1ʸ, on sig. b2ᵛ.

15. W. S. Holdsworth, *A History of English Law*, 3rd ed., 12 vols. (London: Methuen, 1951), vol. XII, p. 174.

16. Giles Jacob, *A New Law-Dictionary: Containing, the Interpretation and Definition of Words and Terms Used in the Law* (London, 1729), sig. A3ʳ⁻ᵛ.

17. Edward Leigh, *A Philologicall Commentary; or, An Illustration of the Most Obvious and Usefull Words in the Law: With Their Distinctions and Diverse Acceptations, as They are Found as Well in Reports Ancient and Modern, as in Records, and Memorials Never Printed* (London, 1652), s.v. *accessorie*. Leigh's definitions are numbered using arabic numerals and French-indented, an early example of the use of such a format to aid vertical scanning.

18. The court ruled that she was an accessory (*ibid.*, pp. 3–4).

19. Cowell, *The Interpreter*, sig. G1ʳ; Blount, *Nomo-Lexicon*, sig. H1ʳ; Thomas Manley, Νομοθετης [*Nomothetes*]: *The Interpreter, Containing the Genuine Signification of Such Obscure Words and Terms Used Either in the Common or Statute Lawes of This Realm* (London, 1672), sig. G2ᵛ. The title page of this fifth edition of *The Interpreter* states it to be "by Tho. Manley," though "first compiled by the learned Dr. Cowell."

20. Allen Reddick, *The Making of Johnson's Dictionary, 1746–1773*, rev. ed. (Cambridge: Cambridge University Press, 1996), p. 54. For a useful review of Johnson's quotations see Rüdiger Schreyer, "Illustrations of Authority: Quotations in Samuel Johnson's *Dictionary of the English Language* (1755)," *Lexicographica* 16 (2000), 58–103, on pp. 60–61.

21. Nancy Wright, "John Cowell and *The Interpreter*: Law, Authority, and Attribution in Seventeenth-Century England," *Australian Journal of Legal History* 1, no. 1 (1995), 11–35, on p. 15.

22. See Tetsuro Hayashi, *The Theory of English Lexicography, 1530–1791*, Amsterdam Studies in the Theory and History of Linguistics, vol. 18 (Amsterdam: John Benjamins, 1978), p. 42.

23. Samuel Johnson, *Letters of Samuel Johnson, LL.D.*, ed. George Birkbeck Hill, 2 vols. (Oxford: Clarendon Press, 1892), vol. II, p. 83 n. 1.

24. J. H. Baker, *Monuments of Endlesse Labours: English Canonists and Their Work, 1300–1900* (London: Hambledon Press, 1998), pp. 80–90, esp. p. 88.

25. Design factors may also come into play. Giles Jacob's entries are consistently formatted as single paragraphs, making long and complex entries difficult to scan, and sub-senses difficult to pick out. In Cowell the distinction between sub-sense and subsequent entry is not always clear, yet as sub-senses regularly entail a new paragraph, vertical scanning is relatively easy.

CHAPTER 10

Hyphenated compounds in Johnson's Dictionary

Noel E. Osselton

It is an odd and unexplained fact that entries for English compound words with a hyphen occur mainly in the earlier part of Johnson's *Dictionary*. There are more than 170 hyphenated compounds under the letter C (*cover-shame, crack-brained, crest-fallen*, and the like) and some 140 under H; but S has only twelve, and W only one (*widow-wail*, with its two adjoining *w*'s). The alphabetical sequence

blue-eyed – eagle-eyed – full-eyed – moon-eyed – oneeyed – paleeyed – squinteyed – walleyed

gives a fair impression of how the hyphens vanished in words put in as the *Dictionary* progressed.[1]

Why should Johnson have changed his mind about the spelling of compound words in the years from 1749 to 1755, when his *Dictionary* was in the make? A study of the likely reasons may provide new insights into how the *Dictionary* was put together – a glimpse of Johnson in the process of devising lexicographical methods as he went along, or (as he puts it in the Preface) "establishing to myself, in the progress of the work, such rules as experience and analogy suggested to me" (1825 *Works*, vol. v, p. 24).

COMPOUNDS AND THE DICTIONARY MAKER

The compilers of English dictionaries have long been confronted with problems in the selection, definition, and spelling of compound terms. They are simply unlike other words: they may be self-explanatory (*garden shed, soap-dish, treetop*) and of hardly any conceivable interest to the user of a monolingual dictionary; if they should be entered for some special reason (to indicate stress, for instance), they may still be not worth defining; and in spelled form they have shown for four centuries now a peculiarly stable pattern of inherent threefold variability, so that even today *soapdish, soap-dish*, and *soap dish* are regarded as perfectly acceptable written forms.

Furthermore, once a compound term has been selected for inclusion, there is still the practical (but also technical) problem of where to put it. What do you do, for instance, about hyphenated items such as *hen-house, ill-favoured*, or *source-book*? Your choices are (1) to enter them as words in their own right in the main alphabetical list, as you more probably would if they were written solid (*henhouse*, etc.); or (2) to tuck them away as run-on structural sub-entries under their first element (*hen, ill, source*), together with derivations and other semantically related compounds. You may then save space in your dictionary, but that is often at the cost of making it harder for the user to find them because of the break in alphabetical order, with run-on items such as *hen-harrier, hennery*, and *hen run* (all under the word *hen*) coming before the entries for words such as *hence, henchman*, and *hendiadys*.[2]

Practice in modern English dictionaries is variable, though there is a clear tendency in newer publications to enter all compounds (whether solid, hyphenated, or two-word) in strict alphabetical order, giving them full entry status. This policy was adopted, for instance, in the ninth edition of the *Concise Oxford Dictionary*,[3] leading to sequences of mixed spelling styles as in *alloy, all-party . . . all right, all-round, all-rounder, All Saints' Day, all-seater, allseed*. The more traditional pattern of run-on entries is to be found in the *Chambers English Dictionary* where, to take only one item from the above sequence, *all-round* will be found (under *all*) two pages and sixty-three items before the entry for *alloy*.[4]

Johnson, who provided a model for so many features of our modern dictionaries, did not establish any steady system for the ordering of compound terms, though his varied treatment of them can be shown to produce patterns which are known to us from the *OED* and other dictionaries today.

HYPHENATED WORDS IN JOHNSON

Compound words with a hyphen became a common feature of English only in the sixteenth century, and the earliest notice of the word *hyphen* itself in the *OED* is as late as 1620. Soon after that, Johnson's predecessor Edward Phillips had been commendably precise in his definition of the word: "*Hyphen, (Greek)* a little stroke between two words or syllables, as a note of *Continuation*, and is used, either when two words are joyned together, for the more conciseness of expression, as *Self-interest*; or when one part of a word concludes the former Line, and the one begins the next."[5] The two dictionaries of Nathan Bailey (1721 and 1730; Johnson used the second edition of the latter, 1736) provide the additional type-examples *House-hold* and *Loving-Kindness.*[6] Johnson's immediate predecessor Benjamin Martin (1749) gives us (somewhat ambiguously) "a little line, set between two words, or syllables, shewing they are to be joined together, or in one, as *inn-keeper,* &c."[7] Johnson himself defines the word simply as "A note of conjunction: as, *vir-tue, ever-living.*"

With so recent a phenomenon it is not surprising that patterns of usage had not yet settled down, nor that dictionary makers (including Johnson) should have been casting around for a way of dealing with it. Users of Johnson's *Dictionary* will have found hyphenated words presented on the page in a number of quite different ways:[8]

1. As normal, independent entries in the main dictionary list, for example in alphabetical sequences such as the following:

armgaunt	archery	crested
arm-hole	arches-court	crest-fallen
armigerous	archetype	crestless

2. In a separate alphabetical cluster with the first entry highlighted by being set in large capitals:

BEE	HEATH	HOAR
Bee-eater	Heath-cock	Hoar-frost
Bee-flower	Heath-pout	HOARD
Bee-garden	Heath-peas	
Bee-hive	Heath-rose	
Bee-master	HEATHEN	
BEECH		

3. Similarly in an alphabetical cluster, but without any highlighting of the initial entry:

bat	market	men
bat-fowling	market-bell . . .	men-pleaser
batable	market-town	menace
	marketable	

4. In a series of entries preceded by a note drawing attention to the word-compounding process.[9] This may come either (a) in the form of a free-standing entry, as "HIGH is much used in composition with variety of meaning" placed before twenty-five hyphenated *high-* compounds, or (b) as a separate item tagged on to the numbered senses of a word. For the word *heaven* five meanings are listed, followed by "6. It is often used in composition," and then entries for *heaven-begot, heaven-born, heaven-bred,* etc.

5. Where the individually defined compound entries are preceded by a general definition of the first compounding element:

BULL, in composition, generally notes the large size of any thing, as *bull-head, bulrush, bull-trout*; and is therefore only an inclusive particle, without much reference to its original signification.

The twelve compound entries following this comment include *bull-baiting, bull-beggar* ("something to fright children with"), and *bull-finch*.

6. Where the hyphenated words which are entered are stated to be a mere selection of possibilities. Compounding with *by-*, for example is said to be "used at pleasure, and will be understood by the examples following" (*by-coffeehouse, by-concernment, by-stander*, etc.).

7. No longer as a dictionary entry complete with definition, but simply in a series of quotations arranged alphabetically within the lemma for the first compounding element: *well-aim'd* (Pope), *well-appointed* (Shakespeare), *well-balanc'd* (Milton), *well-beaten* (Locke) are among those leading off the sixty or more examples given under *well*.

8. Similarly, but where the quotations are arranged in historical order. In a list given under *never-*, Dryden's "*never-opening* gates" comes before Pope's "*never-blushing* head" and Swift's "*never-meaning* face."

These eight styles of presenting hyphenated compound words are listed above in decreasing order of prominence, and of findability for the dictionary user. Words of type 1 rank equally with any other dictionary entry; 2, and still more so 3 with no large capitals to mark the cluster, will be less easily found because of the break in the alphabetical order; in 4 the focus shifts from the individual entry to the linguistic process of compounding; in 5 and 6 attention is on the semantics of the first element, with merely selective examples; and in 7 and 8 we lose sight of dictionary entries proper: the hyphenated words, undefined, occur only in quotations and (especially in cases where they are arranged by date order) they are not going to be found very readily by the enquiring user.

JOHNSON'S SYSTEM OF RUN-ON ALPHABETICAL CLUSTERS

Among the first entries in Johnson's *Dictionary* the ordering of hyphenated compounds is sometimes alphabetical, and sometimes not. *Account-book* comes between *accountant* and *accounting*, and *action-taking* is to be found between between *actionary* and *actitation*. On the other hand, *answer-jobber* is inserted (in defiance of the alphabet) immediately after the entry for its first element *answer*, and before the derivations *answerable, answerer*, etc.[10] So also *ant-hill* follows *ant*, and comes before *antagonist*. In many cases, two-word and solid compounds are similarly shifted back: in a batch of twenty-two compounds after the entry for *all* (and preceding *allantois* and *to allay*) we find the mixed spelling styles of *all-conquering, all fours*, and *allhallowtide*.

As the *Dictionary* progresses, this somewhat haphazard treatment of compound words gives way to a steadier pattern in which it is only (or mainly) those compounds written with a hyphen which are clustered after their first element (types 2 and 3 above), while solid ones appear later in the main alphabetical list (two-word compounds, always infrequent in Johnson, become increasingly rare). Typical of this pattern is the entry for the noun *bear* ("A rough savage animal") followed by seven compounds with hyphens, *bear-bind, bear-fly, bear-garden, bear's-breech, bear's-ear, bear's-foot, bear's-wort*; then an entry for the semantically unrelated *beard*, followed in due course by the solid *bear-* compounds *bearherd* ("A man that tends bears") and *bearward* ("A keeper of bears"). Similarly there are nine hyphenated *black*-compounds (*black-cattle, black-mail*, etc., ending with *black-rod*) before the entries for *blackamoor, blackberried*, etc. One-off hyphenated items are also regularly shunted up to their first element: *bat-fowling* is moved forward by nine entries to be placed next to *bat*; *bog-trotter* is after *bog* and before *boggle, boggy*, and *boghouse*.

This innovative ordering of entries on the page shows clearly enough that for Johnson the very presence of a hyphen carried with it the implication of a distinctive structural category: *bear-garden* "belonged" to *bear* – it was a particular order of compound – whereas the solid *bearherd* did not; it was a word in its own right, with its own place in the alphabet.

Though complete consistency is never attained, this pattern (types 2 and 3) becomes the dominant one for the first half of the *Dictionary*: under the letter C (from *commendably* to *crooked*) only two of the sixty-four compound words with hyphens are not entered immediately following their first element (whether that is their natural alphabetical position or not); under G it is only one (*gilt-tail*) out of nineteen; and for H only three (*hand-bell, hand-gallop, hand-gun*) out of more than 140.

Johnson's distinctive arrangement in alphabetical clusters – in which hyphenated compound words are sited as a separate group on the page, sometimes with a "composition" note (types 4 to 6) – may reasonably be seen as some kind of a precursor of the modern dictionary lemma with its run-on entries. Gabriele Stein ("Word-formation in Dr. Johnson's *Dictionary*," p. 89) goes so far as to say that a compounding element such as *heaven* or *hell* (given above as type 4b) is "listed as a run-on entry." There are, however, great differences between Johnson's practice and that of modern lexicographers: the clusters of compounds in Johnson are *alphabetical* run-ons, standing on the page as individual entries, and even those of type 4b are all left-justified.

In the English dictionaries of his predecessors Johnson would have found no distinctive pattern for dealing with compound words. Blount's *Glosso-graphia* (the only English dictionary before Johnson with any literary aspirations) is more concerned with the recondite vocabulary of the authors cited than with either poetic or everyday compounds.[11] In later editions of Phillips's *New World of Words* (1671, 1678) odd examples crop up such as *high-crested* and *high-rigged* (both are, however, labeled "Terms in Archery"). Bailey (1736) has entries for *heaven* and *heavenly*, but (unlike Johnson) had no call to accommodate Dryden's *heav'n-begot*, Shakespeare's *heav'n-bred*, or Pope's *heav'n-directed* and hosts of like poetic terms; and where clutches of compounds do occur in Bailey (as in the sequence Bull *Feast*, Bull-Head, Bullated, Bull-finch, Bull *Weed*, Bullace, Bull-*Beggar*) little attempt is made to pick them out of the general typographical and alphabetical chaos. For the word *triple* Benjamin Martin has in his second edition (1754) a rare example from Milton in the entry for *triple-coloured bow* ("the rainbow"), distinguished as a poetical term by having a fleur-de-lys device placed before it.[12]

Though the monolingual English dictionaries would then have been of little or no help, a useful model for the Johnsonian alphabetical clusters was to hand in the foreign-language and Latin dictionaries of the day. For sound pedagogical reasons bilingual dictionaries will always tend to take up more compound words: even when an item is self-explanatory the learner may still need to be given the equivalent term in the target language.[13] We know furthermore that Johnson had in his library a number of substantial bilingual dictionaries, including Sewel for Dutch and Boyer for French, as well as Ainsworth's English–Latin, Latin–English dictionary.[14] There is also evidence that he turned to the last of these for his solution to a quite different (but equally intractable) problem of dictionary compilation: what to do about the host of phrasal verbs in English such as *break down, break forth, break off* or *call back, call for, call in.*[15]

Almost any bilingual dictionary of the time would have provided him with a pattern in which compounds (whether hyphenated or not) are clustered under the entry for their first element: at *market*, for instance, Ainsworth has fourteen loosely arranged *market* idioms and compounds, including *a market man* ("Nundinator"), *a market place, above the market price*, and *a market town* ("Emporium"), all corresponding to items in Johnson, and all similarly occurring before the alphabetically displaced adjective *marketable*.[16]

Johnson was the first compiler of an English dictionary to make use of different type sizes for the headwords – in his case, large capitals and small capitals – so as to distinguish major and minor entries.[17] This typographical distinction may well have come from his observation of practice in Latin and foreign-language dictionaries. Even the sixteenth-century *Bibliotheca Scholastica* of John Rider had main entries ("a Peare") in large roman, with smaller roman for compounds ("a muske peare") and other idioms or derivations which the learner might expect to find there.[18] In the first edition of Sewel's Dutch dictionary (1691)[19] all entry words had been printed in lower case, but if the copy in Johnson's library was one of the editions between 1708 and 1754 he would have found groups of compounds there with the first element highlighted in capitals at their head (see type 2 above). At the word *bee*, for instance, Sewel has

BEE . . .
a Bee-hive
a Bee-master
BEECH.

A similar typographical (and alphabetical) arrangement was introduced in later editions of the Boyer French dictionary with an explanation in the Preface: "and to facilitate the ready finding out of every Thing, I have . . . printed in fair Capitals, not only the *Radical* and remarkable Words, but also those *English Particles*, which, being join'd to a *Verb*, do often change its Signification."[20]

A model for Johnson's numerous "composition" notes on productive compound elements (in types 4, 5, and 6 above) is also to be found in contemporary bilingual dictionaries. Where Johnson has the comment "AFTER is compounded with many words . . . some, which occurred, will follow, by which others may be explained" (these include *after acceptation, afterages, after-dinner, aftermath*, etc.), Boyer prefaces a somewhat similar list more briefly with "R[emarquez]. Cet adverbe se compose avec plusieurs noms substantifs, comme . . ." (*after-ages, after-math, after-burthen*, etc.).

Johnson took up far more compounds than his monolingual predecessors had done; he frequently put them in separate alphabetical clusters; he commented on the more productive types; and he sometimes distinguished them typographically. For all these innovations we know that there were models to hand in bilingual dictionaries such as were in his library.

A SYSTEM ABANDONED

The striking arrangement Johnson introduced into his *Dictionary* so as to bring together groups of hyphenated words becomes more erratic in mid-dictionary, and is in the end virtually abandoned. The following table shows the number of clustered (that is, alphabetically displaced) entries for hyphenated compound words in eight passages spaced out through the *Dictionary*. Each passage consists of one complete series of twenty-three signatures (e.g., for *feefarm–fy*, sig. 9A1^r–9Z2^v, with a total of forty-six leaves). The middle column shows the corresponding number of compounds which are not clustered, but are segregated from their headword and entered alphabetically as normal words in the main list. The total number of hyphenated entries for each passage (right-hand column) includes those where the option of alphabetic reordering simply never arose, since the compound stood next to its headword anyway.

Entry	Clustered placement	Alphabetic	Total
antiquity–bent	29	7	56
commendably–crooked	40	2	65
feefarm–fy	28	1	36
harmful–impracticable	96	2	121
man–mutton	36	16	81
to pack–poll	8	0	23
shrimp–stagger	0	2	2
untruly–wring	0	1	1

This illustrates clearly enough how the alphabetical clusters were given up, and it provides incidentally a further indication of the general decline in the total number of hyphenated words referred to at the beginning of this essay.

The eight passages in the above table have been chosen so as to cover the stages in the printing of Johnson's *Dictionary* identified by Allen Reddick. Of these, the first four (here, *antiquity–impracticable*) were printed at various dates between 1750 and October 1753.[21] Then, after a break until the autumn of 1754, the remaining four groups (*man–wring*) were printed by various presses and pressmen: "the composing, printing, and proofreading were carried out in a very short and intensive span of time, with all hands turning to the project" (Reddick, *The Making of Johnson's Dictionary*, p. 75). Can it be, then, that the abandonment of the system in Johnson's *Dictionary* must in part be laid at the door of his printers? It might be instructive to look for other shifts in spelling practice or entry structure which correspond to this break in the printing process.

THE DOWNGRADING OF HYPHENATED COMPOUNDS

The abandonment of alphabetically clustered entries and the virtual disappearance of entries for words with a hyphen (as shown in the table above) can indeed be seen to go with at least one other mid-dictionary change in lexicographical practice: a switch from defined entries to mere illustrative quotations.

In her wide-ranging study of Johnson's word-formation, Stein ("Word-formation in Dr. Johnson's *Dictionary*," pp. 87–92) analyzes in some detail the more productive English word-formation elements (such as *full-* and *over-*) which are variously commented on by Johnson as being "much used in composition," "sometimes used in composition," etc.; that is, the first elements occurring in types 4 to 6 above.

The words listed in her study can, however, be shown to fall into two groups:

(i) compounding elements with hyphens (running from A to M) where each compound appears in Johnson as a full dictionary entry with definition:

> *after-, all-, bull-, by-, dog-, full-, ground-, half-, hand-, heart-, heaven-, hedge-, hell-, high-, moon-.*

> (Exceptions are the compounding elements *best-* and *bottle-*, each illustrated by two quotations, and *bosom-* with six quotations, *bosom-friends, bosom-int'rest,* etc.).

(ii) Compounding elements from the letter M onwards, where the hyphenated words are given not as entries, but merely as quotations within the lemma:

> *marriage-, never-, over-, out-, self-, smock-, twice-, two-, water-, well-, winter.*

The entry for *water* provides a typical example of how such common compounding elements are treated toward the end of the alphabet: *water-flood, water-snakes,* and twenty-one other hyphenated words are entered in the lemma simply as quotations, but these are followed by full, separate alphabetical entries for the *water* compounds without hyphens (*waterfall, water-fowl,* etc.). Stein observes of Johnson's spellings without a hyphen that "it would be difficult to argue that spellings in one word reflect in all cases a higher degree of lexicalisation or conventionality" ("Word-formation in

Dr. Johnson's *Dictionary,*" p. 76). A more detailed semantic study of John-son's compounds is still needed, but with examples such as these from *water* it would indeed be hard to discover any reason for the difference in arrangement on the dictionary page other than the presence of the hyphen.

The two lists above (overlapping at the letter M) show that for the com-moner compounding elements there is in the latter part of the *Dictionary* a clear switch from types 4 and 5 to types 7 and 8: that is, the hyphenated compounds are effectively downgraded from being fully defined entries in their own right to become mere quotations listed alphabetically (type 7) or even in date order (type 8) within the lemma.

At the same time, the occasional one-off compounds (such as *walleyed,* referred to at the beginning of this essay) tend to be entered solid where analogous entries earlier in the alphabet – *blue-eyed, eagle-eyed* – had been with the hyphen. Other examples are:

Early Entry	Late Entry
addle-pated	*shatterpated*
black-lead	*readlead, whitelead*
cream-faced	*smoothfaced*
double-dealing	*plaindealing*
fin-footed	*surefooted*
hen-hearted	*stiffhearted*
high-spirited	*poorspirited*

With *smoothfaced* (quoting "*smoothfac'd* wo(o)ers" from *Love's Labour's Lost* and "*smoothfac'd* peace" from *Richard III*) as against *cream-faced* (quot-ing the "*cream-fac'd* lown" from *Macbeth*), a casual user might think that authorial (or textual, or copyist) spellings in the quotations could have played a part in determining the form of the word Johnson chose to enter in his *Dictionary.* There is, however, evidence that the spellings in the quo-tations themselves underwent the same process of dehyphenation in later entries: the Shakespearean *orange-wife* and *fosset-seller* had been given their hyphens under the letter F in a passage from *Coriolanus* (2.1.79) s.v. *faucet* ("hearing a cause between an orange-wife and a *fosset-seller*"), but when the same quotation was used later on under the letter O at *orangewife* they appeared without hyphens as *orangewife* and *fosset seller.*

Indeed, the tendency seems rather to have been for spellings in printed quotations to follow that of the entry-word rather than to influence it. For the word *timepleaser* ("One who complies with prevailing notions whatever they be") there is a single Shakespearean quotation:

> Scandal, the suppliants for the people, call them
> *Timepleasers*, flatterers, foes to nobleness.

The same quotation is, however, also used to illustrate the words *scandal* (as a verb, with the more satisfactory reading of *Coriolanus* 3.1.46 as *scandal'd*) and *suppliant*; but on both these occasions the word appears with a hyphen as *time-pleaser*. Then the very next item in the *Dictionary* is entered solid as *timeserving* and is similarly written solid in its quotation from South's *Sermons*; but a few pages later it appears with a hyphen (as *time-serving*) when the same passage from South is used to illustrate the verb *to trim*.

The expected range of English hyphenated compounds so noticeably absent from the latter half of Johnson had then not disappeared completely from the *Dictionary*: many of them no longer feature in the main dictionary word list but are taken up (without definitions) in lists of quotations given as specimens of the compounding process; and if we may go by analogous spelling patterns in the earlier part of the *Dictionary* it looks as though for many other fully defined entries the hyphen has been quietly dropped.

SPELLING PREFERENCES AND LEXICOGRAPHICAL CONSTRAINTS

Johnson makes no specific reference in the Preface to the use of hyphens in English, and "compound or double words" are dealt with, rather curiously, in two quite separate paragraphs. In one of them he explains that he has "seldom noted them, except when they obtain a signification different from that which they have in their simple state" – a sound enough principle, which most dictionary makers would embrace today. But in the other he says he has inserted "great numbers," in order to make good the shortcomings of the dictionaries before him, and so as to illustrate this feature of the language: "These, numerous as they are, might be multiplied, but that use and curiosity are here satisfied, and the frame of our language and modes of our combination are amply discovered" (1825 *Works*, vol. v, p. 33). Stein notes the disparity between the two statements ("Word-formation in Dr. Johnson's *Dictionary*," p. 71), putting it down to Johnson's lexicographical realism on the one hand, and an understandable desire to outdo all his rivals on the other. But the stated intentions of the two paragraphs may rather be seen to reflect the change in lexicographical practice which occurs between the earlier and the later part of the *Dictionary*: the long lists of hyphenated items inserted later in the alphabet as mere quotations (types 7, 8) certainly served to illustrate the "modes of our combination" while (especially when placed in historical order) they would hardly function at all as dictionary look-up words.

In creating a historical dictionary based on literary usage, Johnson – unlike his predecessors – was confronted with the need to accommodate the large numbers of (especially poetic) compounds belonging to his and the foregoing age. The very presence of hyphens was evidently cause enough for him to attempt a display of them separately on the dictionary page, even though hyphen use was then (as always in English) extremely unstable.

For this, the user needed a visually effective pattern, but the lexicographical device which Johnson adopted initially for segregating compounds with a hyphen (*corn-master, cow-herd*) from those without (*cornchandler, cowkeeper*) is a far from satisfactory one. Typographically, his clusters do not stand out well on the page, since they are neither indented nor fully embedded, and for the most part the user had only a break in alphabetical order to go by: a consistent use of large capitals (as in type 2) *solely* for the purpose of heading such a group of compounds could have been an effective presentational device, but the large capitals occur too diversely for this to be a good visual aid. Since each hyphenated entry stands alone, unembedded, the system required that all should be provided with a full definition, even when the word entered is pretty self-explanatory (*hell-black*, "Black as hell"). Sometimes (type 5) there is even a general definition into the bargain. Further, the presence everywhere of quotations with spellings different from the form given in the headword would constantly point up the arbitrariness of the whole arrangement.

In his account of the compiling process Reddick refers to the problems of the amanuenses "in organizing the word entries" (*The Making of Johnson's Dictionary*, p. 44 and n), and there are indications that the system of hyphenated clusters may have been among them. In the sequence

MALT *n.s.*
MALTDUST
MALTFLOOR
MALT *v.n.*
MALTDRINK
MALTHORSE

the two items *maltdust* and *maltfloor* are placed as an alphabetic cluster typically employed for hyphenated compounds (i.e., as for type 2). They are in fact entered solid in the *Dictionary*, but it looks very much as though the compiler intended them to have hyphens (as indeed they have in the quotations which illustrate them).

Similar manuscript-to-print problems may also be indicated by the sudden switch from hyphen to solid part-way through the total of 140 compounds entered at *over:* the first fifty-four entries from *over-abound* to *over-joy* are hyphenated (with the exception only of *overcome(r), overdo, overfal, overgrow*), while the remaining seventy-eight from *overlaboured* to *overyeared* (with the three exceptions *over-measure, over-match*, and *over-mix*) are written solid. This crude switch in spelling style happens at the bottom of a page (between sig. 18T2ᵛ and 18U1ʳ), after a single wildly erratic entry for *over-ripen*, and it is very hard to believe that the way in which the whole batch of examples is set up can have represented Johnson's intention. Such practical difficulties in imposing the system for entering compound words could only add to any dissatisfaction with the system itself.

DICTIONARY SPELLINGS AND AUTHORIAL SPELLINGS

Johnson says in his Preface that he has "laboured to settle the orthography" of English (1825 *Works*, vol. v, p. 41). Can this be said to apply to compounds as well? Stein comes to the conclusion that "he was not concerned with spelling in composition" ("Word-formation in Dr. Johnson's *Dictionary*," p. 76), and indeed when he refers to "composition" in the *Dictionary* itself the term is sometimes used to cover compounds written solid, sometimes those with hyphens, and sometimes those written as two separate words. Yet, despite this blanket use of the term, his innovative arrangement of hyphenated items such as *bell-fashioned* or *heart-robbing* shows clearly enough that hyphens mattered to him, and were meant to matter to those who used his *Dictionary*. He saw the presence of a hyphen as a linguistically distinctive feature, setting its compound word apart. Just as the enquiring user was to spell *entire*, not *intire*, so also was he to write *cow-herd*, not *cowherd*.

Also in the Preface he makes clear his intended distinction between the status of entry-word spellings and quotation-spellings: the former were the ones recommended to the user – spellings "to which I give, perhaps not often rashly, the preference," whereas in the latter (in intention at least) he had left "to every authour his own practice unmolested" (vol. v, p. 26). In the switch from types 2 and 3 (clustered entry spellings) to types 7 and 8 (lists of quotations) he therefore effectively gave up a specific recommendation to his users to spell certain English compounds with hyphens, even though many hundreds of them were still tolerated in quotations within the lemma right down to the letter Z (over eighty of them under *self-* alone).

Historical dictionaries (and Johnson's is the first English dictionary with some measure of historical coverage) must always in their very nature be hybrids: largely descriptive in their record of the language of the past (and down to the present), but inevitably also taken to be prescriptive, in as far as the compiler must put forward a chosen modern spelling for each of his entry-words. Johnson's striking mid-alphabet change in lexicographical method thus enabled him to abandon a (somewhat defective) scheme for prescribing the use of the hyphen, while still retaining an impressive display of historical practice – practice which (in its inherent variability at least) was to last down to our own time. The vanishing hyphens of Johnson's word list may then be taken as one small instance of how his desire to regulate the language gave way in the light of experience to the more modest aim of recording it.

NOTES

1. All quotations are from *1755*.
2. General principles for the use of sub-entries in dictionaries are set out in Ladislav Zgusta, *Manual of Lexicography* (The Hague: Mouton, 1971), pp. 268–70, and Wolfgang Rettig, "Die Wortbildungszusammenhänge im allgemeinen einsprachigen Wörterbuch," in *Wörterbücher – Dictionaries – Dictionnaires: Ein internationales Handbuch zur Lexikographie*, ed. Franz Josef Hausmann *et al.* (Berlin: Walter de Gruyter, 1989), vol. 1, pp. 642–49.
3. *The Concise Oxford Dictionary*, ed. Della Thompson, 9th ed. (Oxford: Clarendon Press, 1995). The change of policy is discussed in the Preface, p. vii.
4. *Chambers English Dictionary*, 7th ed. (Cambridge: Chambers, 1988).
5. Edward Phillips, *The New World of Words; or, A General English Dictionary*, 4th ed. (London, 1678). There is no entry for *hyphen* in earlier editions.
6. N. Bailey, *An Universal Etymological English Dictionary* (London, 1721); and *Dictionarium Britannicum; or, A More Compleat Universal Etymological English Dictionary*, 2nd ed. (London, 1736).
7. Benjamin Martin, *Lingua Britannica Reformata; or, A New English Dictionary* (London, 1749).
8. In Johnson's *Dictionary* all entry-words are set in capitals (whether large or small); the original typography is represented here only for type 2.
9. Types 4, 5, and 6 are discussed extensively by Gabriele Stein in "Word-formation in Dr. Johnson's *Dictionary of the English Language,*" *Dictionaries: Journal of the Dictionary Society of North America* 6 (1984), 66–112, on pp. 87–92.
10. Johnson's treatment of derivations is not discussed here. The systems for entering them evolved by him and other early lexicographers would merit further investigation.

11. N. E. Osselton, "Authenticating the Vocabulary: A Study in Seventeenth-Century Lexicographical Practice," *Lexikos* 6 (1996), 215–32.

12. A similar use of the fleur-de-lys device is to be found in some Latin dictionaries of the time, and in his *Plan* (1747) Johnson himself had entertained the idea that poetic words might be "distinguished by some mark prefixed." See N. E. Osselton, *Branded Words in English Dictionaries before Johnson* (Groningen: J. B. Wolters, 1958), pp. 117–19.

13. Bo Svénsen, *Practical Lexicography: Principles and Methods of Dictionary-Making* (Oxford: Oxford University Press, 1993), p. 44.

14. J. D. Fleeman, *The Sale Catalogue of Samuel Johnson's Library: A Facsimile Edition* (Victoria, B.C.: University of Victoria, 1975).

15. N. E. Osselton, "Dr Johnson and the English Phrasal Verb," in *Lexicography: An Emerging International Profession*, ed. Robert Ilson (Manchester: Manchester University Press, 1986), pp. 7–16.

16. Robert Ainsworth, *Thesaurus Linguae Latinae Compendiarius; or, A Compendious Dictionary of the Latin Tongue*, 2nd ed. (London, 1746).

17. An account of printing types in early English dictionaries is given in Paul Luna, "Clearly Defined: Continuity and Innovation in the Typography of English Dictionaries," *Typography Papers* 4 (2000), 5–56. Luna refers to the use of large and small capitals for entry-words and observes that both styles had been used in Bailey's dictionaries (p. 19). But (unlike Johnson) Bailey does not combine them to differentiate words: the large capitals are used for all entries in his *Universal Etymological English Dictionary* (1721), and the small capitals in the *Dictionarium Britannicum* (1730).

18. John Rider, *Bibliotheca Scholastica: A Double Dictionarie* (Oxford, 1589).

19. Willem Sewel, *A New Dictionary English and Dutch . . . Nieuw Woordenboek der Engelsche en Nederduytsche Taale* (Amsterdam, 1691). See also N. E. Osselton, *The Dumb Linguists: A Study of the Earliest English and Dutch Dictionaries* (Leiden: Leiden University Press, 1973), chapter 4 and Appendix 1.

20. *The Royal Dictionary, French and English, and English and French, by Mr. A. Boyer, but Now Revised and Improved by DD. F.R.S.* (London, 1752), Preface, sig. A4ᵛ.

21. Allen Reddick, *The Making of Johnson's Dictionary, 1746–1773*, rev. ed. (Cambridge: Cambridge University Press, 1996), p. 40.

CHAPTER II

The typographic design of Johnson's Dictionary

Paul Luna

DICTIONARIES AS AN AREA OF TYPOGRAPHIC STUDY

How does a typographer look at a dictionary? In particular, how does a typographer look a dictionary that is also a cultural artifact, as Samuel Johnson's *Dictionary of the English Language* undoubtedly is? "Typography" has been variously defined as a method of printing (letterpress) or the art of laying out printed matter; here the more wide-ranging definition of the configuration of verbal graphic language is used. So in looking at Johnson's *Dictionary*, the main concern of this essay is not the quality of the printing, nor the nature of the paper, nor even the origin of the founts of type used to compose the *Dictionary*, but how its visual presentation reflects the structure of the text, its usability, and perhaps even its compiler's intentions.

The printing of English dictionaries from 1604 has paradoxically combined innovation in the production of the text, ranging from Minsheu's first use of subscription publishing for *Ductor in Linguas* to the development of congers in the eighteenth century, with a conservative approach to typographical developments. Printers of dictionaries were slow to adopt the use of variant founts (italic, small capitals) or spacing to articulate their contents graphically. While Johnson's *Dictionary* was a significant piece of typography as well as a literary and lexicographical milestone, its typographical qualities have not been seriously discussed. In 1922 D. B. Updike dismissed the *Dictionary* as set "in a monotonous old style type, in size rather small for the folio double column pages," complaining "these pages . . . seem old-fashioned to us now."[1] James Cochrane in 1964 considered it a "worthy piece of bookwork," but the only feature he cites is the lack of "the disfiguring use of bold type."[2] These approaches concentrate on the surface appearance of the printed page. But if we look at how the *Dictionary*'s typography articulates its underlying structure, we can see that Johnson's page was genuinely innovative and set the standard for English dictionaries for a century. Furthermore, the early variant editions (folio, quarto, and octavo) also provide the typographer with an opportunity to compare different typographic presentations of what is essentially the same structure.

Approaching the history of dictionaries from the standpoint of typographic design is not a well-trodden path.[3] Perhaps this is because of the utilitarian nature of dictionaries, which are books intended to have active readers with a problem to solve, rather than contemplative readers who have an interest in the aesthetics of the book as an object. Book design is intended to serve the reader, by making the structure of the author's text clear in visual form, and books fall into clear genres. Typographic genres have been described by Robert Waller as a combination of a particular authorial or textual requirement (the "topic structure"), a physical format (the "artifact structure"), and a typographic presentation that allows reader access to the information ("access structure"), and on this basis dictionaries constitute a clear typographic genre.[4] Dictionary topic structure is generally an alphabetical sequence of entries, with further levels of information nested within them; the artifact structure is generally a relatively compact book with a multi-column structure; the access structure is provided at one level by the alphabetic sequence and page elements (alphabetic sections, headlines, headwords), which assist navigation and the location of an entry, and at another by the differentiation of the various elements within an entry, which enable the significance of the information to be understood (through the use of variant typefaces and paragraphing).

The whole focus of dictionary typography is to allow the reader rapid access to the relevant piece of information, not to provide for continuous reading; dictionaries are "access" devices. Because they are by their nature structure-rich, dictionaries require a potentially complex typography. A repertory of normal typographic features has developed, and it is possible to describe how these map onto commonly found structural elements in current dictionaries, at least in general terms – boldface type for headwords, for example, and italics for cited words.[5] As if to prove this, advertising regularly calls on the typographic forms associated with dictionary entries, often when it wants to imply an authoritative standard for, or an unimpeachable description of, a product.[6]

But typography also develops over time, and the repertory of effects available in the eighteenth century differed from those available today. So the first questions a typographer might pose of the *Dictionary* are: to what degree is the mapping of structure to typographic form logical, consistent, and revealing to the reader? And to what extent does it use (or even expand) the repertory of typographic resources available for this kind of text?

Imprimer.Imprimeur.
Imprimer,Imprimere,Excudere.
Imprimer en l'entendement, Affigere animis.
Imprimeur,Scriptor, Excufor, Librarius, Typographus.
Improprement.
Improprement,Improprie.
Imprudent.Imprudemment.
Imprudent,Imprudens.
Imprudent confeil,Confilium inconfultum.
Imprudemment,Inconfulte.

Figure 1. Robert Estienne, *Dictionaire francoislatin* (1539). Headwords are set in a larger type, indented. In the definitions, French words are set in italic type, Latin words in roman type (reproduced at 100%).

THE DEVELOPMENT OF TYPOGRAPHIC RESOURCES FOR DICTIONARIES

The foundations of dictionary typography were laid by the Parisian scholar-printer Robert Estienne (1498–1559), who printed the *Thesaurus linguae latinae* (1531) and the *Dictionaire francoislatin* (1539) (figure 1). Estienne's spatial organization of the page was exemplary, precisely because he mapped visual appearance to structural significance: he differentiated headwords by setting them on separate lines, in a larger point-size, deeply indented; definitions were set full out (unindented), and examples of usage indented one em. Significantly, he introduced the differentiation of language by typeface, using italic type for French words and roman type for Latin ones.[7] In other words, he used paragraphing and changes in type size to assist navigation, and changes of typeface to indicate structural elements within a paragraph.[8] Estienne's achievement looks even more significant when compared to the edition of *Ortus Vocabulorum* printed in London by Richard Pynson some thirty years earlier, which has only one typeface for both Latin and English text, and no indentation to articulate entries.[9] Subsequent printed English dictionaries remained slow to aspire to such accessible typography, and were conservative in their use of new typographic forms, only gradually adopting different typefaces and indentation systems.

To navigate a dictionary effectively, a reader needs to know the range of words discussed on a page, and how to locate the start of each entry. It is interesting to note that the use of full headwords in headlines did not replace guide-letters until well into the nineteenth century.[10] To articulate entries on the page, and to assist the look-up of specific headwords, the

ANGEL, a Gold Coin, in Value Ten Shillings, having the Figure of an Angel ſtampt on it.
ANGEL SHOT, Chain Shot, being a Cannon Bullet cut in two, and the Halves being joined together by a Chain.
ANGEL *Bed*, an open Bed without Bed-poſts.
ANGE'LICA [*Botany*] an Herb.
ANGE'LICAL [ἀγγελικη', Gr.] a famous Dance among the *Greeks*.
ANGE'LICAL [*angelicus*, L.] pertaining to, partaking of the Nature of Angels.
ANGELICAL *Garment*, a Monkiſh Garment wHich Men put on a little before their Death, that they may receive the Benefit of the Prayers of the Monks.
ANGE'LICALNESS [of *angelique*, F. *angelicus*, L.] the being angelical, angelical Nature, *&c.*

Figure 2. Nathan Bailey, *Dictionarium Britannicum* (1730). Entries are a single paragraph, and headwords are set in cap and small caps. Etymologies and subject-field labels are set within square brackets. Italics are used for cited forms and subject-field labels (77%).

norm today is to use a boldface type. But no boldface types were available in Johnson's time. Updike's description of the *Dictionary's* pages as "of mild colour and easy air" reflects the lack of color contrast available from types of the eighteenth century (*Printing Types*, vol. II, p. 140). The use of bold type for headwords in English dictionaries seems not to have come about until the 1870s, some thirty years after the introduction of the first boldface types, called Clarendon, by a London type-foundry.[11] In the sixteenth and early seventeenth centuries, black-letter had provided a color contrast analogous to the use of boldface with roman;[12] but black-letter already appears dated when used for the headwords in Thomas Blount's *Glossographia* of 1656. The addition of white space between entries to reinforce their boundaries did not appear until 1817.[13]

For differentiation of significant items within an entry, roman, italic, and small capitals were the only fount variants available to Johnson's printers in the 1750s. The first English dictionary to use roman and italic types, as opposed to black-letter, was John Bullokar's *English Expositor* (1616). Small caps (reduced-height capital letters designed to provide a variant to both capitals and lower case) had been used to differentiate individual words in a text from at least 1519, and had been produced by typefounders as purpose-made founts from the first half of the sixteenth century.[14] They were certainly established as part of the typographic repertoire by the seventeenth and eighteenth centuries,[15] but their use in English dictionaries dates only from Nathan Bailey's *Dictionarium Britannicum* (1730), where headwords were set in elegantly letter-spaced cap and small caps (figure 2).

This lack of typographic resources to differentiate structural elements was not a problem when dictionary structures were relatively simple. Bailey's *Dictionarium Britannicum* seems to function quite well with its three-fount repertory and with single indented paragraphs for the great majority of entries. While in many ways the presentation of Bailey's dictionary can be considered a model for Johnson (the double-column folio page, the use of indented all-cap or cap-and-small-cap headwords), the typographic requirements of the *Dictionary* are far greater, and the spatial arrangement of the page had to be used in a much more dynamic way to overcome the limitations of fount choice.

In type design, the faces cut by William Caslon in the 1720s and 1730s provided a systematic (though not wholly uniform) set of related roman, italic, and small-cap founts in a full range of sizes. Although the concept of a single typeface design did not exist at the time (designs varied in detail from size to size), the relative overall regularity of Caslon's types can be seen by comparing them to the heterogeneous collection of "Fell" types used by the University Press, Oxford, at this period.[16] Johnson's printer, William Strahan,[17] bought his types from the Scottish typefounder Alexander Wilson,[18] who offered faces "conformable to the London types," in other words close in design to those of Caslon.[19]

THE *PLAN* AND THE TYPOGRAPHY OF THE *DICTIONARY*

The folio editions of the *Dictionary* (*1755, 1765, 1773, 1784*) can be considered as a single typographic design, but there are design differences between the smaller-format abridged editions. The two London octavos (*1756* and *1760*) share the same design, which is different from that of the Dublin octavo *1758*. The quarto *1777* represents a fourth design, and the quarto *1785Q* and folio *1785F* share a fifth design, also used by by the octavo *1805*. These will be described as the folio, the London octavo, the Dublin octavo, the Dublin quarto, and the 1785 designs.[20]

The folio design naturally represents not only the most familiar, but also the most developed design of the *Dictionary*; it can be compared with the proposals in *The Plan of a Dictionary*, where Johnson indicates the ideal structure and differentiation of elements envisaged at the start of his enterprise. His argument about the inclusion of scientific and "professional" words clearly indicates an appreciation of the dictionary maker's obligation of utility to the reader: "The value of a work must be estimated by its use: it is not enough that a dictionary delights the critic, unless at the same time it instructs the learner . . . It seems necessary to the completion of

C A S   C A T

CA'SKET (of *caſſette*, F.) a little cabinet or cheſt.

CASSA'VE, an American root, whoſe juice is poiſon, but its ſubſtance being dried, is the common bread of the country.

CASSAWA'RE, a large bird, whoſe feathers are like camels hair.

CA'SSIA, L. a ſweet ſhrub, whoſe bark is ſpicy like cinnamon, and is often uſed inſtead of it.

CASSIA fiſtula, L. caſſia in the cane, a reed whoſe pulp is of a purging quality.

CASSI'NE, It. a farm houſe, where a number of people have poſted themſelves to make a ſtand againſt the enemy.

CASTOR and *POLLUX*, L. are two meteors, that ſometimes in a great ſtorm at ſea, appear ſticking to ſome part of the ſhip, in the ſhape of fiery balls ; and when but one of them is ſeen, it is called *Helena*, and both of them are ſometimes called *Tyndarides*.

CASTOR and *POLLUX*. See *Gemini*.

CASTO'REUM, L. a drug much uſed in medicine, and is commonly taken for the beaver's teſticles ; but this is a vulgar error, for it is contained in a glandule whereof two grow in the hinder parts of both the male and female beaver.

To CA'STRATE (of *caſtro*, L. to geld) 1 to

SPI'RIT, (of *ſpiritus*, L. of *ſpiro* to breathe)
1 a ſubſtance diſtinct from matter.
2 virtue, or ſupernatural power that animates the ſoul.
3 ſoul.
4 ghoſt of a dead body.
5 genius, humour, or nature.
6 principle, as to do any thing out of a ſpirit of charity.
7 wit, or livelineſs.
8 courage, or pride.

SPI'SSITY, or SPI'SSITUDE, thickneſs.
To SPIT, 1 to put on the ſpit.
2 to throw out of one's mouth.
SPIT, a utenſil to roaſt meat withal.
SPITE, malice, grudge, ſpleen.
SPI'TEFUL, full of malice, ill-natured.
SPI'TTLE, 1 a moiſture ariſing in the mouth.
2 a contraction of hoſpital.
SPI'TTER, 1 one that ſpits often.
         2 (among

Figure 3. Benjamin Martin, *Lingua Britannica Reformata* (1749). These entries show italic headwords, the use of primes, and the separate sub-paragraphs for numbered senses. Note the style and alignment of sense numbers, which range on the inside. The first sense is sometimes allowed to run on from the headword (e.g. *spittle*) (100%).

---

‡ Marque un Mot, ou une Expreſſion qui a vieilli, & qui eſt hors d'Uſage.

† Un Mot, ou une Expreſſion baſſe, ou dont on ſe ſert dans le Stile comique & burleſque.

D † Un Mot ou une Expreſſion Douteuſe, c'eſt-à-dire, dont l'Uſage n'eſt pas établi, & ſur laquelle les Auteurs ſont partagez.

☞ Les differentes Significations d'un Mot.

* Un Mot ou une Expreſſion figurée.

* † Mot ou Expreſſion baſſe, dont on ſe ſert dans le Figuré.

P. Un Proverbe, ou une Expreſſion Proverbiale.

R. Une Remarque.

V. Signifie *Vide*, Voyez.

S. ou Subſt. Subſtantif.

S. ou Subſt. M. Subſtantif du Genre Maſculin.

‡ *Marks an Obſolete Word or Expreſſion.*

† *A Mean or Vulgar Word or Expreſſion.*

D † *A Dubious Word or Expreſſion; that is, an Expreſſion of no general Uſe, and about which Authors are divided.*

☞ *The Different Significations of a Word.*

* *A Figurative Word or Expreſſion.*

* † *A Mean Word or Expreſſion uſed in a Figurative Senſe.*

P. or Prov. *Proverb or Proverbial Expreſſion.*

R. *A Remark.*

V. *Stands for Vide, See.*

S. or Subſt. *a Subſtantive.*

S. or Subſt. M. *a Subſtantive of the Maſculine*

Figure 4. Abel Boyer, *The Royal Dictionary* (1727). The page facing the start of letter A explains the symbols and abbreviations used. The same abbreviations work in both English and French (75%).

a dictionary designed not merely for critics but for popular use, that it should comprise, in some degree, the peculiar words of every profession" (1825 *Works*, vol. v, pp. 3, 5). Johnson discusses the structural distinctions within the proposed dictionary. These relate to discrimination: "words are to be distinguished according to the different classes, whether simple, as *day, light*, or compound as *day-light*" (1825 *Works*, vol. v, p. 9), and to the sequence of senses within an entry: "it seems necessary to sort the several senses of each word, and to exhibit first its natural and primitive signification" (1825 *Works*, vol. v, p. 14). He does not (with one exception) discuss the typographic implementation of his structure: "But there ought, however, to be some distinction made between the different classes of words, and therefore it will be proper to print those which are incorporated into the language in the usual character, and those which are still considered as foreign in the Italick letter" (1825 *Works*, vol. v, p. 5). And in discussing the explanation of the status of words, he is not explicit about the form that any "marking" of the text (in a typographical sense) might take:

Words of general use will be known by having no sign of particularity . . .
   The words appropriate to poetry will be differentiated by some mark prefixed . . .
   Of antiquated or obsolete words . . . These will likewise be pointed out by some note of exclusion, but not of disgrace . . .
   Words used in burlesque and familiar compositions . . . will be diligently characterised by marks of distinction.
   Barbarous or impure words and expressions, may be branded with some note of infamy. (1825 *Works*, vol. v, pp. 18–19)

The "marking" of such categories of words by specifically graphic means had clear precedents by Johnson's day, in Benjamin Martin's *Lingua Britannica Reformata* and in Abel Boyer's *Royal Dictionary*.[21] Martin used a dagger to indicate words "not to be used in common Discourse, or the genteel Diction,"[22] and italics for alien words. He marked headwords with a single prime to indicate the stress, a double prime to indicate the pronunciation, and a superior numeral to show the number of syllables in ambiguous words (figure 3).[23]

   A more extensive use of symbols and abbreviations had been used in the 1727 Amsterdam edition of Boyer's French–English, English–French dictionary, reflecting the more developed typography of bilingual dictionaries. The list of the symbols includes those for obsolete (‡) or vulgar (†) words, figurative uses (*), and a symbol to indicate each separate sense (☞) (figure 4).

But there is no developed symbol system in Johnson's *Dictionary*. The only symbol used there is the single prime to indicate stress position in the headword. "Marking" of words by typographic means is only done by fount variation, as follows:

ALL CAPS
   headwords which are base forms (e.g. CEREMONY)

CAP AND SMALL CAPS
   derived headwords (e.g. CEREMONIAL, CEREMONIALNESS, CEREMONIOUS, etc.)[24]

Italic

  1. part-of-speech labels and the particle "*To*" preceding verb headwords
  2. cited forms in etymologies (both English and other languages)
  3. the headword when it appears in the illustrative quotations
  4. the names of authors and their works in the sources to the illustrative quotations
  5. derivatives, compounds, phrasal verbs, idioms, and phrases based on the headword.

Etymologies and subject-field labels are differentiated by being set within square brackets, following the style of Bailey's *Dictionarium Britannicum*. A single, steeply angled prime is inserted into headwords to indicate stress; this interferes little with the shape of the headword. The cap-and-small-caps headwords appear to be slightly letter-spaced. The all-cap headwords are not particularly strong in color but, because they fill the type body, they crowd the line above: the cap-and-small-caps style introduces a useful amount of white space which separates those headwords from the entries above them. Headwords are followed by a part-of-speech abbreviation, in italic lower case. Then comes the etymology, in roman with cited words italicized, the whole enclosed within square brackets. (Johnson, like Phillips,[25] also uses this style to provide subject-field label information.) Cross-references to headwords are in the form of the target headword, whether all-cap or cap-and-small-caps, since there was as yet no conventional form for a cross-reference.

NUMBERED SENSES AND ILLUSTRATIVE QUOTATIONS

Benjamin Martin's *Lingua Britannica Reformata* predates Johnson's use of numbered senses in each entry; indeed it is "the first English dictionary to provide numbered, multiple meanings arranged according to a logically delineated system" (Reddick, *The Making of Johnson's Dictionary*, p. 59). An interesting comparison can be made between the two dictionaries. The sense divisions in Martin's typography have a startlingly modern appearance: not only are sense numbers set without a following full point, there is no capitalization of the first letter of the defining phrase – features which did not recur until well into the twentieth century. Johnson's page is more traditional: sense numbers are followed by a full point, and the start of each definition is capitalized. Each of Martin's senses, however, is a simple definition, with no subsidiary element, and there are no associated illustrative quotations.

The shortness of the individual sense definitions allows Martin's sense numbers to be indented, reinforcing their subsidiary status, and allowing them to range on the inside, which gives a much neater appearance at the change from one- to two-digit numbers. Johnson's longer definitions, and the presence of quotations, prevent this useful feature: in the folio design sense numbers are the only other element set full out and aligning with the headwords.

Johnson's folio page depends on strict typographic regularity of paragraph styling to articulate its text, because it has so few other typographic resources. As well as eschewing symbols, there is only one size of type used, and no use is made of vertical spacing. Johnson allocated a separate paragraph to each sense and each quotation within each entry. This generous style of setting reinforces the innovative features of the *Dictionary*, connecting each quotation with the relevant sense, but it is space-consuming. The single type size used forces the folio design to differentiate items by paragraph format, leaving differences of indentation and alignment, rather than type size, to help the reader understand the structure of entries (figure 5).

Although at first glance this use of roman, italic, and small caps in a single size may seem an underdeveloped typography, in practice it does give prominence to the headwords and to the two innovative features of the text, the sense numbering and the sources of the illustrative quotations, because these are the only elements thrown fully to the left and right of the column respectively. The multiple senses of the verb *to carry* (thirty-two are given), for instance, are immediately obvious; the ranged-right italic sources are as prominent as the headwords, and can be seen as providing an alternative access system – the reader can scan down the right-hand edge of the column to locate specific authors (figure 6).

C E R

4. Civil; according to the ſtrict rules of civility; formally reſpectful.
They have a ſet of *ceremonious* phraſes, that run through all
ranks and degrees among them.   *Addiſon. Guard.* N° 104.
5. Obſervant of the rules of civility.
Then let us take a *ceremonious* leave,
And loving farewel of our ſeveral friends. *Shakeſp. R. III.*
6. Civil and formal to a fault.
The old caitiff was grown ſo *ceremonious*, as he would needs
accompany me ſome miles in my way.   *Sidney, b.* ii.
CEREMO'NIOUSLY. *adv.* [from *ceremonious.*]   In a ceremonious
manner; formally; reſpectful.
Ceremoniouſly let us prepare
Some welcome for the miſtreſs of the houſe.
                              Shakeſp. Two Gentlemen of Verona.
CEREMO'NIOUSNESS. *n. ſ.* [from *ceremonious.*]   Fondneſs of ce-
remony; uſing too much ceremony.
CE'REMONY. *n. ſ.* [*ceremonia,* Lat.]
1. Outward rite; external form in religion.
Bring her up to the high altar, that ſhe may
The ſacred *ceremonies* partake.   *Spenſer's Epithalamium.*
He is ſuperſtitious grown of late,
Quite from the main opinion he held once
Of fantaſy, of dreams, and *ceremonies.* *Shakeſp. J. Cæſar.*
Diſrobe the images,
If you find them deck'd with *ceremony.* *Shakeſp. J. Cæſar.*
2. Forms of civility.
The ſauce to meat is *ceremony*;
Meeting were bare without it.   *Shakeſp. Macbeth.*
Not to uſe *ceremonies* at all, is to teach others not to uſe them
again, and ſo diminiſh reſpect to himſelf.   *Bacon.*
3. Outward forms of ſtate.
What art thou, thou idle *ceremony?*
What kind of god art thou, that ſuffer'ſt more
Of mortal grief, than do thy worſhippers?
Art thou aught elſe but place, degree, and form?
                              Shakeſp. Henry V.
A coarſer place,
Where pomp and *ceremonies* enter'd not,
Where greatneſs was ſhut out, and bigneſs well forgot.
                              Dryden's Fables.
CE'ROTE. *n. ſ.* The ſame with *cerate*; which ſee.
In thoſe which are critical, a *cerote* of oil of olives, with
white wax, hath hitherto ſerved my purpoſe.   *Wiſeman.*
CE'RTAIN. *adj.* [*certus,* Lat.]

Figure 5. Johnson, *1755*. Compare the style of headwords with Bailey, and the style of sense numbers with Martin. *1755* has fuller author and work citations than *1765* or *1773* (93%).

Nor all thy tricks and flights to cheat,
Sell all thy *carrion* for good meat. *Hudibras.*
The wolves will get a breakfast by my death,
Yet scarce enough their hunger to supply,
For love has made me *carrion* ere I die. *Dryden.*

CA'RRION. *adj.* [from the subst.] Relating to carcases; feeding upon carcases.
    Match to match I have encounter'd him,
And made a prey for *carrion* kites and crows,
Ev'n of the bonny beasts he lov'd so well. *Shakespeare.*
    The charity of our death-bed visits from one another, is much at a rate with that of a *carrion* crow to a sheep; we smell a carcase. *L'Estrange.*

CA'RROT. *n. s.* [*carote*, Fr. *daucus*, Lat.]
    It hath a fleshy root; the leaves are divided into narrow segments; the petals of the flower are unequal, and shaped like a heart; the umbel, when ripe, is hollowed and contracted, appearing somewhat like a bird's nest; the seeds are hairy, and in shape of lice. The species are; 1. Common wild *carrot.* 2. Dwarf wild *carrot*, with broader leaves. 3. Dark red-rooted garden *carrot.* 4. The orange coloured *carrot.* 5. The white *carrot.* The first grows wild upon arable land, and is seldom cultivated. This is the particular sort which should be used in medicine, and for which the druggists commonly sell the seeds of the garden *carrot.* The third and fourth sorts are commonly cultivated for the kitchen; as is the fifth sort, though not so common in England. The white is generally preferred for the sweetest. But, in order to preserve *carrots* for use all the winter and spring, about the beginning of November, when the green leaves are decayed, dig them up, and lay them in sand in a dry place, where the frost cannot come to them. *Miller.*
    Carrots, though garden roots, yet they do well in the fields for feed, though the land for them should rather be digged than plowed. *Mortimer.*
    His spouse orders the sack to be immediately opened, and greedily pulls out of it half a dozen bunches of *carrots.* *Dennis.*

CA'RROTINESS. *n. s.* [from *carrots.*] Redness of hair.

CA'RROTY. *adj.* [from *carrot.*] Spoken of red hair, on account of its resemblance in colour to carrots.

CA'RROWS. *n. s.* [an Irish word.]
    The *carrows* are a kind of people that wander up and down to gentlemens houses, living only upon cards and dice; who, though they have little or nothing of their own, yet will they play for much money. *Spenser.*

To CA'RRY. *v. a.* [*charier*, Fr. from *currus*, Lat. See CAR.]
1. To convey *from* a place; opposed to *bring*, or convey *to* a place.
    When he dieth, he shall *carry* nothing away. *Psalms.*
    And devout men *carried* Stephen to his burial. *Acts.*
    I mean to *carry* her away this evening, by the help of these two soldiers. *Dryden.*
    As in a hive's viminous dome,
Ten thousand bees enjoy their home;
Each does her studious action vary,
To go and come, to fetch and *carry.* *Prior.*
    They exposed their goods with the price marked upon them, then retired; the merchants came, left the price which they would give upon the goods, and likewise retired; the Seres returning, *carried* off either their goods or money, as they liked best. *Arbuthnot.*
2. To transport.
    They began to *carry* about in beds those that were sick. *Mark, vi. 55.*
    The species of audibles seem to be *carried* more manifestly through the air, than the species of visibles. *Bacon.*
    Where many great ordnance are shot off together, the sound will be *carried*, at the least, twenty miles upon the land. *Bacon.*
3. To bear; to have about one.
    Do not take out bones like surgeons I have met with, who *carry* them about in their pockets. *Wiseman.*
4. To take; to have with one.
    If the ideas of liberty and volition were *carried* along with us in our minds, a great part of the difficulties that perplex mens thoughts would be easier resolved. *Locke.*
    I have listened with my utmost attention for half an hour to an orator, without being able to *carry* away one single sentence out of a whole sermon. *Swift.*
5. To convey by force.
    Go, *carry* Sir John Falstaff to the Fleet;
Take all his company along with him. *Shakespeare.*
6. To effect any thing.
    There are some vain persons, that whatsoever goeth alone, or moveth upon greater means, if they have never so little hand in it, they think it is they that *carry* it. *Bacon.*
    Oft-times we lose the occasion of *carrying* a business well thoroughly by our too much haste. *Ben. Johnson.*
    These advantages will be of no use, unless we improve them to words, in the *carrying* of our main point. *Addison.*
7. To gain in competition.
    And hardly shall I *carry* out my side,
Her husband being alive. *Shakespeare.*
    How many stand for consulships?—Three, they say; but it is thought of every one Coriolanus will *carry* it. *Shakesp.*

I see not yet how many of these six reasons can be fairly avoided; and yet if any of them hold good, it is enough to *carry* the cause. *Saunderson.*
    The latter still enjoying his place, and continuing a joint commissioner of the treasury, still opposed, and commonly *carried* away every thing against him. *Clarendon.*
8. To gain after resistance.
    The count wooes your daughter,
Lays down his wanton siege before her beauty;
Resolves to *carry* her; let her consent,
As we'll direct her now, 'tis best to bear it. *Shakesp.*
    What a fortune does the thick lips owe,
If he can *carry* her thus? *Shakespeare.*
    The town was distressed, and ready for an assault, which, if it had been given, would have cost much blood; but yet the town would have been *carried* in the end. *Bacon.*
9. To prevail: with it. [*le porter*, Fr.]
    Are you all resolved to give your voices?
    But that's no matter; the greater part *carries* it. *Shakesp.*
    By these, and the like arts, they promised themselves, that they should *carry* it; so that they entertained the house all the morning with other debates. *Clarendon.*
    If the numerousness of a train must *carry* it, virtue may go follow Astræa, and vice only will be worth the courting. *Glanv.*
    Children, who live together, often strive for mastery, whose wills shall *carry* it over the rest. *Locke.*
    In pleasures and pains, the present is apt to *carry* it, and those at a distance have the disadvantage in the comparison. *Locke.*
10. To bear out; to face through; to outface.
    If a man *carries* it off, there is so much money saved; and if he be detected, there will be something pleasant in the frolick. *L'Estrange.*
11. To preserve external appearance.
    My niece is already in the belief that he's mad; we may *carry* it thus for our pleasure, and his penance. *Shakesp.*
12. To manage; to transact.
    The senate is generally as numerous as our house of commons; and yet *carries* its resolutions so privately, that they are seldom known. *Addison.*
13. To behave; to conduct; with the reciprocal pronoun.
    Neglect not also the examples of those that have *carried* themselves ill in the same place. *Bacon.*
    He attended the king into Scotland, where he did *carry* himself with much singular sweetness and temper. *Wotton.*
    He *carried* himself so insolently in the house, and out of the house, to all persons, that he became odious. *Clarendon.*
14. To bring forward; to advance in any progress.
    It is not to be imagined how far constancy will *carry* a man; however, it is better walking slowly in a rugged way, than to break a leg and be a cripple. *Locke.*
    This plain natural way, without grammar, can *carry* them to a great degree of elegancy and politeness in their language. *Locke on Education.*
    There is no vice which mankind *carries* to such wild extremes, as that of avarice. *Swift.*
15. To urge; to bear on with some kind of external impulse.
    Men are strongly *carried* out to, and hardly took off from, the practice of vice. *South.*
    He that the world, or flesh, or devil, can *carry* away from the profession of an obedience to Christ, is no son of the faithful Abraham. *Hammond.*
    Ill nature, passion, and revenge, will *carry* them too far in punishing others; and therefore God hath certainly appointed government to restrain the partiality and violence of men. *Locke.*
16. To bear; to have; to obtain.
    In some vegetables, we see something that *carries* a kind of analogy to sense; they contract their leaves against the cold; they open them to the favourable heat. *Hale.*
17. To exhibit; to show; to display on the outside; to set to view.
    The aspect of every one in the family *carries* so much satisfaction, that it appears he knows his happy lot. *Addison.*
18. To imply; to import.
    It *carries* some great an imputation of ignorance, lightness or folly, for men to quit and renounce their former tenets, presently upon the offer of an argument, which they cannot immediately answer. *Locke.*
19. To contain.
    He thought it *carried* something of argument in it, to prove that doctrine. *Watts.*
20. To have annexed; to have any thing joined.
    There was a righteous and a searching law, directly forbidding such practices; and they knew that it *carried* with it the divine stamp. *South.*
    There are many expressions, which *carry* with them to my mind no clear ideas. *Locke.*
    The obvious portions of extension, that affect our senses, *carry* with them into the mind the idea of finite. *Locke.*
21. To convey or bear any thing united or adhering, by communication of motion.
    We see also manifestly, that sounds are *carried* with wind;
2   and

Figure 6. Johnson, *1765*, showing the entry for *to carry* with thirty-two senses (53%).

The indentation and alignment structure used is as follows:

Headword: full out on a one-em hanging indentation; grammatical category (italic) and etymology or subject-field label (in square brackets)
run on from headword. If there is a single definition sense, this also
runs on.

Numbered senses: full out on a one-em hanging indentation.

Quotations, prose: first line indented two ems, turned line indented one
em.

Quotations, poetry: first line indented three ems, subsequent lines
indented two ems. If the quotation starts with a part-line, the indentation is increased. Otherwise poetry is set observing the lineation of
the original.[26]

Sources: ranged right on the measure; usually in the break-line of the
quotation, otherwise on a line of its own.

While the indentation structure is carefully observed, flexibility is shown
in the composition of some elements. In verse quotations, part lines are
sometimes reinforced with em rules, sometimes not, and the space value
varies from an indentation to apparent centering of the line. Abbreviations
in sources vary considerably: they can be as complete as "*Milton's Par. Lost,
b. ix, l. 953*" or as bald as "*Shak.*"

If there is a problem with the folio design it is that the paragraphing tends
to break up the coherence of longer entries – they do not form strong visual
units on the page. A number of features contribute to this. One, already
mentioned, is the relative weakness of the color of the headwords, and the
fact that they share an alignment with the sense numbers, and so do not
sufficiently dominate them. Although the setting is admirably consistent in
observing the different indentation structures of definition, and verse and
prose quotations, a certain nervousness results from the constant shifting
of alignments. The very positive graphic shape of the poetry quotations
gives them prominence – the reader sees the shape of each poem – and the
varying amount of white space between the (left-aligned) verse lines and
the (right-aligned) source lines dilutes the page.

DESIGN VARIATIONS

The octavo and quarto editions provide useful comparisons with the folio
design, because to some degree all the smaller editions have to compromise
the text and its presentation in order to fit a smaller page size. Between them,
they show significant differences in design, and differences in effectiveness
for the reader.

London octavo design

As stated above, the two London octavo editions (*1756* and *1760*) are similar enough to be considered as one design, which differs significantly from that of the Dublin octavo (*1758*). Johnson's Preface to *1758* explains its relation to the folio: while the folio edition was "for the use of such as aspire to exactness of criticism or elegance of style," the "greater number of readers, who, seldom intending to write or presuming to judge, turn over books only to amuse their leisure" could use the octavo edition to "gain degrees of knowledge suitable to lower characters, or necessary for the business of life: these know not any other use of a dictionary than that of adjusting orthography, or explaining terms of science or words of infrequent occurrence, or remote derivation." Among the several advantages of his work, Johnson explained his innovative features as follows:

v. The senses of each word are more copiously enumerated, and more clearly explained . . .

vii. To the words, and to the different senses of each word, are subjoined from the large dictionary names of those writers by whom they have been used; so that the reader who knows the different periods of the language, and the time of its authors, may judge of the elegance or prevalence of any word; and without recurring to other books, may know what are antiquated, and what are usual, and what are recommended by the best authority. (*1756*, sig. π2^v)

The octavos condense the folio text by omission of entries, compression of etymologies and definitions, and the removal of all illustrative quotations; however, as implied in the Preface, for each sense the name of an author or source remains. While the text of the London and Dublin octavos may be similar, the appearance of the pages is not.

The London octavo design is effectively a miniaturization of the folio design. It follows the folio (and Benjamin Martin's octavo *Lingua Britannica Reformata*) in retaining paragraphing within entries: each sense has its own paragraph, with sense numbers indented, and the relevant author or source is set flush right on the same line (figure 7). The visual effect of the "stacking" of sense numbers at the left, and of author names at the right of the columns, apparent in the folio, is if anything even more insistent on the smaller page, as senses often occupy only one or two lines, so that there are often no intervening full-measure lines between consecutive author or source names. The London design, like the folio, does not have a center rule. Of course the simplification of the text extends to the typography: the distinction between two classes of headwords is lost, and an all-cap style is used for all headwords, although the italicization of aliens remains. The particle "To"

To CA'RRY. v. a. [charier, Fr.]
1. To convey from a place. Dryden.
2. To transport. Bacon.
3. To bear; to have about one. Wiseman.
4. To convey by force. Shakespeare.
5. To effect any thing. Ben. Johnson.
6. To gain in competition. Shakespeare.
7. To gain after resistance. Shakespeare.
8. To manage; to transact. Addison.
9. To behave; to conduct. Clarendon.
10. To bring forward. Locke.
11. To urge; to bear. Hammond.
12. To have; to obtain. Hale.
13. To display on the outside. Addison.
14. To imply; to import. Locke.
15. To have annexed. South.
16. To move any thing. Addison.
17. To push on ideas in a train. Hale.
18. To receive; to endure. Bacon.
19. To support; to sustain. Bacon.
20. To bear, as trees. Bacon.
21. To fetch and bring, as dogs. Ascham.
22. To carry off. To kill. Temple.
23. To carry on. To promote; to help forward. Addison.
24. To carry through. To keep from failing. Hammond.
To CA'RRY. v. n. A horse is said to carry well, when his neck is arched, and holds his head high.

CERE MONIAL. a. [from ceremony.]
1. Relating to ceremony, or outward rite. Stillingfleet.
2. Formal; observant of old forms. Donne.
CEREMO'NIAL. s. [from ceremony.]
1. Outward form; external rite. Swift.
2. The order for rites and forms in the Roman church.
CEREMO'NIALNESS. s. The quality of being ceremonial.
CEREMO'NIOUS. a. [from ceremony.]
1. Consisting of outward rites. South.
2. Full of ceremony; awful. Shakesp.
3. Attentive to the outward rites of religion. Shakespeare.
4. Civil; according to the strict rules of civility. Addison.
5. Civil and formal to a fault. Sidney.
CEREMO'NIOUSLY. ad. In a ceremonious manner; formally. Shakespeare.
CEREMO'NIOUSNESS. s. Fondness of ceremony.
CE'REMONY. s. [ceremonia, Lat.]
1. Outward rite; external form in religion. Spenser.
2. Forms of civility. Bacon.
3. Outward forms of state. Dryden.
CE'ROTE. s. The same with cerate. Wiseman.
CE'RTAIN. a. [certus, Lat.]

Figure 7. Johnson, *1760*, entries for *to carry* and *ceremony*. Compare the style of sense numbers with Martin (figure 3) and the folio design (figures 5 and 6) (90%).

is no longer italicized, but other elements, such as part-of-speech labels and cited forms, remain set in italic.

Dublin octavo design

The Dublin octavo design adopts a more obviously space-saving approach, and runs on all the items, including senses, within a single entry paragraph (figure 8). By dispensing with the folio design's intra-entry paragraphing altogether it destroys any immediate graphic sense of structure. While the entry in the London octavo design is articulated by paragraphing, the Dublin octavo design relies less satisfactorily on horizontal spacing and typeface differentiation within the line. Extra space is set between the end of each sense and the number for the next, and also between each sense number and its sense. Sense numbers are, irritatingly, allowed to fall at the ends of lines. Compactness is achieved in this edition at the expense of providing the reader with an instant overview of the structure of each entry, which is maintained in the London design. The Dublin design follows the London design in details such as the capitalization of headwords, the reduction of etymologies, and the romanization of the particle "To."

CA'RROTINESS. *f.* [from *carroty*.] Rednefs of hair.
CA'RROTY. *a.* [from *carrot*.] Spoken of red hair.
To CA'RRY. *v. a.* [*charier*, Fr.] 1. To convey *from* a place. *Dryden*. 2. To tranfport. *Bacon.* 3. To bear; to have about one. *Wifeman.* 4. To convey by force. *Shakefp.* 5. To effect any thing. *Ben. Johnfon.* 6. To gain in competition. *Shakefp.* 7. To gain after refiftance. *Shakefp.* 8. To manage; to tranfact. *Addifon.* 9. To behave; to conduct. *Clarendon.* 10. To bring forward. *Locke.* 11. To urge; to bear. *Hammond.* 12. To have; to obtain. *Hale.* 13. To difplay on the outfide. *Addifon.* 14. To imply; to import. *Locke.* 15. To have annexed. *South.* 16. To move any thing. *Addifon.* 17. To pufh on ideas in a train. *Hale.* 18. To receive; to endure. *Bacon.* 19. To fupport; to fuftain. *Bacon.* 20. To bear, as trees. *Bacon.* 21. To fetch and bring, as dogs. *Afcham.* 22. *To carry off.* To kill. *Temple.* 23. *To carry on.* To promote; to help forward. *Addifon.* 24. *To carry through.* To keep from falling. *Hammond.*
To CARRY. *v. n.* A horfe is faid to *carry well*, when his neck is arched, and he holds his head high.

CERE'MONIAL. *a.* [from *ceremony*.] 1. Relating to ceremony, or outward rite. *Stillingfl.* 2. Formal; obfervant of old forms. *Donne.*
CEREMO'NIAL. *f.* [from *ceremony*.] 1. Outward form; external rite. *Swift.* 2. The order for rites and forms in the Roman church.
CEREMO'NIALNESS. *f.* The quality of being ceremonial.
CEREMO'NIOUS. *a.* [from *ceremony*.] 1. Confifting of outward rites. *South.* 2. Full of ceremony; awful. *Shakefp.* 3. Attentive to the outward rites of religion. *Shakefp.* 4. Civil; according to the ftrict rules of civility. *Addifon.* 5. Civil and formal to a fault. *Sidney.*
CEREMO'NIOUSLY. *adv.* In a ceremonious manner; formally. *Shakefp.*
CEREMO'NIOUSNESS. *f.* Fondnefs of ceremony.
CE'REMONY. *f.* [*ceremonia*, Lat.] 1. Outward rite; external form in religion. *Spenfer.* 2. Forms of civility. *Bacon.* 3. Outward forms of ftate. *Dryden.*
CE'ROTE. *f.* The fame with *cerate*. *Wifeman.*
CE'RTAIN. *a.* [*certus*, Lat.] 1. Sure; indubitable; unqueftionable. *Tillotfon.* 2. Refolved; determined. *Milton.* 3. In an indefinite fenfe, fome; as, a *certain* man told me this. *Wilkins.* 4. Undoubting; put paft doubt.

Figure 8. Johnson, *1758*, entries for *to carry* and *ceremony*. The unnecessarily thick column rule has a precedent in Bailey's *Universal Etymological Dictionary* (1727) (90%).

Dublin quarto design

The quarto design of *1777* is a hybrid, compressing the folio content rather than radically abridging it. As a result, it is altogether more of a compromise. In the folio design illustrative quotations immediately follow the relevant sense definition. In the quarto design, each entry is divided into a bank of definitions and a separate bank of quotations (figure 9). All the numbered sense definitions are given first, run on, in a larger size of type. The quotations are then set in smaller type. Each quotation is given its own paragraph, and cross-referenced to the relevant sense by its number in parentheses. While the differentiation of type size reinforces the difference between definitions and illustrative quotations, compactness has been achieved at the expense of a clumsy cross-reference system, which reduces the status of the illustrations as an integral part of the plan and purpose of the *Dictionary*.

Prose and verse quotations are differentiated as in the folio design: prose is em-indented, with turns full out; the first line of a poetry quotation is indented two ems, with subsequent lines indented one em. The sense numbers are the first item in each quotation paragraph, and therefore have to follow the relevant indentation, leading to an uneven alignment

Figure 9. Johnson, *1777*, entries for *to carry* and *ceremony*. Larger type is used for the definition bank, smaller type for the illustrative quotations (65%).

at the left. The smaller type size emphasizes the difference between prose and poetry, as a proportionally greater amount of white space is left to the right of poetry, detaching (and emphasizing) the sources. The quarto follows the folio in distinguishing two headword classes, although its cap and small caps headwords are more widely letter-spaced, and in the use of italics. All in all the quarto succeeds in making whole entries more coherent than they are in the folio, because they are more compact, but at the expense of forcing the reader to cross-refer between definition and quotations.

To CA'RRY. *v. a.* [*charier*, Fr. from *cur-rus*, Lat.]

1. To convey *from* a place : oppofed to *bring*, or convey *to* a place : often with a particle, fignifying departure, as *away, off.*

 When he dieth, he fhall *carry* nothing *away.*
  Pfalm xlix. 18.
 And devout men *carried* Stephen to his burial.
  Acts, viii. 2.
 I mean to *carry* her *away* this evening by the help of thefe two foldiers. *Dryden's Spanifh Friar.*
 As in a hive's vimineous dome,
 Ten thoufand bees enjoy their home;
 Each does her ftudious action vary,
  To go and come, to fetch and *carry.* *Prior.*
 They expofed their goods with the price mark-ed, then retired ; the merchants came, left the price which they would give upon the goods, and retired ; the Seres returning, *carried off* either their goods or money, as they liked beft. *Arbuthnot.*

2. To tranfport.
 They began to *carry* about in beds thofe that were fick. *Mark,* vi. 55.
 The fpecies of audibles feem to be *carried* more manifeftly through the air, than the fpecies of vifibles. *Bacon.*
 Where many great ordnance are fhot off toge-ther, the found will be *carried,* at the leaft, twenty miles upon the land. *Bacon.*

3. To bear ; to have about one.
 Do not take out bones like furgeons I have met with, who *carry* them about in their pockets.
  Wifeman's Surgery.

To CA'RRY. *v. a.* [*charier*, Fr. from *currus*, Lat.]

1. To convey *from* a place : opposed to *bring*, or convey *to* a place : often with a particle, signifying departure, as *away, off.*

 When he dieth he shall *carry* nothing *away.*
  Psalms.
 And devout men *carried* Stephen to his burial.
  Acts.
 I mean to *carry* her *away* this evening by the help of these two soldiers. *Dryden's Span. Friar.*
 As in a hive's vimineous dome,
 Ten thousand bees enjoy their home;
 Each does her studious action vary,
 To go and come, to fetch and *carry.* *Prior.*
 They exposed their goods with the price marked, then retired ; the merchants came, left the price which they would give upon the goods, and retired; the Seres returning, *carried off* either their goods or money, as they liked best. *Arbuth.*

2. To transport.
 They began to *carry* about in beds those that were sick. *Mark.*
 The species of audibles seem to be *carried* more manifestly through the air, than the species of visibles. *Bacon.*
 Where many great ordnance are shot off to-gether, the sound will be *carried,* at the least, twenty miles upon the land. *Bacon.*

3. To bear ; to have about one.
 Do not take out bones like surgeons I have met with, who *carry* them about in their pockets.
  Wiseman's Surgery.

4. To take ; to have with one.
 If the ideas of liberty and volition were *carried* along with us in our minds, a great part of the difficulties that perplex men's thoughts would be

Figure 10. Johnson, *1785Q* and *1805*, entries for *to carry*. This entry from *1785Q* shows a short-line verse quotation deeply indented; verse quotations with longer lines are not differentiated by indent from prose quotations (90%).

The 1785 design

The quarto and folio editions published shortly after Johnson's death share a basic design using two sizes of type, which is also used by a later octavo edition. This design resolves some of the issues raised by the earlier designs, and can be regarded as the direct precursor for the design of later English dictionaries.

The quarto *1785Q* is set in three columns, with rather heavy column rules. The original folio design is followed, except that all the illustrative quotations are set in small type, and the differentiation of verse from prose quotations by the use of a deeper indent is not observed. One inconsistency arises: sources are set in small type when they follow quotations, but in the large size when a definition is given a source (figure 10).

The folio *1785F* follows *1785Q* almost exactly, using the same founts, set in three columns with column rules.[27] The greater width of the columns on the folio page allows verse to be differentiated from prose quotations by the use of a deeper indent – deeper in fact that that of the original folio design.

This basic design was also used in the octavo *1805*; however, the larger of the founts used is on a smaller body. Again, verse and prose quotations are not differentiated by indent. There are no column rules, and the long "s" has been abandoned.

For these unabridged editions, the 1785 design combines clarity with relative compactness. It drives a course between earlier designs: the clear but sprawling folio and the problematic Dublin quarto. *1785F* is still an unwieldy tome, but *1785Q* is a manageable two volumes, and *1805* has a particularly elegant octavo page, in spite of running to four volumes. There are gains and losses over the original folio design: the clear division of senses is maintained, and possibly improved, because quotations are now visually subservient to the entry as a whole. This improves the reader's immediate grasp of the shape of an entry, but reduces the status of the quotations; and the small-type italic sources perform less well as an alternative access system, because it is less easy to scan the more tightly packed pages for them. Subsequent editions (for example *1824*) would retain the basic 1785 design, but use modern-face types.

THE TYPOGRAPHIC INFLUENCE OF
JOHNSON'S *DICTIONARY*

While certain design features of Johnson's *Dictionary* became standard, some had a limited life. Johnson's division of headwords into two classes was abandoned by all subsequent major dictionaries with the exception of Richardson's.[28] All-cap headwords remained the norm until the introduction of boldface headwords in the late nineteenth century. The layout of Noah Webster's *American Dictionary of the English Language* (1828) owes much to *1785Q* and *1824*, but has the advantage that its all-cap headwords are distinctly dark and therefore more prominent, because the typeface used is a "Scotch" modern roman, where the capitals have a considerably heavier stroke weight than the lower case. Webster followed the folio design in the paragraphing and alignment of sense numbers. He too used a smaller type size for quotations, making them subsidiary to the entry as a whole, and this was the style that continued in the *Imperial Dictionary*, Worcester's dictionary, and the *Century Dictionary* (figure 11).[29] Indeed, it was not until James Murray was faced with a much larger number of

ABAN'DON, *v. t.* [Fr. *abandonner*; Sp. and Port. *abandonar*; It. *abbandonare*; said to be from *ban*, and *donner*, to give over to the ban or proscription; or from *a* or *ab* and *bandum*, a flag or ensign.] 1. To forsake entirely; as to *abandon* a hopeless enterprize. Wo to that generation by which the testimony of God shall be *abandoned*. *Dr. Mason.* 2. To renounce and forsake; to leave with a view never to return; to desert as lost or desperate; as to *abandon* a country; to *abandon* a cause or party. 3. To give up or resign without control, as when a person yields himself, without restraint, to a propensity; as to *abandon* one's self *to* intemperance. Abandoned *over* and abandoned *of* are obsolete. 4. To resign; to yield, relinquish, or give over entirely. Verus *abandoned* the cares of empire to his wiser colleague. *Gibbon.* ABAN'DON, *n.* One who totally forsakes or deserts. *Obs.* 2. A relinquishment. [*Not used.*] *Kames.* ABAN'DONED, *pp.* Wholly forsaken or deserted. 2. Given up, as to a vice; hence, extremely wicked, or sinning without restraint; irreclaimably wicked.	abandon (ạ-ban'dọn), *v. t.* [< ME. *abandonen, abandounen*, < OF. *abanduner, abandoner* (F. *abandonner* = It. *abandonnare*), abandon, equiv. to *mettre a bandon*, put under any one's jurisdiction, leave to any one's discretion or mercy, etc., < *a bandon*, in ME. as an adv. *abandon, abandoun*, under one's jurisdiction, in one's discretion or power: *a* (< L. *ad*), at, to; *bandon*, a proclamation, decree, order, jurisdiction, = Pr. *bandon*, < ML. **bando(n-)*, extended form of *bandum*, more correctly *bannum*, a proclamation, decree, ban: see *ban¹, n.*] **1.** To detach or withdraw one's self from; leave. (*a*) To desert; forsake utterly: as, to *abandon* one's home; to *aban-don* fear; to strength and counsel join'd Think nothing hard, much less to be despair'd. *Milton*, P. L., vi. 494. (*b*) To give up; cease to occupy one's self with; cease to use, follow, etc.: as, to *abandon* an enterprise; this custom was long ago *abandoned*. (*c*) To resign, forego, or renounce; relinquish all concern in: as, to *abandon* the cares of empire. To understand him, and to be charitable to him, we should remember that he *abandons* the vantage-ground of authorship, and allows his readers to see him without any decorous disguise or show of dignity. *Whipple*, Ess. and Rev., I. 167. (*d*) To relinquish the control of; yield up without restraint: as, he *abandoned* the city to the conqueror. **2†.** To outlaw; banish; drive out or away. Being all this time *abandon'd* from your bed. *Shak.*, T. of the S., Ind., 2. **3†.** To reject or renounce. Blessed shall ye be when men shall hate you and *abandon* your name as evil. *Rheims N. T.*, Luke vi. 22.

Figure 11. Entries from Noah Webster, *An American Dictionary of the English Language* (1828, left), and the *Century Dictionary* (1889, right), showing sense-numbered paragraphs and small-type quotations (83%).

quotations in the *OED* that a new system of running on quotations within a single paragraph was introduced, which solved both the issue of space consumption and that of making quotations subsidiary to the entry as a whole.

Johnson's *Dictionary* brought together for the first time key conventions for future dictionary presentation: the folio design is a system of typography that displays the structure of each entry, though there are inconsistencies of abbreviation and ambiguities. There are successes and failures in its presentation. Importantly, it graphically highlights the innovative features of the *Dictionary*: sense divisions are clear and provide a basis for future development and the illustrative quotation has been introduced into English dictionaries. In the 1785 design quotations are immediately distinguishable by size from the rest of the entry. This design provided a clear model for later dictionaries. In the same way that Johnson's *Dictionary* should not be seen as just a "literary" dictionary but also as a precursor of the systematic and "scientific" dictionaries of the nineteenth century, its typography can be seen as both a culmination and a springboard.

NOTES

The writing of this chapter was made possible by a grant from the Arts and Humanities Research Board (UK) under their Research Leave scheme. Figures 1 and 10 are reproduced from books in Reading University Library; figures 2, 5, and 11 from books in the Oxford English Dictionary library; figure 3 from a book in the English Faculty Library, University of Oxford; figures 4 and 6–9 from books in the Bodleian Library, Oxford.

1. Daniel Berkeley Updike, *Printing Types: Their History, Forms, and Use*, 2 vols. (Cambridge, Mass.: Harvard University Press, 1922), vol. II, p. 140.

2. James Aikman Cochrane, *Dr. Johnson's Printer: The Life of William Strahan* (London: Routledge & Kegan Paul, 1964), p. 29.

3. The work of Michael Hancher in considering the graphic and cultural qualities of nineteenth-century dictionaries is a significant exception. See Michael Hancher, "['The Century Dictionary':] Illustrations," *Dictionaries: Journal of the Dictionary Society of North America* 17 (1996), 79–115; and "Gazing at the Imperial Dictionary," *Book History* 1 (1998), 156–81. See also Paul Luna, "Clearly Defined: Continuity and Innovation in the Design of English Dictionaries," *Typography Papers* 4 (2000), 5–56, for a bibliography of writing on lexicography which relates to design.

4. Robert Waller, "The Typographic Contribution to Language: Towards a Model of Typographic Genres and their Underlying Structures," unpublished Ph.D. thesis, University of Reading (1987), pp. 172–182 (available at www.gem.stir.ac.uk/robwaller.html, 12 February 2004).

5. Bo Svensén, *Practical Lexicography: Principles and Methods of Dictionary-Making* (Oxford: Oxford University Press, 1993), pp. 218–19, provides a list of the fount variants currently considered normal for different structural elements.

6. The text of a recent UK press advertisement for a Honda car "defined" the vehicle's qualities as if they were dictionary entries, complete with "headwords," "phonetics," and "sense numbers." The typefaces used were very similar to those used in Oxford dictionaries.

7. Michael Twyman, "The Graphic Presentation of Language," *Information Design Journal* 3 (1982), 12.

8. Estienne's Preface to the *Thesaurus* includes the following comment on its design, which holds good for the *Dictionnaire*:

> Here the different senses of words have not been indiscriminately piled into one confused heap, but distinguished by making each one start on a new line throughout, even in cases of twenty or more variant meanings. Here, as a result of this elegant differentiation in sequential form, the variety not only of constructions but also of expressions has been noted, by the observation of a regular manner of expression in authoritative writers. (cited in Edgar Ewing Brandon, *Robert Estienne et le Dictionnaire française au xvie siècle* [Baltimore: J. H. Furst, 1904], p. 42 n. 3), passage translated by Leofranc Holford-Strevens

9. *Ortus Vocabulorum* (London, 1509).

10. John Ogilvie's *Imperial Dictionary* (Glasgow, 1850) sets the first headword in each column in full at the top of that column; explicit headlines had previously been used in Riddle's *Complete Latin–English Dictionary* (London, 1836). Webster's *American Dictionary of the English Language* (Springfield, Mass., 1854) still used guide letters at the top of each column.

11. Robert Hunter's *Encyclopædic Dictionary* (London, 1879) is the earliest use of bold headwords I have located (Luna, "Clearly Defined," p. 25). Michael Twyman, "The Bold Idea: The Use of Bold-Looking Types in the Nineteenth Century," *Journal of the Printing Historical Society* 22 (1993), 107–43, discusses the introduction and development of boldface types in general. Luna ("Clearly Defined," pp. 24–35) and John A. Simpson, "English Lexicography after Johnson to 1945," in *Wörterbücher – Dictionaries – Dictionnaires*, ed. Franz Josef Hausmann *et al.* (Berlin: Walter de Gruyter, 1990), p. 1964, identify later popular dictionaries with boldface headwords.

12. Joseph Moxon, discussing fount variation in relation to title-page copy, states, "And what Words of Emphasis come in that precedent Matter; that he [the compositor] may *Set* them either in *Capitals, Roman, Italick*, or *English* [black letter]." See Moxon, *Mechanick Exercises on the Whole Art of Printing*, ed. Herbert Davies and Harry Carter (London: Oxford University Press, 1958), §22, ¶5.

13. Charles Richardson, *A New Dictionary of the English Language* (London, serial publication 1817–; 1836).

14. Margaret M. Smith, "The Prehistory of 'Small Caps': From All Caps to Smaller Capitals to Small Caps," *Journal of the Printing Historical Society* 22 (1993), 103–06. The Egenolff–Berner specimen sheet of 1592, which includes types cut by Garamond, Granjon, and Le Bé, shows small capitals for all text sizes except for the smallest. The 1734 specimen issued by William Caslon, who revived the art of typefounding in England, shows small caps for all roman sizes from Double Pica to Brevier.

15. See M. Twyman, "Articulating Graphic Language: A Historical Perspective," in *Toward a New Understanding of Literacy*, ed. M. E. Wrolstad and D. E. Fisher (New York: Praeger, 1986), pp. 188–251, on pp. 194–95.

16. The range of roman and italic founts at Oxford represented the work of at least seven different French and Dutch punch-cutters: see Stanley Morison, *John Fell: The University Press and the "Fell" Types* (Oxford: Clarendon Press, 1967).

17. S. H. Steinberg, *Five Hundred Years of Printing*, ed. John Trevitt (London: British Library, 1996), pp. 110–13, includes a brief discussion of the roles of typefounder, printer, author, and bookseller in this period. For William Strahan see R. A. Austen-Leigh, *William Strahan and His Ledgers* (London: London School of Printing, [1923 or 1924]); Robert D. Harlan, "William Strahan: Eighteenth Century London Printer and Publisher," unpublished Ph.D. thesis, University of Michigan (1964); and Cochrane, *Dr. Johnson's Printer*. Allen Reddick, *The Making of Johnson's Dictionary, 1746–1773*, rev. ed. (Cambridge: Cambridge University Press, 1996), discusses the production of the *Dictionary*.

18. Cochrane (*Dr. Johnson's Printer*, p. 15) also notes that Strahan took one of Wilson's sons as his apprentice. Wilson's foundry is discussed in Talbot Baines Reed, *A History of the Old English Letter Foundries*, ed. A. F. Johnson (London: Faber & Faber, 1952), pp. 254–62.

19. Alexander Wilson's 1772 type specimen, cited in Reed *A History of the Old English Letter Foundries*, p. 262.

20. The editions and copies consulted are as follows: *1755 = A Dictionary of the English Language*, 2 vols. folio (London, 1755), Bodleian Library 30253 d.14; *1756 = A Dictionary of the English Language . . . Abstracted from the Folio Edition*, 2 vols. octavo (London, 1756), Bodleian Library 12Theta 508, 509; *1758 = A Dictionary of the English Language . . . Abstracted from the Folio Edition*, 1 vol. octavo (Dublin, 1758), Bodleian Library Vet. A5 e.6606; *1760 = A Dictionary of the English Language . . . Abstracted from the Folio Edition*, "2nd ed.," 2 vols. octavo (London, 1760), Bodleian Library Vet. A5 e.6554; *1765 = A Dictionary of the English Language*, 3rd ed., 2 vols. folio (London, 1765), Bodleian Library 302 z.3; *1773 = A Dictionary of the English Language*, 4th ed., 2 vols. folio (London, 1773), Oxford English Faculty Library W1[1773]; *1777 = A Dictionary of the English Language*, 2 vols. quarto (Dublin, 1777), Bodleian Library Don. d.224; *1784 = A Dictionary of the English Language*, 5th ed., 2 vols. folio (London, 1784), Bodleian Library Vet. A5 b.88,89; *1785Q = A Dictionary of the English Language*, 6th ed., 2 vols. quarto (London, 1785), Reading University Library; *1785F = A Dictionary of the English* Language, 7th ed., 1 vol. folio (London, 1785), Bodleian Library Vet. A5 b.90; *1805 = A Dictionary of the English Language*, 9th ed., 4 vols. octavo (London, 1805), Reading University Library; *1824 = A Dictionary of the English Language*, 2 vols. quarto (London, 1824), Reading University Library.

21. Benjamin Martin, *Lingua Britannica Reformata; or, A New English Dictionary*, 2 vols. (London, 1749); Abel Boyer, *Dictionaire Royal, François–Anglois, et Anglois–François*, 2 vols. (Amsterdam, 1727). The copies examined were Oxford English Faculty Library XW1 [1749] for Martin, and Bodleian Library 30999 d.44 for Boyer.

22. The dagger has had a pejorative meaning in textual annotation since the days of St. Jerome (*OED*, s.v. *obelisk* n. 2).

23. Benjamin Martin, Preface, *Lingua Britannica Reformata*, p. xi;

> Where I have observed the Number of Syllables in a Word to be in any ways doubtful or uncertain to the Unlearned, I have shewn the Number by a Figure at the End of the Word. Thus in the Word *Antipodes*[4], the Figure (4) shews there are *four* Syllables; in the Word *Cycloid*[3], the Figure (3) shews there are *three* Syllables. (p. vii)
>   The single Accent shews the Syllable on which the Emphasis or Stress of the Voice lies, and the double one shews the same Thing if alone. But the Use of the double Accent is every-where to denote that the Letter which begins the Syllable to which it is prefix'd has a double Sound, one of which belongs to the preceding Syllable. Thus the Word *A "nimal.* is sounded with a double *n*, as *An-nimal.* (p. vii)

24. The differentiation of headwords points to a paradox in the organization of the dictionary. To show derivations clearly, the derived headwords would not only

have been typographically distinguished, but also ordered by morphological group or by etymological derivation after the base form. In fact Johnson, unlike Richardson, chose to use a single alphabetical sequence for all headwords, the most useful arrangement for the ordinary reader. The cap-and-small-cap headwords remain as a slightly puzzling feature for the casual reader, an echo of a different way of organizing the *Dictionary.*

25. Edward Phillips, *The New World of English Words; or, A General Dictionary* (London, 1658).

26. An exception can be seen in a quotation from Wotton, s.v. *a* (contraction of *at*) in *1765.* A turn-over line and a two-line chorus are further indented.

27. See R. Carter Hailey's essay in this volume for a discussion of the printing of these two editions.

28. The main volumes of Richardson's dictionary were beautifully printed by Richard Clay, the Supplement by Charles Whittingham at the Chiswick Press. Richardson's desire to establish the "radical etymology" of words led him to compact definitions which sought to integrate, rather than differentiate, senses, and to group headwords under their "root." The entry for *ordain* begins with the following bank of headwords: ORDAIN. ORDAINABLE. ORDAINER. ORDINABLE. ORDINABILITY. ORDINAL, *adj.* ORDINAL, *n.* ORDINANT. ORDINANCE. ORDINARY, *adj.* ORDINARY, *n.* ORDINARILY. ORDINATE, *v.* ORDINATE, *adj.* ORDINATELY. ORDINATION. ORDONNANCE. Richardson's system reflects his standpoint, but provides little help for the reader to access individual words: words which are included in the headword banks do not have a cross-referring entry at their correct position in the alphabetic sequence, making access without etymological knowledge impossible.

29. Joseph Worcester, *A Dictionary of the English Language* (Boston, 1864); William Dwight Whitney, ed., *The Century Dictionary* (New York, 1889).

CHAPTER 12

The Dictionary *in abstract: Johnson's abridgments of the* Dictionary of the English Language *for the common reader*

Catherine Dille

Recent critical focus on Johnson's *Dictionary* has centered almost exclusively on the folio editions of the work, particularly the first edition of 1755 and the fourth edition of 1773. But the dictionary that most of Johnson's contemporaries used was not the familiar folio but the "abstracted" *Dictionary*, the two-volume octavo that Johnson abridged from the folio for the benefit of the "common reader." During the twenty-eight-year period of copyright, approximately 5,000 copies of the folio edition were printed and distributed, compared with 35,000 copies of the abstracted edition (*Bibliography*, vol. 1, pp. 410–500). These are only the editions printed in London, initially by the bookseller's consortium that had financed the folio *Dictionary*; were one to take into account the bastard offspring of Johnson's book printed in Dublin and elsewhere, the disparity would be even greater. Continuing to outpace demand for the folio edition after Johnson's death, the abstracted edition, in various guises, had a vigorous existence well into the nineteenth century. After the 14th edition of 1815, J. D. Fleeman's bibliography lists numerous impressions of Wilson's edition (1812), Tegg's (1813), Jameson's (1827), Kay's (1836), and Latham's (1876). The Johnson brand name spawned countless miniature dictionaries, some shrunk to the size of matchboxes, all claiming on their title pages some form of patrimony to Johnson's original. By the mid nineteenth century the book had spread across the English-speaking world, with editions appearing in Dublin, Glasgow, Philadelphia, and New York. The text was incorporated into bilingual dictionaries, supplying the word list for the English half of dictionaries of French, German, Italian, and Bengali. Of these, however, only the abstracted *Dictionary*, abridged by the author himself, can make any claim to being Johnson's text.

But the abstracted *Dictionary* has a phantom historical existence, merging in the cultural record with the folio under the all-embracing designation of "Johnson's *Dictionary*," or sometimes merely "Johnson." Thousands of copies were printed and bought, given as presents and left to relatives, according to inscriptions.[1] But recorded comments on the *Dictionary* usually simply refer to "Johnson's dictionary." We must assume that when Thackeray's Becky Sharp launches her copy of Johnson's "Dixonary" out the coach window in the direction of Miss Pinkerton's academy, it is some form of the lighter, more easily projected abridged edition;[2] or that when Stephen Austin, the founder of Texas, brought west with him early in the nineteenth century his father's copy of Johnson's *Dictionary* it was more likely the abstracted edition than the weightier folio.[3] When James Fenimore Cooper called upon "the definitions of Johnson that come nearest to the matter at hand" in the New York *Evening Post* in 1835, it might well have been the abstracted edition that he had close by.[4] And yet after the great public fanfare over the folio *Dictionary*'s publication in April 1755, the appearance of the octavo edition in January 1756 attracted little notice.[5]

The extent to which Johnson was necessarily involved in the process of abridgment is uncertain, and he could have delegated some of the work. But several circumstances point to Johnson having carried out the abridgment himself. The work was advertised as being "Abridged from the Folio Edition, by the Author, SAMUEL JOHNSON, A.M.," and the title page announces it as having been "Abstracted from the FOLIO EDITION, By the AUTHOR SAMUEL JOHNSON, A.M."[6] It seems unlikely that Johnson, who was deeply uneasy about having misled the public over his authorship of the "Debates in the Parliament of Lilliput" for *The Gentleman's Magazine*, would have allowed his name to appear prominently on a work in which he had little or no involvement.[7] J. D. Fleeman, moreover, has noted that a rare variant title leaf for the first abstracted edition without the words "by the author" points to this line having been added while the book was at press (*Bibliography*, vol. 1, p. 487). This added emphasis on Johnson's editorial responsibility highlights for potential purchasers his involvement in the abridgment and capitalizes on the critical success of the folio *Dictionary*. It should also be noted that Johnson was in straitened circumstances at this time; he had received no additional payment on completion of the folio *Dictionary* and, in March 1756, he was arrested for debt.[8] The income from the preparation of the abstracted edition would no doubt have been extremely welcome.

The tone of the succinct two-page Preface Johnson composed expressly for the abstracted edition outlining his intentions for the work is confident and authoritative; here the great literary lexicographer descends Parnassus "to accommodate the nation with a vocabulary of daily use."[9] The folio *Dictionary* stands at the back of this edition, authorizing Johnson's stance towards his audience. His ironically casual opening reference to the folio assumes the reader's familiarity with his recent achievement and recognition of his status as national lexicographer: "having been long employed in the study and cultivation of the English language, I lately published a dictionary like those compiled by the academies of Italy and France" (*1756*, sig. π2^r). The long years of work and delay in bringing out the folio edition are now turned to positive advantage as Johnson asserts that he may "without arrogance claim to myself a longer acquaintance with the lexicography of our language than any other writer has had" (sig. π2^r). But while other dictionaries like Bailey's directed their efforts towards "Students, Artificers, Tradesmen, and Foreigners," Johnson's intention is to provide a dictionary for the user he characterizes as the "common reader."[10]

From the outset of the *Dictionary* project, Johnson clearly conceived of different classes of dictionary users and understood that a significant proportion of the literate populace would not only find the folio dictionary too expensive but also superfluous to its language needs. The abstracted dictionary is intended expressly as a dictionary for "common readers"; or more precisely, as Johnson explains in his Preface, "the greater number of readers, who, seldom intending to write or presuming to judge, turn over books only to amuse their leisure, and to gain degrees of knowledge suitable to lower characters, or necessary to the common business of life" (sig. π2^r). The emphasis here is on facilitating the comprehension of common *readers*.[11] The user of the abstracted dictionary was conceived of as writing but little, aside from "adjusting orthography" in letters and business correspondence, but, in Johnson's view, he or she read widely and voraciously in the vernacular canon. Understanding the abstracted dictionary as a reference work directed specifically at readers sheds light on several unique aspects of the work as well as on Johnson's editorial choices regarding what linguistic information to retain.

The fact that the octavo *Dictionary* is an abstract derived from the folio predetermines several features which make it unique among popular dictionaries.[12] In addition to the usual claims made by lexicographers of the day – that this dictionary would include more words, better etymologies, and more accurate spelling – Johnson also asserts that his dictionary provides better definitions with "more copiously enumerated" senses. He further suggests that the book can serve as a glossary or "expository index" to the poetical writers (sig. π2^r). The most noticeable aspect of the abridgment setting it apart from other dictionaries is the names of authors that accompany the various senses of each entry, typically one per sense. Even though the folio's illustrative passages themselves are eliminated (it is principally this change which enabled the book to be compressed into two volumes octavo), the names of selected authors, disembodied of their quotations, remain. Johnson explains the intended purpose of this unusual aspect of the abridged *Dictionary*:

To the words, and to the different senses of each word, are subjoined from the large dictionary the names of those writers by whom they have been used; so that the reader who knows the different periods of the language, and the time of its authors, may judge of the elegance or prevalence of any word, or meaning of a word; and without recurring to other books, may know what are antiquated, what are unusual, and what are recommended by the best authority. (*1756*, sig. π2^v)

Although this feature is not typical of monolingual popular dictionaries, Johnson would have known it from Latin–English dictionaries, like Ainsworth's *Thesaurus*, which include the names of classical authors to indicate what period of literature a word belonged. This proposed function of the abstracted *Dictionary* strongly points to Johnson's understanding of the "common reader" as one who aspires to familiarity with the best works in the English language, from Shakespeare and Milton to Locke and Swift.

The absence of a regular pattern among the authors chosen to remain in the abstracted edition suggests that Johnson was actively engaged in the process of selection, determining case by case which writer best represented the period associated with each sense. Some generalities regarding his selections, however, can be made; if a word or sense had been branded "obsolete" in the folio, then there is a greater likelihood that Spenser (or "Fairy Q."), Sidney, or Shakespeare is the author retained in the abstracted edition. One effect of this process of discrimination is that while Shakespeare is still frequently cited in the abstracted *Dictionary*, he no longer dominates the list of authors to the degree that he did in the folio. If indeed Johnson was responsible for this aspect of the abridgment, then his selections present an additional perspective on his view of the language: information that is not available outside of the abstracted *Dictionary*.

In order to ensure a substantial return on their investment in the folio edition, the publishers of the abstracted *Dictionary* sought a wide popular consumer base for the work.[13] Daily advertisements, prominently placed on the front page of *The Gazetteer and London Daily Advertiser*, ran during January 1756, and weekly advertisements appeared in the *London Evening-Post*, the *Public Advertiser*, and *Jackson's Oxford Journal* in December 1755 and January 1756 both before and after the publication on 5 January.[14] At £4 10s., the folio *Dictionary* was beyond the means of most readers, whereas the modestly priced ten-shilling abstracted edition would have been within reach of the book's target audience (although still more expensive than Bailey's *Dictionary*, which cost six shillings). The abstracted *Dictionary* appears to have sold reasonably well, and a new edition was called for in 1760. It is not known whether it was indeed purchased by the "lower characters" that Johnson envisioned as his readers, but the traditional purchasers of popular dictionaries – students, foreigners, and women – seem to have been among its early users. In his Preface, Johnson does not expressly include students among his "common readers," but young people and students do appear to have owned copies of the book; a fifteen-year-old Robert Burns, for example, acquired a copy of the fourth edition in 1774, and others appear to have belonged to university students.[15] Johnson presented several copies of the book to new friends and acquaintances, like Donald Maclean, the schoolmaster whose story so impressed him on his visit to Scotland.[16] Parisians would have found the book for sale at Pissot, the bookseller, in 1784.[17] If Johnson had educational intentions for his *Dictionary*, then one might assume that these objectives would likewise be apparent in the abstracted edition of the work, intended not for Johnson's intellectual peers but for the common reader.

Where Johnson assumes that the users of the folio share an advanced level of education and cultural literacy, the general approach of the abstracted *Dictionary* is generally more authoritarian; gone is the tone of uncertainty that occasionally marks the etymologies and definitions of the folio *Dictionary*. An *abyss*, for instance, in the folio is "The body of waters supposed at the center of the earth"; "supposed," however, does not survive in the abstracted edition. Users of the abstracted *Dictionary* discover that *adamant* is "a stone of impenetrable hardness," while folio users are informed that this was "imagined by writers" to be the case. In the folio edition, *to quaffer* is "a low word, I suppose, formed by chance," of which "to feel out . . . seems to be the meaning." In the abstracted edition, it is merely "To feel out." Yet it must be recalled that Johnson's primary concern in abridging the *Dictionary* is to render it considerably shorter while still practically useful; superfluous commentary had no place in a popular dictionary.

The process of abridgment itself appears to have been relatively straightforward. A complete collation of the first folio and abstracted edition for the letter A, with an analysis of 10 percent of the rest of the letters across the alphabet, shows that the abridger had merely to cross out the non-essential parts of the etymology, definitions, and attributions.[18] It seems likely that deletions and alterations were made directly onto a copy of the first edition folio *Dictionary* and then submitted as printer's copy. This is supported by the accidental retention under *birchen* of not only the attribution to Pope, but the quotation as well – "His beaver'd brow a *birchen* garland bears" – an error corrected in later editions, indicating that the compositor is likely to have had the folio text open in front of him as he worked. Additions made to the text in the abstracted edition are brief, usually no more than a few words, suggesting that the abridger is making them principally in the margins, which would be consistent with Johnson's practice in revising the folio text for the fourth edition.[19]

Aside from minor grammatical changes in the definitions, there are in the letter A twelve textual changes that may be authorial, including a Johnsonian dig at the Scots poet David Malloch, who had anglicized his name to Mallet on moving to London, a reference that appears under the word *alias* (*Life*, vol. iv, p. 217 n. 1). A number of definitions are subtly improved; for example, *addle-pated*, "having addled brains," is altered to "having barren brains" in order to avoid repetition of the headword.[20] Similar alterations are made throughout the alphabet, although there appears to be a higher concentration of alterations in the earlier letters. Small additions are also made; the definition of *caret*, "a note which shews where something interlined should be read," is supplemented with an example of the typographical symbol for a caret: "as, ∧." In some cases, definitions are rewritten for brevity. The definition for *gainfulness*, "profit; advantage," for example, is replaced with "lucrativeness," and *badger*, "an animal that earths in the ground, used to be hunted" is simplified to "a brock." Etymologies are occasionally expanded, such as that for *vainglorious*, which is enlarged with the addition of "*vanaglorioso*, Italian." Some new material and information is also included. For instance, a new sense 2 for *canticle* is added, "The song of Solomon," a sense that does not appear in the folio editions. In the case of *ragamuffin* the definition was missing in the folio, and "A paltry mean fellow" is supplied in the abstracted edition.[21]

It is the material eliminated from the abstracted edition, however, not the small additions, that is most suggestive of Johnson's intentions for the abstracted *Dictionary*. Among the material that is sometimes excised are the poetical and figurative senses of words: for instance, *to calve* v.n. 2, which is "used metaphorically for any act of bringing forth," and the poetical usages of *dame* and *dart*. These expulsions might be explained by Johnson's assertion in the Preface that this kind of dictionary is expressly for people "seldom intending to write or presuming to judge." Perhaps less explicable in a dictionary intended for the common reader is the regular elimination of indicators that would guide the usage of the less confident English speaker. Readers of the folio *Dictionary* may discover that *bamboozle* is "a cant word not used in pure or in grave writings" and that *adread* v.a. is "now obsolete," but users of the 1756 abstracted edition are not provided with any such assistance. Neither are they informed that *jeopardy* is "a word not now in use," that *grum* is "a low word," or that *parable* is not in use as an adjective. Since this dictionary was intended for the general rather than the learned reader, Johnson perhaps felt justified in saving space by eliminating such usage indicators, although, as will be discussed below, he may have later rethought the usefulness of this information to the common reader. Not only are senses and comments on usage eliminated in the first abstracted edition; whole entries are excised in an effort to reduce the bulk of the volumes. A consideration of the categories of words that were eliminated might suggest what Johnson considered the level of vocabulary suitable to the "lower characters" for which this "vocabulary of daily use" was intended.

When Dublin booksellers George and Alexander Ewing produced their own one-volume edition of Johnson's abstracted *Dictionary* in 1758, a main selling point for the work, aside from its price of seven shillings, was that the editors claimed to have inserted "in their proper places, above 500 Words from the Folio Edition, none of which are contained in the *London Octavo*."[22] Words like *abalienation, baldachin*, and *holy-ghost* that had been removed from the word list of the London abstracted *Dictionary* are restored in the Dublin edition, with newly abridged definitions based on the folio text. In fact, Johnson had silently trimmed his word list for the abstracted edition by over 1,200 entries, representing about 3 percent of the lexicon of the folio edition. Of the roughly 1,200 deleted words, the letters A, B, and U/V together account for 60 percent. This anomaly can be explained partly by the fact that in A and B Johnson had originally included a higher proportion of obscure and latinate terms, like *agrestick* and *balbucinate*, than he did in later letters. The large reduction in the letter U/V is accounted for by the fact that Johnson eliminated as unnecessary many words beginning with the prefix *un-*, like *uncommonly* and *undutiful*, since they could be consulted in the *Dictionary* under their roots. The same holds true for words with the prefix *mis-*, as *to misconjecture* and *to mispel*. Compound words, including *goatsmilk* and *moneybox*, are also often omitted, presumably because readers could deduce their meaning from their constituent parts.

In his Preface, Johnson asserts that "Many barbarous terms and phrases by which other dictionaries may vitiate the style are rejected from this" (*1756*, sig. π2ᵛ), but only a handful of the excised words had been so branded in the folio edition.[23] Among the deleted words, a noticeable proportion had been designated "obsolete," "not now in use," or "little in use" in the folio *Dictionary*, or were only included on the authority of earlier dictionaries, like Bailey's and Phillips's *New World of Words*, but most frequently merely attributed to "*Dict.*" These together account for approximately 15 percent of the deleted words and suggest that Johnson thought that words suitable for contemporary use were more appropriate for a popular dictionary.

Terms designated as being specific to particular trades and professions or in use only in particular geographical regions of the country are occasionally excised, as are words belonging to specifically designated areas of discourse – including legal, musical, and architectural terms, nautical terminology, and words specific to heraldry. Writers of practical dictionaries at this time seem to be divided on the question of inclusivity. While John Wesley claimed that his *Complete English Dictionary* (2nd ed., 1764) did not include "a croud of *technical* terms, the meaning whereof is to be sought in books expressly wrote on the subjects to which they belong," Daniel Fenning made a virtue of including technical terms in his *Royal English Dictionary* (1761?) in order "to unite these scattered rays, as it were, into one focus."[24] Johnson may have removed these terms on the grounds that they could have been found in dictionaries of specialized vocabulary, like *The Builder's Dictionary* (1734) or Richard Rolt's *New Dictionary of Trade* (1756), and he was economizing on space by excluding the less useful of these.[25] Johnson also deletes from his *Dictionary* some words designated as peculiarly Scots usages; *by-past, to narrate* v.a., *luff,* and *loppered* are deleted, as are the Irish words *booly, brehon, carrows, coigne, coshering,* and *tanist,* but so also are the "provincial" English words *scottering, spewy,* and *whitsul.* The Dublin edition of the abstracted *Dictionary,* incidentally, replaces none of the Irish words that Johnson omitted.

At the risk of warranting the censure that Johnson is by tradition supposed to have directed at Frances Brooke and her sister, who on commending Johnson for having expunged all "*naughty* words" from the folio *Dictionary* were challenged as to whether they had been looking for them, it is worth noting Johnson's treatment in the abstracted *Dictionary* of terms that are neither demotic nor cant, but were accepted anatomical terms in contemporary usage.[26] In the folio *Dictionary,* Johnson excludes outright "those ancient obscenities referring to excremental or sexual functions," as Donald Siebert has noted, but he also omits other less objectionable terms found in Bailey, who maintained an inclusive policy with regard to his lexicon.[27] *Pizzle* and *fundament*, although they appear in the folio *Dictionary*, are rejected from the abstracted edition. Johnson also shows considerable reluctance to provide clear definitions for those anatomical terms that he does admit. In the folio edition confusion arising from Johnson's reticence to supply clear definitions for some words is relieved in some cases by the descriptive quotations, while the less informed among the abridged *Dictionary*'s users remain in the dark. *Testicle*, defined in both Kersey's and Bailey's abridged dictionaries as "the Organs of Seed in Men and Women," is defined without further elaboration as "stone" in both the folio and abstracted editions of Johnson's *Dictionary*. The folio user will no doubt receive immediate edification from the succeeding quotations from Brown's *Vulgar Errors* – "That a bever, to escape the hunter, bites off his *testicles* or stones, is a tenet very antient" – and Wiseman's *Surgery* – "The more certain sign from the pains reaching to the groins and *testicles*." *Priapism* is similarly treated. The common reader seeking a definition for the medical term is informed that it is "a preternatural tension" on the authority of Bacon. This obscure definition is helped in the folio by Bacon's citation that "lust causeth a flagrancy in the eyes and *priapism*," which at least links the word to lust, and Floyer additionally informs the reader that "the person every night has a *priapism* in his sleep." It would be implausible to suggest that Johnson is actively seeking to limit his common reader's knowledge of such subjects, but his reluctance to define these words adequately, in addition to his removal of the citations from the abstracted *Dictionary*, potentially has this effect.

Although such editorial exclusions from the abridgment might initially appear an attempt to restrict the common reader's knowledge (both of the body and the word), in many cases these can be more plausibly attributed to Johnson's concern over limitations of space in the octavo. In fact, Johnson appears to include an increasing amount of additional material from the folio *Dictionary* as he progresses with the abridgment. While in the early letters of the octavo notes on usage like "obsolete" or "not now in use" are eliminated, such comments are more frequently retained in the later letters, along with the words they gloss. Further, where Johnson typically included only one author attribution per sense in the first part of the alphabet, quite frequently three and sometimes even four or five, and in one case eight (*to take* v.a. 24), names are subjoined to senses in the later letters of the alphabet. Apart from the question of space, Johnson may also have progressively come to the view that such linguistic information as usage indicators provided useful guidance concerning register for the non-learned user. This trend of increasing inclusion can be seen to continue in the 1760 second edition of the abstracted *Dictionary*, which was announced on the title page as having been "corrected."

Aside from the expected correction of numerous compositorial and press errors, the second abstracted edition of 1760 appears to have been in the early part of the alphabet carefully revised by Johnson. James Basker has noted that Johnson "quickly corrected" his definition of *dab-chick* in the second abstracted edition in response to Tobias Smollett's criticisms in *The Critical Review*,[28] but the extent to which Johnson altered the text of the 1760 edition has not previously been recognized. One noticeable change is that some of the comments on usage that were eliminated in the first edition are reintroduced, based loosely on the folio text. *Aleknight* and *algates*, for instance, are once again branded "obsolete" and *bamboozle* regains its status as a "low word."[29] The language is improved in many definitions, and senses and explanations are reintroduced from the folio edition. Significantly, although I have not discovered the inclusion of any new words, a substantial amount of new material and new senses and explanations is included which never appear in a folio edition; for example, a new sense for *to allow* v.a. is added: "To praise, to commend. Obsolete." This sense never appears in the folio editions. The reader of the second abstracted *Dictionary* is informed that *A, B, C* is "pronounced *abece*," an explanation not provided to folio users. The definition for *armgaunt*, "Slender as the arm," is augmented to read "Slender as the arm; or rather, slender with want." *To affect* v.a. 6, "To study the appearance of any thing; with some degree of hypocrisy," is altered to read "To practice the appearance of any thing; with some degree of hypocrisy." This is a small change, but one that subtly improves the definition. Likewise, *to alter* v.n., which had been defined as "to become otherwise than it was," is expanded to read "to become otherwise than it was; to be changed; to suffer change." Additional material is also newly added to the etymologies; *hamper* is derived from "*hanaperium*, low Lat.," one first learns in the second abstracted edition. Usage notes are also added which do not appear in the folio editions. *Alternate* as a nominative, Johnson explains, is "Not generally used," *to blare* is "not in use," and *bagatelle*, "a trifle," is "Not English."[30] The adjective *amatory*, "relating to love," one may be surprised to discover, is also "Little used." In the 1756 edition, the *basilisk* is a "serpent; a cockatrice; said to kill by looking." In the second abstracted edition it is additionally noted that "He is called *basilisk*, or little king, from a comb or crest on his head." This information is not provided in any of the citations, nor does it appear in later editions of the folio. It should be noted, however, that a high proportion of these changes occur in the early letters of the alphabet, which might suggest that Johnson's revisionist zeal abated some way into the work.

While there is no clear evidence to suggest that the abstracted *Dictionary* served materially as a step in the process of Johnson's revisions for the folio, since changes made to the abstracted editions were not consistently applied to the folio editions, yet the process of abridging the *Dictionary* perhaps encouraged Johnson to rethink some aspects of his lexicographical practice. An early example might be his decision to break *a*, the article, into its various senses. While the first folio edition features a discursive paragraph on the article *a*, in the first abstracted edition this is broken down into ten senses, a change that is applied to later editions of the folio.[31] The usage indicators, such as "obsolete" and "not in use" in the second edition of the abstracted edition, also occasionally find their way into Johnson's revisions for the fourth folio edition of the *Dictionary*. Whether this is coincidental or not is uncertain; it is possible that Johnson, having made the changes in the abstracted edition in 1760, recalled what he had previously done when he came to revise the fourth edition. Since the changes are seldom verbatim, it would not appear that the abstracted *Dictionary* was strictly followed.

The letter B, which contains at least four such changes, may, however, be a special case. The prepared printer's copy for the fourth-edition revisions to this letter was lost before it reached the printer, and since new copy had to be prepared quickly, it seems possible that the abstracted edition was consulted, or at least called to Johnson's mind.[32] One example is *to bedizen*, which was defined simply as "to dress out" in the first three folio editions, but in the second abstracted edition it is also described as "a low term." In the fourth edition it is described as "a low word." *Bombard* is defined as "a great gun" in the first folio edition and additionally as "a barrel for wine" in the second abstracted edition. In the fourth folio edition, the definition "a barrell. Obsolete" is added.[33]

Alterations to the second abstracted *Dictionary* – significant ones numbering about one hundred, based on a collation of 10 percent of each letter – are not changes that will radically alter our view of Johnson's *Dictionary*. But they clearly show the extent to which he remained interested in and actively involved with the fate of his abstracted *Dictionary* and its accuracy and continued success. Only further investigation will reveal whether the description "corrected" on later editions of the abstracted edition means that Johnson continued to alter his text. One realization that emerges from this study of the abstracted edition is that there is not one monolithic Johnson's *Dictionary of the English Language*, but in a sense two parallel dictionaries, the abstracted edition deriving from the folio as its source, but each work evolving independently and developing its own textual history with each successive edition. While the folio edition remains the primary focus of scholarly attention, a full assessment of Johnson's views on language and language users cannot be made without consulting his other *Dictionary of the English Language*.

NOTES

1. A copy of the 2nd ed. (1760), for instance, is inscribed by William Badley: "My Aunt Sarah gave me this Dictionary, 1769" (Birmingham Central Library, Store A824.6321).

2. William Makepeace Thackeray, *Vanity Fair*, ed. Peter L. Shillingsburg (New York and London: Garland, 1989), p. 8. Thackeray perhaps had in mind one of the many "miniature" versions of the *Dictionary* in 12°, 16°, or 18°.

3. Rebecca Smith Lee, *Mary Austin Holley, A Biography* (Austin: University of Texas Press, 1962), pp. 293–94. Austin's "father's old copy of Doctor Johnson's *Dictionary*" to which Lee refers was in fact the 3rd Dublin ed. of the abstracted *Dictionary* (Center for American History, University of Texas at Austin Library, TZZ 097.9 AU77J).

4. *The Letters and Journals of James Fenimore Cooper*, ed. James Franklin Beard (Cambridge, Mass.: Belknap Press, 1960–68), vol. III, p. 126. I have not been able to identify the edition Cooper used.

5. The book was noticed in *The Gentleman's Magazine* 26 (Jan. 1756), 45, but it does not appear to have been reviewed anywhere.

6. *Public Advertiser*, 20 December 1755. See below, note 14, for further advertising details.

7. See *Life*, vol. I, pp. 151–52.

8. *Life*, vol. I, p. 303 n. 1; *Letters*, vol. I, p. 132.

9. *A Dictionary of the English Language*, 2 vols. (London, 1756), vol. I, sig. π2^r. Allen Reddick describes it as "a bookseller's preface, intended to catch a particular share of the market," in *The Making of Johnson's Dictionary, 1746–1773*, rev. ed. (Cambridge: Cambridge University Press, 1996), p. 87.

10. Nathan Bailey, *An Universal Etymological English Dictionary*, 20th ed. (London, 1763), title page.

11. I owe this suggestion to Anne McDermott.

12. As opposed to *abridgement*, "the contraction of a larger work into a small compass," Johnson's definition for *abstract* in *1755* connotes distillation rather than merely truncation: an "abstract" is "a smaller quantity, containing the virtue or power of a greater," an "epitome."

13. The publishers were "J[ohn] Knapton, C[harles] Hitch and L[acey] Hawes, A[ndrew] Millar, R[obert] and J[ames] Dodsley, and M. and T[homas]

Longman." Of these, Knapton, Hitch, and Millar were members of the conger of booksellers who sponsored the first folio *Dictionary*, along with Paul Knapton and Thomas Longman's uncle, also Thomas.

14. *Public Advertiser*, 20 and 27 December 1755; *London Evening-Post*, 20–23 December 1755, 27–30 December 1755, 1–3 January 1756, 3–6 January 1756, 6–8 January 1756, 8–10 January 1756; *Jackson's Oxford Journal*, 20 and 27 December 1755; *The Gazetteer and London Daily Advertiser*, daily advertisements 1–27 January 1756.

15. This copy (4th ed., 1770) is signed and dated "August 31 1774" (Houghton *EC75.B9375.Zz770j).

16. Johnson inscribed this copy "To Mr Maclean Teacher of Languages in the Island of Coll, from the Authour" (*Bibliography*, vol. 1, p. 495). Other copies given by Johnson as gifts include a 3rd edition (1766) to James Drummond (*Bibliography*, vol. 1, p. 493) and possibly a first edition to Ann Gardner, although the inscription is not in Johnson's hand (*Bibliography*, vol. 1, p. 487). Copies belonging to women include a 5th ed. (1773) signed "Eliz. Inge" (Johnson Birthplace Museum, 2001.570.1–2), which may have belonged to Elizabeth Inge (d. 1784), the wife of William Inge, canon-residentiary of Lichfield Cathedral, who is described on her memorial stone in Thorpe-Constantine church as "studioque in liberos verè præclara." See Stebbing Shaw, *The History and Antiquities of Staffordshire*, 2 vols., ed. M. W. Greenslade and G. C. Baugh (Wakefield: EP Publishers, 1976), vol. 1, p. 407. I am grateful to Graham Nicholls for this possible identification.

17. *A Catalogue of English Books Sold by Pissot, Bookseller, Quai des Augustins, Paris* (Paris, 1784), p. 7.

18. The letter A was collated using the CD-ROM text of *1755: A Dictionary of the English Language on CD-ROM*, ed. Anne McDermott (Cambridge: Cambridge University Press, 1996). I have proceeded by comparing it with the 1756 abstracted edition and striking through material not contained in the abstracted edition, thus reenacting to a degree the process by which the text was originally abridged. The first 10 percent of the text of each letter was analyzed, excluding the letters K, Q, Y, and Z as not statistically relevant.

19. Although Johnson used an interleaved copy for revising the fourth edition folio, his changes to the printed text are typically made on the printed page, the interleaf being reserved mainly for new quotations. See Reddick, *The Making of Johnson's Dictionary*, pp. 190–91.

20. The definition for *to amble* 1, "to move upon an amble," is similarly improved by the addition of "to pace."

21. Neither is the word defined in the second (1755–56) or third (1765) folio editions, although in the fourth edition (1773), the newly added definition "a paltry mean fellow" follows the abstracted edition, suggesting the possibility that Johnson returned to the abstracted edition to supply the deficiency.

22. Samuel Johnson, *A Dictionary of the English Language . . . Abstracted from the Folio Edition* (Dublin: Geo. and Alex. Ewing, 1758), Preface, sig. A2ᵛ. The Dublin edition in fact only replaces about half this number. The history of

the Dublin editions of the *Dictionary* is described in Richard Cargill Cole, *Irish Booksellers and English Writers, 1740–1800* (London: Manswell, 1986), pp. 89–93.

23. For instance, *irresistless, to denshire, spinny,* and *worser.*

24. John Wesley, *The Complete English Dictionary, Explaining Most of Those Hard Words, Which Are Found in the Best English Writers,* 2nd ed. (Bristol, 1764), "To the Reader," sig. A2^r; Daniel Fenning, *The Royal English Dictionary; or, A Treasury of the English Language* (London, 1761?), Preface, p. vii.

25. Some terms attributed to "Builders Dict" and "Sea Dict." are retained in the abstracted dictionary.

26. Henry Digby Best, *Personal and Literary Memorials* (London, 1829), pp. 11–12.

27. Donald T. Siebert, "*Bubbled, Bamboozled,* and *Bit*: 'Low Bad' Words in Johnson's *Dictionary,*" *Studies in English Literature 1500–1900* 26 (1986), 485–509, on p. 492.

28. James G. Basker, *Tobias Smollett, Critic and Journalist* (Newark: University of Delaware Press, 1988), p. 178.

29. *Aleknight* had been labeled "a word now out of use" in the folio.

30. In the fourth folio edition Johnson adds that this is "a word not naturalised."

31. Similarly, *to act* v.a. from the first folio is divided into v.a. and v.n. in the abstracted edition, a change which also appears in the next folio edition.

32. See Reddick, *The Making of Johnson's Dictionary,* chapters 1, 5, and Appendix A.

33. *Bagatelle,* mentioned above, and *barbarick* are the other instances.

CHAPTER 13

Revision and the limits of collaboration: hands and texts in Johnson's Dictionary

Allen Reddick

Collaboration in the production of literary and other written works has in the last thirty years emerged as an area of study with significant theoretical and historical implications. With the putative death of the author and increasing interest in the social construction of authorship and of texts in general, it has been asserted, with some reason, that an exclusive focus upon single authorship denies the true nature of the creation of works; they should be more accurately considered as social, communal, dynamic, the result of a process of exchange.

Significant studies have engaged in Marxist-oriented and other "constructivist" readings of literary creation, with ideological justifications for dismantling the single-author construction. The study of sixteenth- and seventeenth-century practices in the theatre has emphasized the various ways in which collaboration, both contemporary and across time, was taken for granted as part of the production of theatrical texts. The notion of the single author has been called a Romantic construction, masking earlier forms of collective authorship, particularly the medieval and early-modern notion of collective compilation, *scholia*, and commentary. Conversely, it has been suggested that it is only with the eighteenth century that we have a publishing and consuming world in which society to a large extent, through the publishers, distributors, purchasers, readers, and critics, shapes the product or artifact as never before.[1] Imaginative historical and theoretical investigations into publishing history, transmission, and reception have particularly enabled scholars to expand their understanding of the range and importance of collaborative creation.

Collaboration is of particular interest in relation to Johnson's *Dictionary*, in part because authority in the *Dictionary* is a vexed concept and bound up necessarily in the work's creation. Is Johnson simply a compiler, a booksellers' man? – or is he an author? – if so, in what sense? – and is he the only author? Thomas Edwards complained that Johnson's *Dictionary* was "nothing but a Bookseller's Jobb," crammed with materials from the print record that Johnson simply compiled and assembled, at the direction of the consortium of booksellers. Horne Tooke would later dismiss it as "a publication of a set of booksellers, owing its success to that very circumstance which alone must make it impossible that it should deserve success."[2] Edwards, Tooke, and others were determined to deflate the idea that the *Dictionary* might be the work of individual genius.

And what of "inherited assistance" or diachronic "collaborative" impact through the inclusion of texts from the past in the work? Because past authored texts, the thousands of quotations from other authors, and textual borrowings and examples from former lexicographers are subsumed into Johnson's own work, it has been said that Johnson's role could more accurately be seen as a compiler and commentator upon the products of writers from the past.[3] In what sense does this increase the shared responsibility for authorship in the work? Jeffrey Masten, in his provocative book *Textual Intercourse: Collaboration, Authorship, and Sexualities in Renaissance Drama*, has referred to "the frequent revision of play-texts, itself a diachronic form of collaboration" (p. 14). If this characterization can be altered slightly and adapted to Johnson's "diachronic" borrowing, which takes over texts from the past and reworks them into his own text, it might illuminate the process of incorporation of past authors in the construction of his own authority, revising them by decontextualizing, then partly re-contextualizing them in his text. Masten stresses the "historical and theoretical challenges collaboration poses to the ideology of the Author. Collaboration is . . . a dispersal of author/ity, rather than a simple doubling of it; to revise the aphorism, two heads are different than one" (*Textual Intercourse*, p. 19). If we see Johnson's incorporating of these texts and voices as a kind of collaboration, must we accept that his authority is dispersed throughout and among the "contributors"? As one of the *Dictionary*'s critics scathingly put it in 1785, "the joke is, that with [Johnson] every body is an authority."[4]

The specific nature of Johnson's *Dictionary* and its process of compilation, as with many large dictionaries and other books of reference, have encouraged speculation concerning the nature of the work, Johnson's authority, and the nature of the collaboration involved. The team of amanuenses working with Johnson on the first edition in whom, in several cases, he took a personal interest, has naturally drawn our attention to the kinds of contributions to the work they might have made. Their own published endeavors show that they could have contributed much to the composition apart from mere copying.[5] Johnson continued his connection with the surviving amanuenses through the years, assisting them materially and probably employing two of them again on the revision of the work in the early 1770s. One can almost imagine the work as a "family" industry or, more accurately, a patriarchal enterprise: the relationship is obviously social and domestic as well as textual. Moreover, comments from Johnson and others that learned friends from his circle made suggestions or even significant contributions to one or more editions of the *Dictionary* encourage us to imagine a collaborative effort with others.[6]

Much of the discussion to this point has been merely speculative principally because it is impossible to say with certainty, with reference to the printed pages primarily, what parts might have been contributed by others, or in tandem with Johnson. Where are the individual *hands*, in other words, that might delineate the contributed parts? The mechanism of print obliterates the written hand, whether or not the trace of style survives. Parts of manuscript and archival material related to the making and revising of the *Dictionary* have survived, however, and some cursory examinations of this material have prompted imaginative speculation on this topic in the last few years. The presence of other hands in the so-called Sneyd-Gimbel copy at Yale – a partial copy of annotated printed first-edition sheets bound with manuscript slips containing material used in the revision of the *Dictionary* as well as material dating from the original composition – has encouraged the conclusion that they could be those of collaborators, or near-collaborators, with Johnson.[7] One study concludes that the work was the product of a mechanized production line, a "modern" work, yet impersonal, like Diderot's *Encyclopédie*: each member of the team adding his piece, each step more or less equivalent to the one before (DeMaria and Kolb, "Johnson's *Dictionary*," p. 20).

Fortunately, however, other evidence survives which provides much more specific information on Johnson's work with his assistants on the *Dictionary*, revealing specific functions in the production of final copy. Annotated and interleaved first-edition sheets, prepared by Johnson and at least one amanuensis as printer's copy for the major revision of his work, undertaken between 1771 and 1773, have survived in the collections of British Library. In this case, uniquely, the *hand* is preserved in what was intended to be the *text* of the *Dictionary* – the printer's copy for text covering entries for the letter B, comprising 122 printed pages with interleaves. It provides a unique opportunity for seeing into the process of revision.[8]

A brief review of the process Johnson followed both in compiling and later in revising his work will enable us to identify and describe the materials which have survived.[9] In the late 1740s, Johnson eventually settled upon his method of marking quotations in printed books illustrating certain words, then having his amanuenses copy them out for possible use in the *Dictionary*. These illustrations would eventually be copied into notebooks under alphabetical entries. The first attempt at a manuscript was abandoned in the late 1740s or 1750, when Johnson altered his procedures and reset his handwritten materials. When he undertook the extensive revision of 1771–73, while preparing the fourth folio edition, he returned to this abandoned manuscript material and extracted quotations, which he had originally used in the first edition, to illustrate different words in the new edition. Someone (Johnson or an amanuensis) would mark a passage, and the amanuensis would copy it out onto a slip or onto paper later cut into a slip. Some of the illustrations appear to have been simply clipped out from their places in the early manuscript. These slips, bound into the Sneyd-Gimbel copy at Yale, represent one step in the revision process, providing hundreds of added illustrations and notes on usage or definitions in the hands of amanuenses. In preparing the final copy, a portion of which, for the letter B, survives in the BL copy, another amanuensis subsequently copied verbatim these handwritten texts onto the interleaves inserted in another set of first-edition sheets.[10] Johnson then reviewed the material on the interleaf, edited it, keyed it into the printed text of the first-edition sheets he was using, or excised the suggestion completely.

Johnson reviewed the interleaved material and prepared it clearly and carefully for printer's copy. Because his preferences and indications to the printer are clearly marked, the manuscript is unusually unambiguous in its record of his intentions and his relationship to the work of others involved in the project. The fact that so much material is rejected – and that so much of it is, as we shall see, atypical of Johnson's text and his desires for it – strongly suggests that the quotations, extracted from the abandoned first-edition manuscript, were chosen, gathered, and proposed for inclusion in the fourth edition not by Johnson, but by the amanuenses, and that all of the definitions they included were their own.[11] The amanuenses, for example, took the liberty of providing many notes on dialect, Scottish usage, custom, and history, as well as quotations and notes from Thomas Tusser on rural and antiquated words. Yet in *every case* the notes, as well as the material from Tusser, are excised by Johnson. Furthermore, notes on Scots usage in the margins of the printed text (both Sneyd-Gimbel and British Library) were clearly proposed independently by the amanuensis and in every case were excised by Johnson. It would appear that Johnson turned them loose to gather material, presumably fully intending to take advantage of their linguistic and literary expertise, then severely curtailed and edited their proposed additions. He acted as a tight bottleneck, altering the modest number of additions proposed which were not excised and marking them for insertion into the printed text. We might wonder whether the amanuensis took it upon himself to offer his specific knowledge of dialect and literature with dialect words, and particularly Scots usage, or was encouraged to do so by Johnson; we cannot know this for certain. Judging from the final result, it is hard to believe that Johnson encouraged this particular source of additions, though he must have at least given the amanuensis the freedom to make some independent decisions on what would be proposed. It has recently been asserted that the writing down of these notes in the Sneyd-Gimbel material in the preparation of copy may be a sign that the amanuenses were involved in a more important joint-authorial effort with Johnson late in the revision process than has been thought. In fact it illustrates the opposite: Johnson rejects every single usage note in the end.[12]

The editorial rigor of Johnson's practice as exercised upon the contributions of the amanuenses exhibits his firm control over the final version of what would be presented to the printers. Contrast the role of Johnson's amanuenses with the earlier scribal practice of Ralph Crane, the scribe almost certainly involved in the preparation of some of Shakespeare's works for the First Folio, as well as plays by Jonson, Fletcher, Massinger, and others, in which the amanuensis had the final or near-final say. Existing manuscripts reveal Crane (working from the author's manuscript or from the foul papers) altering the author's or company's text, changing stage directions, wording, possibly excising profanity, and altering spelling. His interventions – and, we can assume, those of other contemporary scribes – have led scholars to emphasize the collaborative nature of such preparation of copy, as his changes found their way into the printed versions, apparently without authorial or editorial intervention.[13] In the case of the preparation of Johnson's *Dictionary*, however, we can see a clearly divergent practice, moving away from the collaborative, as Johnson is the one reviewing the work of the amanuensis and making his own changes in *his* handwritten text, not the other way around. Johnson's amanuenses, despite their abilities, are excluded from the final freedom of preparation. That responsibility is left to the author and compiler – the *final* compiler and the author who leaves his mark.

There is considerable evidence in the BL materials to suggest not only the nature of the contributions from the amanuenses, but also the ways in which they worked.[14] Many examples conclusively demonstrate that the material was proposed independently of Johnson. One of the ways of illuminating the method and role of the amanuenses is by examining errors made in the processing of this material. One such case is the addition for *blown*, copied onto the interleaf facing sig. 3G^v, written opposite the printed entry *to blow* v.n.:

To spread or publish with a view to betray
  Is a man betrayd lost & <u>blown</u> by such agents
  as he employs in his greatest & nearest concerns
The cause of it is from this that he misplaced
his confidence & took hypocrisy for fidelity
    South

The passage is followed on the interleaf by further additions to *blow*. In this case, the definition appears to be little more than a guess at South's meaning, and is completely insufficient as a definition; Johnson crosses through it. Johnson's practice is to incorporate all illustrations containing the past participle of a verb under the entry for the past participle, not the entry for the verb; the quotation is therefore copied in the wrong place in the prepared materials, for it should be facing the text for *blown* on the following page, not, as here, facing *to blow* v.n.

Another mistake by the amanuensis is interesting for its use of Scottish material. The handwritten passage reads as follows:

6 To blow nails: a proverbial expression
for poor Comfort, akin to that in Scotland
He blaws a cald coal
        Our love is not so great Hortensius
But we may blow our nails together
And fast it fairly out Shak
When isicles hang down from wall
And Dick the shepherd blows his nail. Idem.

The entire passage is crossed out with two vertical strokes by Johnson. The amanuensis presumably originally gathered the quotations, or at least the first one, with an eye to the printed text of the *Dictionary*, because he applies it, by giving it the number, to definition 6, in this case *to blow* v.a. ("To warm with the breath"), which already contains the quotation ("And Dick the shepherd" plus two more lines) from *Love's Labour's Lost*, but with no indication in the definition of the particular idiomatic nature of the expression. When it came time to insert the addition, however, the amanuensis copied it in the wrong place, on a different interleaf facing the entry *blow* v.n. Johnson then reviewed it and struck through the entire handwritten text, as he did all of the Scottish additions elsewhere proposed.

Handwritten passages on the interleaf facing sig. 3H2^r, completely struck through by Johnson, provide a particularly characteristic selection from the amanuenses:

1 Bodle n.s.
Is a small scotish coin of copper as big as a doit, three of which make a babee or halfpenny It is otherwise called twa pennies [daa pheign Erse] This coin is now wore out to make way for the English Copper, as the Scottish Silver and gold coins have before done for the Sterling money of England.

Boddle is a weed like the mayweed, but bears a large yellow flower: tis hardy and will grow again, unless the roots are clean pulld up. The seed is also very spreading
Tuss. Notes
The brake & the cockle be noisome too much
Yet like unto boddle now weed there is such
                              Tuss. husb. for May

The amanuensis offers his own knowledge of the Scottish coin and its progress, citing no written source. The following additions from Tusser concerning the rural name for the corn marigold, *boddle*, lack contextual notes and were probably newly selected. All of this material is consistent with the amanuensis's philological and lexicological interests, but none of it with Johnson's. He consistently deletes Scottish usage, both oral and written, as well as rural or dialectical usage.

In another example (interleaf facing sig. 2N1^v), the amanuensis copies from a note on Scottish usage without a quotation:

Baby [Babée]
In Scotland denotes a halfpenny, as alluding to the Head impressed on the copper coin

This is a slavish copying of what he found on the slip, in another amanuensis's hand, with "Baby" written at the top. Johnson strikes it out.

Another Scottish note is the following, copied by the amanuensis from the slip, where the text is written in another amanuensis's hand. It is typical of other examples in its reliance upon native knowledge for Scots usage; it is also typical in that Johnson completely deletes it:

Bandog, may be a dog of a bad omen
the schreich owl which is reckond so being added

For in Scotland the common people observe that before a persons death happens some dog and generally it is a strange dog comes at the dead of night, & howles three or four times at the door & goes off quietly.

In *1755*, Johnson explicitly expresses his uncertainty as to the etymology and provides a vague definition ("A kind of large dog"); the amanuensis who copied it onto the slip may be attempting to correct this inconclusiveness.

In the next example, the amanuensis copied the following note and quotation from the slip, where the text is written in the hand of a different amanuensis: "Baldrick, is very probably derived from the inventer or first wearer of this belt, who was called Balderic, baldric. It was worn by women as well as men across the breast." A quotation from *The Faerie Queene* then follows. Here is a case in which the first amanuensis presumably offered his own expertise as a way of assisting in filling gaps in the printed text. In *1755*, s.v. *baldrick* n.s. 1, Johnson had provided the following: "A girdle. By some *Dictionaries* it is explained a *bracelet*; but I have not found it in that sense." Johnson remained unimpressed with the entire proposed text, however, and struck through it. This is consistent with his practice in the fourth edition of not adding, and instead abbreviating, such discursive information, particularly related to dialect or word derivation in English. This is a patent indication that the amanuenses' activities and interests were often contrary to Johnson's sense of his work.

Elsewhere the amanuensis wrote a series of nine additional quotations illustrating *to bring* in its various forms, plus definitions and notes on usage. Johnson deletes them all with two downward strokes of his pen. The following is an example of a proposed addition, deleted by Johnson:

To bring. In the following passage the distinction now a days made betwixt bringing from a place and carrying to another is not regarded. Bring is used in both.

> He who <u>brought</u> me hither
> Will bring me hence, no other guide I seek
> Parad. regd. 1

The comment is certainly not Johnson's: "betwixt" is not a characteristic Johnsonian word, and he does not use the word form in this way in the *Dictionary*; equally telling is the fact that the note on usage is entirely out of character with the other senses for this word listed in the printed work. It is more expansive and explicit about language change, entirely uncharacteristic of the *Dictionary* entries. This amanuensis, however, is interested in the history and development of expressions of spoken English, very likely because of the retention of expressions in Scotland. Johnson has little such interest, and excludes it. The evidence supports the view that all of this material was collected and prepared by the amanuensis, culling through material gathered for the first edition.

One example should suffice for demonstrating Johnson's careful adapting
of some of the illustrative material for use in the printer's copy. Opposite
the printed entry for *to bark* v.a., the amanuensis has written the following,
copied from the Sneyd-Gimbel slip:

To cover with bark, to encase with bark; to encrust.
    A most instant tetter *bark'd* about
Most lazar like, with vile & loathsome crust
All my smooth body   Shak.

Johnson corrects the mistaken definition to, simply, "To cover as with
bark." The amanuensis who first copied the material onto the slip had
badly misunderstood the passage he found in the abandoned first-edition
manuscript – a misunderstanding impossible for anyone with knowledge of
the Ghost's speech in *Hamlet*. This clumsy mistake makes clear that Johnson
was unlikely to have been involved with the selection of quotations to be
recycled for the fourth edition, or at least that he had nothing to do with
the added glosses.

It is instructive to compare handwritten material written by Johnson on
the interleaves with that written by the amanuensis. In general, Johnson's
notations are characteristic of the printed text, economical and clear; the
amanuensis's, on the other hand, deviate often from the usual method and
are vague or discursive. On the interleaf facing sig. $2Y1^r$, for example, the
amanuensis has written:

Begone in composition, as woebegone, depressd with woe
    A man so spiritless
So dull, so dead in look, so woebegone
Drew Priams curtain in the dead of night
And would have told him all his Troy was burn'd
But Priam found the fire, 'ere he his Tongue
    Shak. H.4.2.
    Begone Opprest
Tancred be sure his life's Joy set at nought
So woebegone was he with pains of love
    Fairf. 1.9.
Of before the thing beguiled of
    Other mens insatiable desire of revenge, wholly beguiled church & state of the
benefit of all my retractions & concessions
    K. Charles.

Johnson crosses out all of the material with a vertical pen-stroke.

The copied material is confused. The amanuensis found this material in
the abandoned manuscript (the first two quotations appear under *wobegon*

in the first edition, the third under *retraction*). When the BL amanuensis copied it out from the slip onto the interleaf, he misread the handwriting and miscopied "Tancred be sure" for "Tancred he saw" on the slip. The first "definition" is actually little more than a direction on compounds, with "begone" as the second element in the compound; Johnson does not include such information in the *Dictionary* for second elements in a compound. The second "definition," "Begone Opprest" (on the Sneyd-Gimbel slip, "Begone, oppresst"), would appear to be the gloss for the word *woebegone* in the passage, yet it is unusable as it is under the *Dictionary* entry for *begone*. The final addition, "Of before the thing beguiled of," with the subsequent quotation, is unusable as it reads, and uncharacteristic of Johnson's delineations of usage.

Contrast this instance with the addition of a handwritten entry added by Johnson a few pages earlier, on the interleaf facing sig. 2U2^r:

Be is an inseparable particle placed before verbs of which it seldom augments or changes the signification as to bedeck, and before nouns which it changes into verbs. As dew, to bedew.

Johnson keys this new entry into the printed text in its alphabetical place. The precision, accuracy, and economy of Johnson's entry render it ready for inclusion; and this note on compounds, this time regarding the *first* element in the compound, is consistent with Johnson's practice elsewhere in the *Dictionary* and allows him to insert it into alphabetical order.

Perhaps the clearest sign that the amanuenses are working completely independently of Johnson's wishes is that quotations from James Thomson were gathered and proposed for inclusion. Far from adding new Thomson quotations to the *Dictionary*, Johnson systematically excised many between the first and fourth editions.[15] The two Thomson quotations proposed on the BL material (for *to broaden* and *to blush*) are both deleted. On the interleaf facing sig. 3P2^v, for example, the amanuensis has written:

To broaden v.a. [from broad]
    To make any thing spacious & wide.
    Tis used in Scotland and perhaps in no other place to be found but in the following passage unless he mistook it for browden'd which in the Scotish dialect denotes louring frightful, alluding to knitting the brows
    Whence glaring oft with many a broaden'd orb
He frights the Nations   Thoms. Aut. 780.

The same amanuensis who is interested in Scots usage provides the example from Thomson, which in this case exemplifies it.

A similar example appears on the interleaf facing sig. 3T1^r, where a quotation from Sidney is cited as part of a statement on the history of the language and the usage in Scotland. This quotation is recycled from *interrogatory* n.s. in *1755*:

10 A fantastic unnecessary intermeddling, in the same sense with busy body & is still retaind in Scotland
He with no more civility, tho with much more business than those under fellows had shewd began in a captious manner to put interrogatories unto him Sidney

Johnson has crossed out the definition and note on usage, retaining the quotation, and written above it a new definition – "1 State of being busy" – and keyed it into its place in the printed text.

It seems clear, as the evidence reviewed above illustrates, that the amanuenses were given more freedom in gathering and presenting material for inclusion in the text than has previously been thought; yet the evidence also demonstrates that they were allowed no say in the final copy. In fact, it is not overstating the case to conclude from the evidence in the B material that Johnson adopts a hostile attitude towards the amanuenses' contributions. He is certainly completely unconvinced of the more personal contributions on Scots or dialect usage. Nor does he trust the proffered new definitions, and often for good reason. Expansive commentary, glossing of passages, and usage notes are also dismissed. The evidence presented in this unique source leads one to conclude that Johnson's control of his final text is more strongly reserved to himself than could previously be demonstrated. In short, the "collaborative" role of the amanuenses, judging from the surviving evidence related to the revised edition of the *Dictionary*, is limited to gathering quotations in bulk from the first edition – material chosen originally by Johnson – for possible reuse under other entries in the fourth. Most commentary upon these quotations is struck out, any broader collaborative role extinguished. We can surmise that Johnson instructed the amanuenses to contextualize the material they reprocessed in some way, adding glosses or notes, although we cannot know this for certain. In the test of preparing the final copy, however, there can be no question but that he found their work wanting or inappropriate. Johnson's inhabiting of the place of authority is particularly noteworthy because he insists on retaining his own final authorizing hand even in the face of potentially useful "collaborating" action. Boswell recorded that Johnson had told him "it was remarkable that when he revised & improved the last [fourth] edition of his Dict[iona]ry the Printer was never kept waiting."[16] Certainly, it was the material he had his amanuenses gather, copy, gloss, and annotate that enabled him to proceed quickly and smoothly. But it is striking that so little of it, judging from the evidence for the letter B, actually makes it into the printed text without change.

The evidence concerning Scottish and dialect usage is of considerable importance in that it supports the view that, at least in the revision, Johnson tends to suppress linguistic difference within English, actively and repeatedly rejecting dialect or regional variations which pluralize the conception of the national and accepted language.[17] This has been a point of great interest to linguists and critics of Johnson's attitude towards the "national tongue" and its many variations, in particular Scots dialect. The astonishing fact that so many of Johnson's helpers on the *Dictionary* were themselves Scots seems to open up the possibility that they were employed, not only for their obvious skills, but also in an attempt for Johnson to include a wide range of linguistic variation. Scottish writers and critics such as Robert Fergusson and Archibald Campbell savaged Johnson's *Dictionary* for, in part, including so much latinate English and excluding Scots usage.[18] The amanuenses, in the course of the revision, may well be trying to address criticisms of the *Dictionary* by proposing material from Scots dialect and quotations from Scottish authors. In October 1769, Johnson even insisted that Boswell should "complete a Dictionary of words peculiar to Scotland, of which [Boswell] shewed him a specimen . . . By collecting those of your country, you will do a useful thing towards the history of the language" (*Life*, vol. II, pp. 91–92). Whether or not he thought of Boswell's efforts as related to his own lexicographic project, the revision of which would begin in less than two years, he demonstrates, at least, that he is aware of the importance of Scots dialect in its historical relation to English. It is significant, however, that he does not consider it of *current* relevance.

The material that has survived in the British Library collections also leads us to understand a further aspect of collaboration in the *Dictionary*, concerning other friends or contemporaries who might have contributed. It is still undetermined why the BL material covering the entries for the letter B was not used when setting printer's copy for the fourth edition, despite being prepared in the same manner as the rest of the printer's copy. In *The Making of Johnson's Dictionary* I provided an account of what was used in their stead, detailing how Johnson rapidly collected material to fill the gap when his original materials were, for whatever reason, not to be found. This description is valid, however, only in part; as R. Carter Hailey has recently demonstrated, once Johnson missed the materials he had prepared for the printer for the letter B, he first incorporated new material which had already been prepared by George Steevens, his collaborator on the 1773 edition of Shakespeare.[19] The part of the text of the fourth edition *Dictionary* covering entries beginning with the letter B is the only part of the fourth edition set from pages of the third edition *Dictionary* from 1765; the remainder of the printed sheets besides the B material in the BL copy are from the third edition and are annotated by Steevens. Whether or not Steevens undertook these revisions at Johnson's request, and whether or not Steevens originally thought they would be included in the final copy, Johnson clearly knew of their existence and turned to them in an emergency. Yet he did not use other Steevens contributions written on the other pages. The collaboration would appear to have been undertaken only under extreme circumstances. In contrast, Steevens was engaged in active collaboration with Johnson at this time on the edition of Shakespeare, and took the initiative in making additions and changes to the edition.

If Johnson exhibits what we might call a "collective" instinct in his work on the *Dictionary*, it is less persuasive to think of it as collaborative. He looked for assistance in his great work where he could find it. Johnson demonstrates his possible collaborative instincts when he has the amanuenses gather material and propose readings, notes, and definitions for the fourth edition, but he severely truncates the material actually transcribed. He incorporated Steevens's additions and changes gratefully, we can imagine, but only, apparently, in an emergency. The quoted voices from literary texts (his "authorities") compete in ways with Johnson's own, but remain, to a large extent, subservient to his own overarching authority as both author and compiler. He remained the authority, with other voices, past and present, clamoring for attention, some subsumed within the teeming work, others excluded. The *Dictionary* is in many ways a battleground for authority; in the manuscript material that exists for the making of the work, Johnson's persistent determination to control the material, incorporate authorities, and simultaneously exclude "other" voices can be clearly traced.

NOTES

1. A select list of relevant scholarship includes Martha Woodmansee, "On the Author Effect: Recovering Collectivity," in *The Construction of Authorship: Textual Appropriation in Law and Literature*, ed. Martha Woodmansee and Peter Jaszi (Durham, N.C.: Duke University Press, 1994), pp. 15–28 (this essay includes a discussion of Johnson), and "The Genius and the Copyright:

Economic and Legal Conditions of the Emergence of the 'Author,'" *Eighteenth-Century Studies* 17 (1983–84), 425–48, revised in *The Author, Art, and the Market: Rereading the History of Aesthetics* (New York: Columbia University Press, 1994), chapter 2; Jerome J. McGann, *A Critique of Modern Textual Criticism,* 2nd ed. (Charlottesville: University Press of Virginia, 1992), and *The Textual Condition* (Princeton: Princeton University Press, 1991); and David McKitterick, *Print, Manuscript and the Search for Order, 1450–1830* (Cambridge: Cambridge University Press, 2003), chapter 9. The following studies of Renaissance authorship address and build upon previous studies of collaboration in the period: Lukas Erne, *Shakespeare as Literary Dramatist* (Cambridge: Cambridge University Press, 2003), and Jeffrey Masten, *Textual Intercourse: Collaboration, Authorship, and Sexualities in Renaissance Drama* (New York: Cambridge University Press, 1997), p. 14; see also Brian Vickers, *Shakespeare, Co-Author: A Historical Study of the Five Collaborative Plays* (Oxford: Oxford University Press, 2002).

2. Thomas Edwards to Daniel Wray, Bodleian Library MS Bodl. 1012, p. 211; John Horne Tooke, *Diversions of Purley* (London, 1786), p. 268 n.

3. Robert DeMaria, Jr., and Gwin J. Kolb, "Johnson's *Dictionary* and Dictionary Johnson," *Yearbook of English Studies* 28 (1998), 19–43.

4. Robert Heron (John Pinkerton), *Letters of Literature* (London, 1785), p. 265.

5. There appear to have been six amanuenses who worked, at one time or another, for Johnson on the *Dictionary*: Francis Stewart; Robert Shiels, the real author of Cibber's *Lives of the Poets*; Alexander Macbean, author of dictionaries of the Bible (1779) and of ancient geography (1773) and former amanuensis for Ephraim Chambers's *Cyclopædia*; his brother, William Macbean; V. J. Peyton, the only Englishman in the group and author of several works on the English language in his own right; and a man known only by the name of Maitland. The five we know about were seasoned in the world of literary compilation or journalism. It was probably Peyton and William Macbean who assisted with the fourth edition.

6. Samuel Dyer and Bennet Langton are likely figures. According to Sir Joshua Reynolds, Dyer had at Johnson's "desire made notes, explanations and corrections of words to be used, in a future edition" of the *Dictionary*: see *Letters of Sir Joshua Reynolds,* ed. F. W. Hilles (Cambridge: Cambridge University Press, 1929), p. 141. Johnson wrote to Bennet Langton on 29 August 1771: "I am engaging in a very great work the revision of my Dictionary from which I know not at present how to get loose. If you have observed or been told any errors or omissions, you will do me a great favor by letting me know them" (*Letters*, vol. 1, pp. 381–82).

7. See DeMaria and Kolb: "Perhaps Johnson's amanuenses have received less credit for the composition of the whole *Dictionary of the English Language* than they deserve" ("Johnson's *Dictionary*," p. 32). For a description of the Sneyd-Gimbel copy at Yale, see Reddick, *The Making of Johnson's Dictionary, 1746–1773,* rev. ed. (Cambridge: Cambridge University Press, 1996), pp. 179–89.

8. British Library shelfmark C.45.k.3. My facsimile edition of this material, with transcription, analysis, and critical commentary, will be published by Cambridge University Press (2005). The collection consists of printed sheets, the entries from *A* through *jailor*, bound in three volumes and interleaved. Only the sheets for the letter B are from the first edition; the remainder are from the third (1765) and have been annotated by George Steevens (see below). For a full description and history of the material, see Reddick, *The Making of Johnson's Dictionary*, pp. 190–94.

9. For a fuller discussion, see Reddick, *The Making of Johnson's Dictionary*, especially chapters 3–5.

10. I have refrained from identifying which amanuensis did what because the handwriting evidence is not yet clear enough to enable me to be certain.

11. In *The Making of Johnson's Dictionary* I thought it possible, even likely, that Johnson marked the quotations to be recycled, and may have provided other entry-material at this early stage of preparing material for the revision. After further review, I no longer believe this to be the case.

12. DeMaria and Kolb "Johnson's *Dictionary*," pp. 33–35. Two cases might be borderline: Johnson accepts *break fast* as an additional use of *break* and a comment on Dryden's use of *boisterous* under that entry. Otherwise, from the handwritten commentary (i.e., non-quoted material), he accepts very short definitions for twenty-seven different entries and three simple "etymologies" (e.g., "bonjour [French]").

13. See Stanley Wells and Gary Taylor, *William Shakespeare: A Textual Companion* (Oxford: Clarendon Press, 1987), pp. 20–23; T. H. Howard-Hill, *Ralph Crane and Some Shakespeare First Folio Comedies* (Charlottesville: University Press of Virginia, 1972); and Erne, *Shakespeare as Literary Dramatist*, p. 214.

14. I use the plural here to refer to the two amanuenses who assisted on the fourth edition, one copying onto slips or clipping out passages, the other transcribing onto the BL interleaves.

15. Johnson drops Thomson quotations disproportionately from the *Dictionary* in his revision primarily because of Thomson's association with "liberty" causes; see also the discussion in Reddick, *The Making of Johnson's Dictionary*, pp. 136–40.

16. Boswell's *Note Book*, reproduced in *The R. B. Adam Library Relating to Dr. Samuel Johnson and His Era*, 3 vols. (London: privately printed, 1929), vol. II, between pp. 51 and 52.

17. Janet Sorenson, *The Grammar of Empire in Eighteenth-Century British Writing* (Cambridge: Cambridge University Press, 2000), chapter 2, contains the most recent and in many ways most articulate expression of this view. For a different perspective, see Nicholas Hudson, "Johnson's *Dictionary* and the Politics of 'Standard English,'" *Yearbook of English Studies* 28 (1998), 77–93. See also James G. Basker, "Scotticisms and the Problem of Cultural Identity in Eighteenth-Century Britain," *Eighteenth-Century Life* 15 (1991), 81–95.

18. Robert Fergusson, "To Dr. Samuel Johnson: Food for a New Edition of His Dictionary," and "To the Principal and Professors of the University of St. Andrews on Their Superb Treat to Dr. Samuel Johnson," in *The Poems of Robert Fergusson*, vol. II, ed. Matthew P. McDiarmid (Edinburgh and London: Blackwood and Sons, 1956), pp. 204–06; Archibald Campbell, *Lexiphanes: A Dialogue* (London, 1767).

19. See R. Carter Hailey, "'This Instance Will Not Do': George Steevens and the Revision(s) of Johnson's *Dictionary*," *Studies in Bibliography* 54 (2001), 243–64.

CHAPTER 14

Hidden quarto editions of Johnson's Dictionary

R. Carter Hailey

The history of Johnson's *Dictionary* following Johnson's revision of the fourth edition in 1773 has received relatively little critical and bibliographical attention. In 1785 two new editions appeared: the sixth edition was the first authorized edition to be printed in quarto, and seventh was the first folio edition in one volume. No new folio edition was ever produced and a new quarto edition did not appear until 1799, creating the longest gap between editions since the *Dictionary's* initial publication in 1755. This gap might seem to indicate diminishing popularity or a saturation of the market. But new bibliographical evidence demonstrates that the sixth edition was actually reprinted several times in large press runs during this period. That eighteenth-century publishers sometimes "puffed" their products by designating such reprints as "new and improved" editions, is indicated by Thomas Percy's comment that in the sixteenth century booksellers "did not ostentatiously affect to multiply editions."[1] By contrast, these reprints of the sixth edition were unacknowledged and therefore constitute hidden editions, although they were in fact improved. Demand for the *Dictionary* clearly remained strong in the 1780s and 1790s, and such was the iconic status of Johnson's authority that the publishers saw fit not just to reprint their profitable product, but also to employ an unnamed editor who worked diligently to honor Johnson's legacy by increasing the accuracy of its text. Despite these anonymous improvements, the editions have been hidden because they are remarkably similar and, as Johnson said of the revisions he made for the fourth edition, most readers "will not, without nice collation, perceive how they differ" (*1773*, vol. I, sig. [C]1ʳ).

In the Preface to his edition of Shakespeare, Johnson conceded that the duty of a collator is indeed dull, yet, like other tedious tasks, very necessary (Yale *Works*, vol. VII, p. 94). But like the harmless drudgery of lexicography itself, the tedium of collation may yield unexpected rewards. Several years ago I attempted a critical edition of the letter K from Johnson's *Dictionary of the English Language.* My procedure was to collate that letter in the first seven authorized and unabridged editions in which Johnson had or might have had a direct hand: the first through fifth editions folio, and the posthumously and concurrently published sixth edition quarto and seventh edition folio.[2] The latter editions were advertised as being printed from a copy of the revised fourth edition, which contained Johnson's final additions and corrections which the author had bequeathed to Sir Joshua Reynolds. The production of the serially published Q6 and F7 resulted not so much from the proprietors' advertised desire "that the publick [might] not be deprived of the last improvements of so consummate a Lexicographer as Dr. Johnson," but rather to preserve a profitable franchise by quashing competition which had arisen when their copyright expired at Johnson's death.[3] While Thomas Longman and the other proprietors were still hawking their fifth edition folio for £4 10s., two substantially cheaper editions had begun to appear in the autumn of 1785: James Harrison offered a folio reprint of the first edition supplemented by a life of the author in one hundred weekly numbers at sixpence each, while John Fielding published the first English quarto edition in forty-eight weekly numbers at a shilling apiece.[4]

Longman reacted quickly, and by 19 November 1785 began issuing competing quarto and folio editions (Q6 and F7) in weekly numbers. The large number of surviving copies, especially of Q6, and the relative scarcity of the Harrison and Fielding editions attest to Longman's marketing savvy. The printing in parts was to have run through 30 June 1787, but by 17 February of that year the *Morning Chronicle and London Advertiser* indicated that both the one-volume folio and two-volume quarto could be had complete, and that "Subscribers to either edition, in numbers, may now complete their books: and any person may begin with Number I. and purchase one or more numbers weekly."

While the consultation of multiple copies within editions was beyond the scope of my editorial project – a procedure which I would later realize to be inadequate – I had acquired photocopies of the letter K from two different copies of Q6, one from the British Library copy, one from the Alderman Library copy at the University of Virginia. One evening I chanced to have the two side by side, and glancing casually back and forth between them, noticed several minor variants in spelling and punctuation in the first few lines. The most curious of these was in the Shakespeare quotation used to illustrate *kalendar,* the first headword under the letter K. In the British Library copy, a line from *Macbeth* read, "Let this pernicious hour stand *as* accursed in the *Kalendar,*" while the Virginia copy read "*ay* accursed" (my emphasis). "As" versus "ay": the difference of a single letter in these two copies was to lead to a complex series of discoveries which revealed both the existence of several "undenominated reprints"[5] – i.e., not separately numbered – of the sixth edition and the intervention of an anonymous corrector who saw to it that the several printings of Q6 were improved in a number of seemingly minor, though cumulatively significant, details.

The problem had initially appeared straightforward enough. Since I knew from my collations that all six of the folio editions read *as*, I at first supposed the variants to have resulted from the stop-press correction of a compositor error, with the British Library copy representing the corrected state of the sheet. The reading *ay* for *as* is a rather unlikely foul case error since the letter-forms are dissimilar and the sorts are not adjacent in the type case, but I made nothing more of it than deciding to use the British Library copy of the letter K for collating against the first edition. A subsequent phase of the project was to check the text of quotations as printed in the *Dictionary* against their probable sources in an attempt to distinguish intentional Johnsonian alterations from copying or typesetting errors.[6] This proved to be an exceptionally challenging task owing both to the difficulty of determining the precise editions Johnson used for selecting his illustrations, and of locating specific passages in lengthy works. But in this case the editor's job is simplified since the copy of the 1747 Warburton edition Johnson marked for selecting his Shakespeare quotations is extant. For the *kalendar* quotation, Warburton's *Macbeth* read "ay accursed" rather than "as accursed."[7] The reading in the UVa copy of Q6, in other words, was correct, while all other editions – including the BL copy of Q6 – had got it wrong. Subsequent collation of the rest of the letter K in the two copies of the sixth edition revealed a second substantive variant in a Shakespeare quotation, this time from *Othello*. Under *to keep* v.n. 2 all other editions, including the BL copy of the sixth, had read:

> What! keep a week away? seven days and nights?
> Eightscore hours? And lovers absent hours!
> Oh weary reckoning!

But in the Alderman copy the period was a bit longer: "Eightscore *eight* hours" (my emphasis) rather than "Eightscore hours" (which would leave one eight hours shy of a week). Again the UVa reading agreed with Warburton.

It was now evident that these were not simply press variants, but active corrections. But what could have been their source? Johnson was dead, and

these were not among the corrections he had noted in the Reynolds copy.[8]
And why should the readings differ in two copies of what were ostensibly the
same edition? I thus began a more detailed comparison of the two and soon
found that the BL and UVa copies, while ostensibly from the same edition,
were from different settings of type throughout. But the most remarkable
discovery was that much of the paper in the UVa copy had as a watermark
the date "1794," nine years *after* the date on the title page, by which time at
least four of the proprietors listed on the title page were dead. I was unable
to collate the full texts of the two copies, but in comparing them page for
page for resettings, I found a number of corrections to column headings
and the alphabetical order of entries in the later setting.[9] At this point I
still had no evidence regarding who the anonymous corrector might be,
but I recalled Sledd and Kolb's description of George Steevens's annota-
tions to a copy of mixed first and third edition sheets of the *Dictionary*
held by the British Library; they remark that "most of [the annotations]
deal in one way or another with Shakespearean quotations," and what I
had found were corrections to Shakespeare quotations.[10] I began to wonder
whether George Steevens might have been their source. As a suspect, he at
least had the advantage of still being alive in 1794. And despite contentions
that Johnson had never made use of Steevens's notes, it seemed unlikely
that someone – even a bibliographer – would undertake so daunting a
project as annotating the *Dictionary* if the work were not to serve some practical use. After transcribing Steevens's notes in the BL copy and comparing
them to readings in F4, I was certain that Johnson had in fact made some
use of them. Equally certain that Steevens must have been the source of
the two corrections in the UVa copy of Q6,[11] I compared his notes in the
BL copy to the text of UVa Q6 and found five additional instances where
suggested corrections had been made, all in Shakespeare quotations.[12] It
now seemed possible that there might be several undenominated reprint
editions.[13]

Some notion of the bibliographical complexity of this edition is indicated
by the ESTC, which provides two separate records for Q6, the first of
which includes the note "Published in 84 parts?," implying that copies
distributed in parts were from a separate issue than those sold as complete
volumes.[14] But as J. D. Fleeman remarked in his magisterial bibliography of
Johnson, "The ESTC discrimination between the vol. and part publication
is reasonable, but difficult in practice" (*Bibliography*, vol. I, p. 440). The
major source of confusion is the presence of multiple and variant sequences
of press figures in copies of Q6; variation is so ubiquitous that Fleeman
found "No complete repeated sequence . . . in the copies examined." He

further observes that "sheets issued as weekly numbers are not consistently figured; sheets published in volumes are equally variable so that the different figures do not yet distinguish the two issues" (*Bibliography*, vol. 1, p. 440). In fact, as I will show, there is no bibliographical distinction between sheets published in parts and sheets published in volumes. The variation in press-figure sequences is owing in fact to the sixth edition of the *Dictionary* having been twice reset, reprinted, and reissued over a period of ten years; each reprinting produced a near facsimile of the original issue of 1785–86, always maintaining the title-page date of 1785. The variation is further multiplied because individual copies may be made up of sheets from more than one printing.

Press figures are numbers, typographic symbols, or occasionally letters – distinct from and in addition to signatures – which sometimes appear at the bottom of the pages of eighteenth-century English books.[15] While their function is still not fully understood, the most plausible explanation is that they were used to designate the press on which the forme had been worked: "In essence the use of press figures was a form of accounting or record-keeping, allowing the pressman to check on the accuracy of his wages and the overseer to identify the pressman responsible for a specific piece of bad workmanship" (McMullin, "Further Observations," pp. 177–78). In books that include press figures, individual gatherings may be figured in one or both of the inner and outer formes and some gatherings may not be figured at all. When different copies from what appears to be the same edition exhibit variant figures it *may* imply resetting, though as will be shown below, figures are sometimes changed in the middle of a press run.

In order to help unravel these difficulties, I not only continued to examine additional copies of Q6, but consulted the Strahan ledgers in the British Library for any additional information they might yield since, as Fleeman notes, they provide the only external source of information about the printing of the sixth edition.[16] On fols. 96–97 of BL Add. MS 48809, in entries dated November 1786, Andrew Strahan records a number of details which concern the production of Q6 and the concurrently produced F7. The production of both editions was shared between several printers, with Strahan printing the History of the English Language in the preliminaries and the letters L–R inclusive, for both the quarto and folio.[17] There appears to have been some haste in printing the preliminaries since Strahan lists an additional charge "To the Men [for] Nightwork and Sunday," though he realized a considerable savings on typesetting the L–R sheets by "overrunning," that is, reimposing the type originally set up for the folio to print off the quarto edition. Both editions were produced in substantial runs: in folio, Strahan printed 1,750 copies of the History and 1,500 of L–R; for the quarto, 3,250 copies of the History and 3,500 of L–R (with the exception of the first sheet, signature B, of which for some reason only 3,000 were printed). Strahan also records charges for printing the blue paper covers in which the parts were issued, again for both formats. While Fleeman's bibliography accounts for all this, he makes no note of a significant entry on fol. 118 of the same ledger. Under the heading "Johnson's Dictionary 4to" dated Nov. 1789, Strahan lists charges for printing another 2,250 copies of the History of the English Language in the prelims of volume I and 2,000 copies of sheets B–3Z from volume II. These charges corresponded to an undenominated reprinting of the *Dictionary* which is implied by the appearance on 21 December 1787 of a new advertisement: "GENUINE EDITIONS . . . On Saturday, January 5, 1788, will be published, Number 1. of the Folio, and Number 1. of the Quarto Edition of A Dictionary of the English Language" (*Morning Chronicle and London Advertiser*). Although in February of 1787 the proprietors announced that both Q6 and F7 could be had complete, barely a year later serial publication had begun again. The quarto was to be issued in seventy-eight parts, which would imply a completion date of early July 1789, a date that, judging from Strahan's entry, was not met. Demand for the *Dictionary* must have been fairly consistent, because entries in another ledger, Add. MS. 48817, indicated that there was yet another printing of the sixth edition, and in this case production seems to have been for some reason attenuated. Again under the heading "Johnson's Dictionary 4to" Strahan lists charges for printing 2,000 copies of the History of the English Language in January 1791; 2,000 of signature B and 1,500 of signature C in July 1793; and 1,275–1,325 copies of signatures D–3Z in December 1795. I now had clear archival evidence that after its initial publication in 1785–86, the text of Q6 had been twice completely reset and republished over the following ten years.

By combining information from the Strahan ledgers with the physical evidence from the examination of multiple copies of the sixth edition – especially that of press figures and watermarks – I am now able to paint a more complete picture of the fate of Johnson's *Dictionary* on the presses of London in the several years following his death. The Strahan ledgers had confirmed my suspicions, based on the physical evidence, that Q6 had been twice reprinted without acknowledgment; these later issues were intended to be indistinguishable from the earlier printings, to the extent that even the anomalous signatures of the earliest printing were replicated although, paradoxically, the text was improved in a number of minor details (see Hailey,

"'This Instance Will Not Do,'" pp. 263–64). But after examining eighteen copies of the sixth edition and recording their press-figure sequences, I had compiled a wealth of apparently contradictory data.[18] While, unlike Fleeman, I did encounter some copies in which press-figure sequences were duplicated, the majority of copies were, at least in minor detail, singular. The bewildering multiplicity of sequences began to make sense only after I displayed the press-figure data on a color-coded spreadsheet: suddenly patterns began to emerge, patterns which corroborated the evidence of the Strahan ledgers, since copies tended to fall in one of three basic groups – in fact only two of the 278 gatherings exist in four settings.[19] I knew from the evidence of the watermark "1794" in the Virginia (V) copy that this must represent the latest printing, and I subsequently examined three additional copies that both contained the same watermark and duplicated the press-figure sequence of the Virginia copy throughout (L^K, O^{24}, and RCH4). A sub-group of two copies, RCH4 and GU, shared the same sequence as these four from the beginning of volume I to sig. 5E, but differed from that point forward (5F–6X), while in volume II, they shared only the initial gathering with the first group, with the clear implication that volume I gatherings 5F–6X and volume II gatherings C–^{2}3Z represented sheets left over from the second printing eked out with sheets from the third to make up complete copies. I also had discovered that a large group of ten copies – L, O^{18}, C^2, LC, JH, NLM, LEH, RCH1, RCH2, and DVM – were invariant in volume II, but had one of two different setting in volume I. A key to determining the priority of the different settings in volume I was provided by the Lincoln College, Oxford copy (C^{13}) which shared the same settings in gatherings *a*, b, g, h, and K–Dd with what I now knew to be the third printing, but otherwise generally matched a sub-group of copies L, C^2, LC and DVM. The Lincoln copies thus provided a sort of missing link between printings that indicated that the other volume I subset of O^{18}, JH, NLM, LEH, RCH1, RCH2 had come from the earliest printing.

What had emerged was a pattern in which the earliest and latest copies of Q6 exhibit relative uniformity, while sheets from the middle printing also figure in various combinations with early and later sheets. The indication from both the Strahan ledgers and the press figures is that the production and re-production of the sixth edition of Johnson's *Dictionary* was the product of a rolling schedule which was permitted by continued demand, dictated by the issuing in parts, and complicated by shared printing. Production could have extended over the seventy-eight weeks it would take to issue the work in parts, but it would have been prudent for a printer to produce as a unit those sheets that were his responsibility,[20] although the precise number of copies needed would have been to some degree a matter of guesswork. Certainly many more customers began subscriptions than kept up with them for the whole seventy-eight weeks. The advertisements indicate that the first printing was completed several months early, while the second appears to have taken several months longer than originally scheduled. For the third printing, while I lack the corroborative evidence from advertisements, production appears to have extended over a considerably longer period, since in January 1791 Strahan produces the third printing of the Q6 History, while the vol. II letters B–R are not completed until December 1795. These factors account for some of the variability in the makeup of individual copies, since it would always make economic sense to use up sheets from a previous printing before starting on the newly printed ones, and they also explain why throughout the series of hidden editions volume II is less variable than volume I. One additional and perplexing factor responsible for press-figure sequence variation is that in the earliest printing of volume I, gatherings 5F–6X frequently have their figures changed during the press run (eighteen of the forty-one). In most such instances figures are invariant in one forme, while the other forme will exhibit one of two different figures (in some cases figures are present in some copies, absent in others). One may only speculate why formes would repeatedly be moved from one press to another during the run; it is a phenomenon I have encountered nowhere else in any of the three printings. No wonder Fleeman was perplexed, concluding of Q6, while it "is undoubtedly a textually significant ed[ition]," that "it would be imprudent to use a single copy as the only source for references" (*Bibliography*, vol. I, p. 440).

Other than to perplex bibliographers, why might the proprietors have chosen to issue undenominated reprints rather than to puff "new and improved" editions of the *Dictionary*? Apparently there was no need. The very fact that the editions were twice reprinted argues for a strong continuing demand, and they were already advertising Q6 and F7 as the "Genuine Editions" which contained numerous "additions, corrections, and improvements" "from a copy bequeathed by the author to Sir Joshua Reynolds."[21] There was little more that Longman *et al.* might have claimed for their *Dictionary*. But what is truly remarkable is that the proprietors felt strongly enough about the fidelity of their text that they engaged George Steevens, for many years Johnson's co-editor on the Shakespeare editions, to oversee these undemoninated republications. Without acknowledgment, Steevens worked not only to prevent new errors from creeping in, but continued actively to correct the text, particularly with regards to Shakespeare quotations. His activities reflect Johnson's contention in his Advertisement for the revised fourth edition that while "Perfection is unattainable . . . nearer and nearer approaches may be made" (*1773*, vol. I, sig. [C]I^r), and argue for the iconic status of the *Dictionary*, which continued in the period following Dr. Johnson's death to appear in "new and improved" versions, although no such claim was ever made for it.

NOTES

1. Thomas Percy, *Reliques of Ancient English Poetry*, 3 vols. (London, 1765), vol. II, p. 262.
2. After the first edition of 1755, the folio *Dictionary* went through two additional editions in 1755–56 and 1765 before the major revision which resulted in the fourth edition of 1773. I will employ the following abbreviations: the first through fifth editions folio, each in two volumes, will be designated F1 (1755), F2 (1755–56), F3 (1765), F4 (1773), and F5 (1784); the sixth edition is a two-volume quarto, designated Q6 (1785); and the seventh edition, a single-volume folio, designated F7 (1785). The changes noted by Johnson in the Reynolds copy number only about 250.
3. From an advertisement appearing in *The Morning Chronicle and London Advertiser*, 24 October 1785. For a more detailed account see James H. Sledd and Gwin J. Kolb, *Dr. Johnson's Dictionary: Essays in the Biography of a Book* (Chicago: University of Chicago Press, 1955), pp. 127–33.
4. Thomas Ewing had published an unauthorized quarto edition in Dublin in 1775.
5. I take the phrase from William B. Todd, who, in discussing the study of printing in the eighteenth century, notes that "undenominated reprints are to be suspected everywhere," and that one may assume "the presence of two or three concealed editions in practically every major production in the eighteenth century." See "Bibliography and the Editorial Problem in the Eighteenth Century," *Studies in Bibliography* 4 (1951–52), 42–43.
6. Johnson intentionally compressed and even altered quotations to save space; as he acknowledged in the Preface, "The examples [i.e. quotations] are too often injudiciously truncated, and perhaps sometimes, I hope very rarely, alleged in a mistaken sense; for in making this collection I trusted more to memory, than, in a state of disquiet and embarrassment, memory can contain, and purposed to supply at the review what was left incomplete in the first transcription" (1825 *Works*, vol. V, p. 42).
7. The copy marked by Johnson is held by the National Library of Wales, Aberystwyth. Unfortunately volume VI, which contains *Macbeth*, is missing; it is impossible to be certain that Johnson used Warburton's text for this play or the others in that volume. See Anne McDermott, "The Defining Language: Johnson's

Dictionary and *Macbeth*," *Review of English Studies* 44, no. 176 (November 1993), 521–38. Nevertheless a check of the Macbeth *Variorum* showed no occurrences of the reading "as" in other editions.

8. See Gwin J. Kolb and James H. Sledd, "The Reynolds Copy of Johnson's *Dictionary*," *Bulletin of the John Rylands Library* 37 (1955), 446–75, and Anne McDermott, "The Reynolds Copy of Johnson's *Dictionary*: A Re-Examination," *Bulletin of the John Rylands Library* 74 (1992), 29–38.

9. In the center column of vol. 1, sig. 4R2^r, the BL copy has the headword *enpierce* wrongly inserted between *to enmesh* and *enneagon*, the order in all previous editions. In the Virginia copy it appears in its proper alphabetical location on sig. 4R2^v, between *en passant* and *to enrage*. This transposition creates a temporary "domino effect" in which the columns of text no longer match and the catchwords on sig. 4R2^r are different. But by the bottom of the first column on sig. 4R2^v the two texts are once again synchronized, with precisely the same words beginning and ending each column, as they do with few exceptions throughout these two copies of Q6. The same thing occurs on sig. 6E2^{r+v} where *honied*, which appears in the BL copy between *honesty* and *honey*, is in the Virginia copy found in its proper location between *honeywort* and *honorary*.

10. See Sledd and Kolb, *Dr. Johnson's Dictionary*, p. 122. The shelfmark of the British Library copy is C.45.k3.

11. A clinching bit of evidence is that Steevens had suggested as an additional illustration for *calendar* (Johnson included both *calendar* and *kalendar* as headwords) the very quotation from *Macbeth* that he was subsequently to correct in the late printing of Q6.

12. Under *censer* n.s. 2, *chamberlain* 3, *farrow* n.s., *to fast* v.n., and *green* adj. 4. The most significant of these is under *farrow* n.s. In the *Macbeth* quotation, "Pour in sow's blood that hath litter'd / Her nine *farrow*," "litter'd" is corrected to "eaten." For a more detailed consideration of Steevens's involvement see see R. Carter Hailey, "'This Instance Will Not Do': George Steevens, Shakespeare, and the Revision(s) of Johnson's *Dictionary*," *Studies in Bibliography* 54 (2001), 243–64.

13. In bibliographical parlance, *edition* refers to "all copies printed from a given setting of type," and *impression* to "those copies of an edition printed at any one time." An *issue* is "a group of published copies of an impression which constitutes a consciously planned publishing unit, distinguishable from other groups of published copies of that impression by one or more differences designed expressly to identify the group as a discrete unit." A *state* is "a copy or a group of copies of a printed sheet or a publisher's casing which differs from other copies (within the same impression or issue) of that sheet or casing in any respect which the publisher does not wish to call to the attention of the public as representing a discrete publishing effort." See G. Thomas Tanselle, "The Bibliographical Concepts of *Issue* and *State*," *Papers of the Bibliographical Society of America* 69 (1975), 18, 65.

14. The record ID numbers are ESTCN18 and ESTCT116655.

15. A classic early study of press figures is William Todd, "Observations on the Incidence and Interpretation of Press Figures," *Studies in Bibliography* 3 (1950–51), 171–205. For a more recent consideration, which addresses the problems of using press figures for the analytic study of printing practices, see B. J. McMullin, "Further Observations on the Incidence and Interpretation of Press Figures," in *Writers, Books, and Trade*, ed. O M Brack, Jr. (New York: AMS Press, 1994), pp. 177–200. McMullin notes that "Press figures are essentially a characteristic of the eighteenth century, though in fact they do extend well beyond both termini of the century, ranging from at least 1628 to at least 1866" (p. 177).

16. William Strahan had a long association with Johnson and printed the first edition of the *Dictionary*. Strahan set up as a printer in London in 1739 and, following his death in July 1785, was succeeded by his son Andrew. A remarkable set of records from Strahan printing house is preserved in the British Library and offers valuable insights into the workings of this prominent London printing house. The complete archive runs to 121 volumes covering the years 1738–1861, with some gaps. Part 1, with which I will be concerned, consists of printing ledgers, cost books, accounts and memoranda, 1739–1815 (British Library Add. MSS. 48800–48861).

17. In F7 the History appears in signatures 'c'–'h', the letters L–R in signatures '7A'–'10A'; in Q6 the History appears in gatherings 'c'–'f' and '[g]'–'[k]' of vol. I, the letters L–R in 'B'–'3Z' of vol. II. Shared printing accounts for anomalies in the sequence of signatures in both Q6 and F7; the indication is that three and possibly four printers were involved. Q6 collates: vol. I. a^4 b^4 c–f^2 '[g]'–'[h]'^{2} '[i]'–'[k]'^{4} g–h^4 B–4E^4 '4F–M'^{4} 4N–6U^4 6X^4 (–6X4=II. A1). Vol. II. A1 (=I. 6X4) B–3Y^4 3Z^2 ^{2}A–3Y^4 ^{2}3Z^2 (slightly adapted from Fleeman). In vol. I the odd signature '4F–M' fills a gap in the sequence, separating what must have been discrete printing units B–4E and 4N–6X. In vol. II, we know from the ledgers that Strahan printed B–3Z, with the following unit a second series beginning A and running to 3Z. There are complimentary discrepancies in the signing of F7.

18. The examined copies are here listed with a reference abbreviation following, using ESTC codes when possible: five copies in private hands, four in my own possession (RCH1, RCH2, RCH3, RCH4), and a copy owned by David Vander Meulen (DVM); The British Library (L); King's College, University of London (L^K); Trinity College, Cambridge (C^2); Bodleian Library (O); Lincoln College, Oxford (C^{13}); Oriel College, Oxford (O^{18}); Pembroke College, Oxford (O^{24}); Library of Congress (LC); University of Virginia (V); National Library of Medicine (NLM); Georgetown University (GU); Johns Hopkins University (JH); Lehigh University (LEH).

19. They are gatherings *a* and 1 in volume 1. Limitations of space prevent the inclusion of these spreadsheets; interested readers may see the full range of press-figure data at http://rchail.people.wm.edu/hidden_editions/endnote.html.

20. This is particularly evident in the sheets Strahan produced for the first printing since, judging from the press figures, two presses, no. 5 and no. 6, were wholly

given over to the production of the *Dictionary*. Nowhere else in either the later printings done by Strahan or in any of the sections done by other printers is there such uniformity of press figures.

21. Such advertisements had appeared regularly beginning with the 11 October 1785 number of the *Morning Chronicle and London Advertiser*. (See Sledd and Kolb, *Dr. Johnson's Dictionary*, p. 234 n. 61.) A new series of advertisements began to appear, in the same venue, on 21 December 1787.

General index

Index of Dictionary *entries*